BROTHERS
IN WAR AND PEACE

Dennis Cruywagen

BROTHERS
IN WAR AND PEACE

Constand and Abraham Viljoen and
the Birth of the New South Africa

Published by Zebra Press
an imprint of Random House Struik (Pty) Ltd
Reg. No. 1966/003153/07
The Estuaries No. 4, Oxbow Crescent, Century Avenue, Century City, 7441
PO Box 1144, Cape Town, 8000, South Africa

www.zebrapress.co.za

First published 2014

1 3 5 7 9 10 8 6 4 2

Publication © Zebra Press 2014
Text © Dennis Cruywagen 2014

All photographs from the personal collection of Abraham Viljoen,
except where indicated

Cover photos:
AWB march: © Doug Lee, SAHA collection
Voting queue: © Denis Farrell/AP Photo/PictureNET Africa
Constand Viljoen: © SANDF Documentation Centre
Abraham Viljoen: UNISA Institutional Repository

All rights reserved. No part of this publication may be reproduced,
stored in a retrieval system or transmitted, in any form or by any means,
electronic, mechanical, photocopying, recording or otherwise,
without the prior written permission of the copyright owners.

PUBLISHER: Marlene Fryer
MANAGING EDITOR: Robert Plummer
EDITOR: Bronwen Leak
PROOFREADER: Lisa Compton
COVER AND TEXT DESIGNER: Jacques Kaiser
TYPESETTER: Monique van den Berg
INDEXER: Sanet le Roux

Set in 11.5 pt on 16.5 pt Adobe Garamond

Printed and bound by CTP Book Printers, Duminy Street, Parow, 7500

ISBN 978 1 77022 600 5 (print)
ISBN 978 1 77022 601 2 (ePub)
ISBN 978 1 77022 602 9 (PDF)

Dedicated to the memory of Henry and Marie Cruywagen.

Contents

Acknowledgements ix
Abbreviations and acronyms xi

Introduction 1
1. The long shadow of the Anglo-Boer War 5
2. Out of the ashes 17
3. Early politics of the Viljoen family 31
4. The dissident Afrikaner 53
5. Military in the blood 73
6. In enemy colours 99
7. Riven by politics 109
8. The general answers the call 131
9. Secret negotiations get under way 143
10. Bridging the divides 157
11. The Freedom Front is born 173
12. The game changer: the Bophuthatswana coup 191
13. The ultimatum 205
14. Time to go 215
    Epilogue 227

Appendix I: Letter from Nelson Mandela to
Constand Viljoen 231
Appendix II: Accord on Afrikaner self-determination ... 233
Notes 237
Bibliography 245
Index 249

Acknowledgements

THIS BOOK WAS supported by a Taco Kuiper Grant for Investigative Journalism, for which I am exceedingly grateful. The majority of the research done outside of Cape Town and the Western Cape was made possible by this grant.

To Robert Plummer, Marlene Fryer and Bronwen Leak of Zebra Press, thank you. Your patience, support and editorial insights are gifts that I treasure.

Louise Korentajer and Margaret Titlestad got me interested in this project, and Louise unselfishly showed me what friendship can mean: Thank you. When writing, one needs sustenance, cajoling and encouragement. Without quiet places to think, write and plan, I would have been at a loss, and Izak and Corné de Wet offered their tranquil stone cottage on the lagoon in Wortelgat at a pivotal time. The solitude was essential.

Thanks also to my wife Lianda, Colin and Lebo Cruywagen, Johan Leibrandt and Anton Harber, and Siobhon Tregoning, for generously opening up 'the Estate' in Paarl. Thank you to Jan and Toekie de Necker: you lived through these times and took the political changes in your stride. Thank you, too, to Ayjay and Maggie Jantjies, Lionel and Rose Roode, Clive and Elsabe Vlotman, Linda Jacobs, Andre

Cruywagen, Marietjie van Zyl, Daphne Engelbrecht, and my children Yasser, Rameez, Fazlin, Ziyaad and Riyaad.

A number of people allowed me to interview them for this book. They include F.W. de Klerk, Jaap Durand, General Tienie Groenewald, Marie Haasbroek, Braam Hanekom, Jürgen Kögl, Augusta Marais, General Georg Meiring, Corné Mulder, General Chris Thirion, Colonel Piet Uys, and the two remarkable and courageous brothers, Abraham and Constand Viljoen. Others asked to remain anonymous but nonetheless spoke to me. Thank you for your time and for your trust. I must add that the book's conclusions are nevertheless my own.

DENNIS CRUYWAGEN
JUNE 2014

Abbreviations and acronyms

ANC: African National Congress
AVF: Afrikaner Volksfront
AWB: Afrikaner Weerstandsbeweging
BOSS: Bureau of State Security
COSAG: Concerned South Africans Group
CP: Conservative Party
DP: Democratic Party
FF: Freedom Front
FNLA: National Front for the Liberation of Angola
HNP: Herstigte Nasionale Party
IDASA: Institute for a Democratic Alternative for South Africa
IEC: Independent Electoral Commission
IFP: Inkatha Freedom Party
MK: Umkhonto we Sizwe
MP: member of Parliament
MPLA: People's Movement for the Liberation of Angola
NP: National Party
PAC: Pan Africanist Congress
PFP: Progressive Federal Party
SABC: South African Broadcasting Corporation
SABRA: South African Bureau for Racial Affairs
SACC: South African Council of Churches
SACP: South African Communist Party
SADF: South African Defence Force

SSC: State Security Council
SWAPO: South West Africa People's Organization
UN: United Nations
UNISA: University of South Africa
UNITA: National Union for the Total Independence of Angola
UWC: University of the Western Cape

Introduction

TWENTY-SEVEN YEARS BEHIND bars is more than enough time for a man to learn how to control and discipline his emotions, facial expressions and thoughts, to give nothing away. During his time as a political prisoner, Nelson Mandela learnt how to mask his feelings, to deny his jailers any advantage, no matter how small.

After his release in 1990, Mandela's life became a frenzied helter-skelter that showed no signs of slowing down. By mid-1993 the president of the African National Congress (ANC) was within sight of the end of his journey to bring political freedom to all South Africans. There had been setbacks, events that threatened to derail the process towards a democratic election, such as the assassination of popular ANC leader Chris Hani by white right-wingers earlier in the year. But through good leadership and political will, the country did not turn to civil war. The constitutional negotiations were back on track and millions of black South Africans were finally beginning to believe that democracy was coming to their land. The rest of the world was also upbeat about the prospect of arguably the most famous political prisoner of the last quarter of the twentieth century becoming president of the only remaining white-ruled country on the African continent. The world wanted Madiba, to pay homage to him, to hear him, to be inspired by this man who had forgiven his persecutors. Outwardly

Mandela epitomised confidence, but inwardly he harboured deep concerns about the Afrikaner right wing, for he knew very well that not all white South Africans were prepared to give up or share political power with the black majority.

A man with a voracious appetite for news, Mandela was closely following the rise of the Afrikaner right wing. Knowing that right-wingers occupied key positions in the civil service from which they could cause chaos in society, he regarded them as fearsome enemies and was acutely aware that they could scupper negotiations for democracy. They were angry and still believed it was their birthright as white Afrikaners to rule over the country's black inhabitants. They were prepared to go to war to ensure that political power remained in their hands. Mandela shared his fears and worries with his inner circle, but he understood that only direct talks between the ANC and the right wing could save the country from plunging into a civil war that would have no winner. He thus tried to reach out to the right wing, but his approaches were always rebuffed. For a while it looked like right-wing leaders had closed the door on any talks with him.

But that all changed one night as Mandela was about to depart on an overseas trip from Jan Smuts International Airport in Johannesburg. Abraham Viljoen, a former lecturer at the University of South Africa (UNISA) and an academic regarded as a leftist, had prevailed upon former student Carl Niehaus to arrange a face-to-face meeting with the ANC president. Although running on a tight schedule, Mandela was intrigued by the possibilities inherent in the request.

It would be no ordinary meeting, for Abraham was the identical twin brother of the former head of the South African Defence Force (SADF), General Constand Viljoen.

At this first meeting, hastily arranged at Jan Smuts, Abraham talked about involving those Afrikaners who were not part of the political negotiations, those seen as part of a lunatic fringe. He thought that the threat from this group could be addressed if the ANC met with his brother and other like-minded leaders to the right of the ruling National Party. Abraham offered to broker these discussions, which, if they ever came off, would not form part of the official constitutional negotiations.

Mandela, who had mastered the art of careful listening and measured words, gave no indication of just how pleased he was with Abraham's suggestion. Of all the groups on the right, he considered the Afrikaner Volksfront, formed by Constand Viljoen and a few other generals in May 1993, the most dangerous. He knew General Viljoen wielded great influence in the SADF and was concerned that if a civil war broke out, an ANC government would not be able to use the army. Abraham had no inkling of these concerns; neither did he know that Mandela had been secretly informed of the right wing's plans for armed rebellion. All Mandela said was, 'Go ahead. It's on.'

With these words, a series of secret meetings between the ANC and the right wing commenced, and South Africa was pulled back from the brink of civil war.

Not much is known about these covert negotiations in which Abraham and Constand Viljoen played a decisive role, one that demanded they cross the political divide that had estranged them to become Mandela's partners in peace.

Not much is known about the early life and family history of the Viljoen twins, or about how they came to follow such different paths.

This book tells their story.

1

The long shadow of the Anglo-Boer War

THE YEAR 1933 was not a good one in South Africa. Besides being the third year of the Great Depression, it was also the second year of a severe drought that had caused widespread crop failures, unemployment and poverty. The price of yellow maize was falling, as had the price of wool. Depression was not only felt in the economy, it was also part of the national mood. In Germany, it was the year in which Adolf Hitler and the Nazis destroyed the last remnants of the Weimar Republic as they seized power to form the Third Reich.

It was three decades since the end of the Second Anglo-Boer War, and, while defeat by Great Britain had been hard, the Afrikaners had slowly managed to recover, to once again become a political force, this time in the new Union of South Africa. But the new threat of the Great Depression, combined with the crippling drought, attacked whatever optimism might have been in their hearts. They felt powerless.

But for some there were still moments of joy. The birth of a child in families that had lost women and children to concentration camps and men to war was one such. So the birth of identical twin boys Abraham Carel and Constand Laubscher at the end of October 1933 on the farm Potfontein in the district of Standerton was a double blessing for the Viljoen family.

These were testing and hostile times to raise children. The drought brought deprivation, poverty, humiliation and dehumanisation to many farms. A huge dust bowl hung over everything and when the wind sprung up it created swirling sandstorms. Animals starved to death and the cattle that did not lacked the strength to pull the ploughs.

Farmers had to make hard decisions if they wanted to survive and protect their families. Many left their beloved land to seek temporary jobs in the cities as part of a rapidly growing poor white community. Those that stayed were invariably broken by the drought sooner or later. In the cities they had to compete against black people who were also suffering the fury of Mother Nature and the Great Depression. Mines, factories and small enterprises were all closing down and unemployment was rising at an alarming rate.

In 1931, the Carnegie Commission of Investigation on the Poor White Question had established that, out of a total white population of 1.8 million, the number of whites who could be classified as very poor had risen to 300 000. The majority of these poor whites were Afrikaans-speaking.[1]

The despondency in the white Afrikaans community was a far cry from the bravado they had shown less than forty years earlier, when the Boer republics of the Transvaal and the Orange Free State declared war on Britain on 11 October 1899, thus beginning the Second Anglo-Boer War. The British public expected it to be a short exchange, which would be over by Christmas. But when the Boers realised that they were not equipped and properly trained, and did not have the numbers to engage the enemy in conventional warfare, they introduced a new concept: guerrilla war, for which the British were not prepared – mentally, militarily or emotionally.

General Louis Botha was in charge of the Transvaal's forces (he later became commander of all the Boer forces), while General Christiaan de Wet led the Free State's army. Between them, the two

Boer republics could not muster more than 55 000 men. By the time the war ended in May 1902, the British had altogether used 250 000 soldiers.[2]

The war lasted two years and eight months and claimed at least 22 000 British, 25 000 Boer and 12 000 African lives. At a total cost of £200 million, it was not only the costliest war Britain had waged in almost a century, but also the bloodiest, longest and most humiliating.[3]

One of the major causes of the war was ostensibly the refusal of the president of the Transvaal Republic, Paul Kruger, to extend the franchise to the British immigrants who had streamed into South Africa lured by the discovery of gold. By 1898, the Transvaal had become the greatest gold power in the world, having overtaken Russia, Australia and America. One British minister declared it to be the richest spot on earth.[4]

However, there were other, more sinister factors at play.

Historian Thomas Pakenham's research into British high commissioner to southern Africa and governor of the Cape Colony Sir Alfred Milner's motivations revealed the real goal: 'His plan was to annex the Transvaal. He would rule it as a Crown Colony, much as his old chief, Cromer, ruled Egypt. It was all part of a larger game of federating the white Empire. He would achieve "a place in history as big as the man who made the American Constitution or the authors of the United Germany".

'Milner was interested in power, not only for himself but for England and the English race as well. This was the love of his life, English "race patriotism" as he defined it.'[5]

The vision of a 'Great Union of South Africa', which he would create, also burnt inside Milner. He confided in his ally Percy FitzPatrick that the ultimate end was a self-governing white community, supported by well-treated and justly governed black labour, extending from Cape Town to the Zambezi. 'Dams, schools, agricultural colleges – all the unglamorous but essential prerequisites of civilization – would overwhelm the veld,' wrote Pakenham. 'British settlers would pour into South Africa. This was the imperial mission. This was the great exercise in remoulding a nation and a landscape, the grand design that would follow the war – his war, as he boasted in private, and the Pax Milneria that would be his monument.'[6]

Grand plans, though, often require rich and influential supporters. To this end, Milner had an informal alliance with the rand millionaires. Known as 'the gold bugs', these were the men who controlled the richest gold mines in the world. By 1899, he had forged an unofficial pact with the firm Wernher, Beit & Co., the dominant mining house of the times. 'It was this secret alliance,' Pakenham suggested, 'that gave Milner the strength to precipitate the war.'[7]

Milner was not about to abandon his dreams and ambitions now because of the stubborn Paul Kruger. Kruger was caught in the middle of a tussle between Milner and Joseph Chamberlain, the colonial secretary and Milner's boss. While Chamberlain wanted Kruger to back down, Milner desired the war that would lead to annexation.[8]

On 31 May 1899, Milner met Kruger at what became known as the Bloemfontein Conference in the Free State capital, in an attempt to resolve the matter of the franchise for immigrants. It was here that Milner showed that although his and Chamberlain's strategies were at odds, the same tactics could serve both men.

Chamberlain was prepared to allow Milner to pressurise Kruger into stepping down. He knew that besides turning the political screw, Milner would argue that the best way to a peaceful settlement was through a show of military force. This dual approach would precipitate the war.[9]

The Bloemfontein Conference was the high commissioner's first step in damning Kruger. His strategy was to pitch his demands very low, and once he had lured Kruger into his deceptive schemes and into publicly seeking a settlement, he would turn the other screw until it became unbearable. The negotiations started on a Wednesday, but by the Saturday the two men were in a stalemate: Milner had failed to outwit Kruger, but he had not been outmanoeuvred himself.[10]

As Milner contemplated breaking off negotiations on the Sunday, a visibly emotional Kruger told him, with tears in his eyes, 'It is our country you want.' The accusation hit its mark and Milner ended the talks, declaring, 'This conference is absolutely at an end, and there is no obligation on either side arising from it.'[11]

The high commissioner realised that he had failed to frighten Kruger sufficiently enough to trap him. For his part, Kruger suspected that war would come. Indeed, he had been preparing for it, purchasing weapons and spreading the word that the independence of the Transvaal Republic was in danger.

On 11 October 1899, the Boers declared war.

War brings out the worst in everyone, and this war certainly brought out the worst in the British. The official British record of the Anglo-Boer War, *The History of the War in South Africa*, edited by General John Frederick Maurice and others, deliberately and conveniently kept silent about the full horror of British war crimes. According to Pakenham, 'All its political chapters were eliminated in draft by the Colonial Secretary, Alfred Lyttelton, for fear of offending the ex-enemy, the Boers – that is, for "fear of impeding the powers of reconciliation", as he recorded in a confidential minute. And, for fears of offending their friends, the War Office staff found it equally impossible to write frankly about many of the "regrettable incidents" which occurred in the war.'[12]

But the Afrikaners were not fooled. They knew the truth: not from hearsay, but from painful, first-hand experience. Their memories, which have subsequently been handed down from generation to generation, were constructed from their own very real pain and loss. Women and children had been forced off their farms. They had watched as their homesteads were looted and burnt to the ground. They had made the sad, humiliating journey to the concentration camps, where they were greeted by abject misery, hunger, disease, hopelessness and, for many thousands of them, death.

When the British realised the Boers could not be so easily defeated in skirmishes, they turned to other methods, scorched earth and concentration camps. The camps were used to strike at the men psychologically: that they could not protect, feed, see or save their immediate families emasculated them. The camps were akin to a death sentence. Of the over 60 000 inmates, about 28 000 Boer women and children were estimated to have died in British concentration camps.

And no one was immune. General Jan Smuts and his wife, Sybella, lost a sixteen-month-old son, Koosie, in August 1900 in a concentration camp. The last time Smuts saw the infant was on 4 June 1900, when he rode off to war, and he only got news of his son's death at the end of the year. Sybella didn't hear a word from her husband until June 1901.[13]

What happened in these camps was kept secret from the British public and Parliament. And it probably would have remained so but for a middle-aged English spinster named Emily Hobhouse, who arrived in Cape Town in December 1900. Little did she know that she was to become an eyewitness to atrocities, human rights abuses and cruelty.

On 24 January 1901, Hobhouse visited Bloemfontein as a member of the South African Women and Children Distress Fund to see first hand what the concentration camps were all about. The biggest was in the Free State and held 1800 people living in white bell-tents that stood out against the brown veld.

'The shelter was totally insufficient,' she reported. 'When the 8, 10 or 12 persons who occupied a bell-tent were all packed into it, either to escape from the fierceness of the sun or dust or rainstorms, there was no room to move, and the atmosphere was indescribable, even with duly lifted flaps. There was *no soap* provided. The water supplied would not go round. No kartels (bedsteads) or mattresses were to be had. Those, and they were the majority, who could not buy these things must go without. Fuel was scanty ... The ration was sufficiently small, but when ... actual amount did not come up to scale, it became a starvation rate.'[14]

In what foreshadowed the mass transportation of Jews by the Nazis during the Second World War, Hobhouse saw people crammed into cattle trucks, waiting to be taken to concentration camps. Hungry, cold and despairing, these wretches had no protection against the elements and were forced to share the trucks with animals. Hobhouse remembered 'frightened animals bellowing and baaing for food and drink, tangled up with wagons ... and a dense crowd of human beings'.[15] To her it was 'war in all its destructiveness, cruelty, stupidity and nakedness'.[16]

She compared the situation to 'a parish I had known at home of about 2000 people where a funeral was an event – and usually of an old person. Here some twenty-five people were carried away daily ... The full realization of the position dawned on me – it was a death-rate such as had never been known except in the times of the Great Plagues ... the whole talk was of death – who died yesterday, who lay dying today, who would be dead tomorrow.'[17]

Hobhouse's report to the South African Women and Children Distress Fund was published in Britain in June 1901, and circulated to all members of Parliament. It caused an uproar, and was discussed in an adjournment debate in the House of Commons, where it was revealed that a total of 61 127 people, white and black, were being held in concentration camps.

Abraham and Constand Viljoen's paternal grandmother, Andriesina Zezilia Viljoen, and her four children – daughters Andresina Cecilia and Magel Margaretha, and sons Francois and Andries – were among the thousands driven off their family farms. They were incarcerated in a concentration camp on the banks of the Vaal River in Standerton. Andriesina's husband, Abraham Carel Viljoen, was a farmer in the Standerton district. During the war he fought in the Standerton commando, a militia that distinguished itself as one of the most formidable Boer fighting units.

In the camp, Andriesina and her children would have lived in overcrowded straw huts owing to a shortage of tents. Even then the number of huts was not enough to house all the prisoners, who became weak from exposure, diseases and malnutrition. Because of the camp's proximity to the Vaal River, it was bitterly cold in winter, while summer was wet and rainy.[18]

It is believed that of the 2 983 prisoners said to have been interned there by the end of May 1901, 1 400 women and children died. Andriesina lost three of her four children: measles claimed seven-month-old Francois and five-year-old Margaretha, while sixteen-month-old Andresina also perished. Only Andries managed to survive along with his mother.

The Viljoens were not alone in their suffering. Near the site of the camp today is a commemorative plaque naming each of Magretha Swart's eight children who died in the Standerton concentration camp between 17 September and 5 October 1901: Johanna (age twelve), Antonie (one), Cornelis (six), Willem (ten), Jacob J. (three), Jacob N.

(three), Gerhardus (fourteen) and Heleje (fifteen). One cannot imagine what Magretha must have felt as one after the other, over a period of eighteen days, she buried her children. The Swart memorial is a reminder of the atrocities committed during the Anglo-Boer War, as well as an indicator of the heavy price exacted from Boer families.

I visited the cemetery in Standerton on two separate occasions. When I saw it for the first time, with Abraham Viljoen, it was neglected. It was also, incidentally, the first time that Abraham, who had been at high school in the town, was seeing it with the knowledge that he had relatives buried there. We did not know the exact location of the Viljoen children's graves, and as his gaze swept over the waist-high brown weeds obscuring the slate gravestones, his eyes misted over. Abraham stood there in silence and grief, thinking about what he did not know about his father's siblings and their tragic deaths, and wondering what it must have been like for those trapped in the camps, starving and diseased.

When he eventually spoke it was to say, 'When you are here and see these graves ... So many children died here. So many women ... Now you can understand why Constand has such strong feelings about the Anglo-Boer War and against the English.'

We had been planning to have a quick lunch after our visit, but the experience of being in that cemetery, where three small bodies lay in unmarked graves, numbed us. Food was the last thing we wanted. We needed solitude, and so we drove off enveloped in a deep sadness.

On my second visit, a veld fire had preceded me, burning away the weeds and blackening the soil. This time I, too, wondered about the graves and the secrets they held.

It is understandable that many who survived the concentration camps did not wish to talk about their experiences, but instead retreated into themselves, trapping their pain and memories, as they tried to hold themselves together. Abraham and Constand's father, Andries, did not share with his children that, contrary to what they believed, his parents had had six, and not three, children. It was a family secret that was only discovered when the Viljoen twins, by now in their seventies, read about it in a book tracing their family's genealogy.

Veldkornet Abraham Viljoen was captured near Drinkwater on 6 February 1900. He was taken to Green Point in Cape Town, where he was held until 11 April 1901, when he was put on the *Roslin Castle* and shipped to a prisoner-of-war camp in Ceylon (now Sri Lanka). The thirty-five-year-old farmer arrived in Ceylon on 24 April and was imprisoned at Bellary camp. It is not certain if he knew at the time that three of his four children had died in the concentration camp. In later years, he and his wife seldom talked about their wartime experiences in front of their children.

The establishment of the concentration camps was just one of the blows dealt to the Boers. As the tide began to turn in Britain's favour, some in their ranks switched sides. These traitor Boers were called joiners, and acted as scouts, guides and transport riders for the enemy. Among the 5 464 joiners was Piet de Wet, brother to the famous Boer general Christiaan de Wet.

The joiners' betrayal went deeper than any bullet could, into the core of the Afrikaner psyche, especially when it was reported that the despicable traitors were ill-treating Boer women and children. The problem was pervasive, with General Louis Botha at one point saying, 'There are men of our own kith and kin who are helping to bring us to ruin. If we continue the war, it may be that Afrikaners against us will outnumber our own men.'[19]

During the war, those convicted of being traitors by Boer military tribunals were executed, but pragmatism emerged after the conflict was over. 'We must be ready to forget and forgive,' said the acting president of the Transvaal Republic, Schalk Burger, referring to the joiners.[20]

After the war, in their efforts to unite their volk, Afrikaner leaders built on the myth of the heroic Boer fighters facing the mighty British Empire, and found it expedient to largely ignore the existence of the joiners who had carried arms for and sworn allegiance to the British Crown. Nurturing a growing Afrikaner nationalism was a priority, and so they chose to keep any Boer treachery from subsequent generations.

By May 1902, Britain's new tactics were having the desired effect and the Boers surrendered. They had various reasons for negotiating peace: some of their ranks were now fighting for the enemy; those Boer women and children not in concentration camps were at the mercy of Africans on their farms; the British were threatening to confiscate Boer land; and they could not keep British prisoners.[21] And so the war was brought to an end with the signing of the Treaty of Vereeniging on 31 May.

But not all Boers were amenable to surrender. Some hardliners, called bittereinders (bitter-enders), wanted to fight until the proverbial last bullet. In trying to persuade them otherwise, General Koos de la Rey said, 'Fight to the bitter end? Do you say that? But has the bitter end not come?'[22]

In the end, 22 000 bittereinders finally surrendered before leaving for the concentration camps to begin the grim task of finding their wives and children, not knowing whether they were alive, sick or buried. It was then back to the desolate ruins that had once been their farms to try to salvage some sort of life.

While it is generally accepted that some 28 000 Afrikaners died in the British concentration camps, no one knows the exact number.

What is known is that horrific atrocities, including rape, were committed there. Those who survived the war were ruined and demoralised. Their farmsteads were gone, their cattle, sheep and horses were dead, and their fields were desolate.

2

Out of the ashes

WHEN ABRAHAM CAREL VILJOEN returned to South Africa from Ceylon, he found a farm in ruins. He had also lost three children. But it appears that he had undergone a spiritual transformation while in prison and had developed a strong faith in God. This focused his mind on reconciliation, between Afrikaner and Afrikaner, and Afrikaner and English. The man who had taken up arms to defend the Transvaal and Free State republics was now a resolute agent for reconciliation.

'My grandfather was an extraordinarily religious person,' recalls his namesake and grandson, Abraham. 'I think he came to his deeply held religious beliefs in Ceylon. On the occasions when we slept over on their farm as children, I recall him getting up at about four in the morning to read his Bible and sing hymns. After his wife died he continued praising God every morning, singing psalms and hymns.'

Accounts of the old Boer's deep spiritual beliefs became legend in the district. Years after his death, some sangomas decided to dig up his grave under the cover of night and remove his remains to use in muti. They found that the tools they had brought along could not make an impression on the soil and left empty-handed. Later, a Viljoen relative encased the site in concrete to foil any other prospective grave robbers.

Despite losing the war, the Boers eventually gained political control of the country in 1910, when the Union of South Africa was formed. General Louis Botha, who had founded the political party Het Volk (People's Party) with General Jan Smuts in Pretoria in January 1904, was appointed the first prime minister of the Union.

It was a political settlement between whites. Blacks were not involved in the birth of the new country, neither as co-founders nor as citizens. They were a people not equal to whites, but one whose labour could be exploited. This political snub would come back to haunt the descendants of those whites in power in 1910.

It was a white man's world and blacks had to know their place, as the laws passed by successive white governments demonstrated. Between 1910 and 1948, when the National Party (NP) came to power, the Union Parliament passed a battery of laws that entrenched white rule and turned blacks into serfs: laws such as the Natives Land Act of 1913, which gave 13 per cent of the country to Africans and which would form the basis of the NP's homelands policy; and the Immorality Act of 1927, which criminalised sex across the colour line.[1]

In launching Het Volk, Botha was following through on his declaration during the peace talks that unity had to be forged between Afrikaners.[2] The party's prime objective was thus the reunion of Afrikanerdom.[3] To this end, in 1910, Het Volk and Boer resistance hero General James Barry Munnik Hertzog's Orangia Unie (Orange Union) merged with the Afrikaner Bond and Cape liberal John X. Merriman's South African Party. Although called the South African Party, the product of the merger was a new political formation with a fusion policy and the patriotic slogan 'South Africa First'.[4]

The slogan belonged to the new national minister of justice, Hertzog, who was 'the first to explicitly advocate a South African nationalism free from Britain's apron strings'.[5] But his was a narrow version of national unity, restricted to Afrikaans- and English-speaking white South Africans only.

As Jan Smuts was in favour of forming a united white front against black capitalism, the new coalition also sought to form an alliance between English capital and Afrikaner farmers. It was thus imperative that those cultural barriers separating whites came down.[6]

It would be more difficult than they imagined. The new party's leaders tried using age-old fears of black people to corral whites into unity, but they had underestimated the Afrikaners' rancour towards the British and ignored the lesson of the treachery within that had bedevilled the Boers during the war.

The coalition was short-lived, as Botha and Hertzog had a falling-out over the latter's virulent anti-British views. Hertzog, a champion of the concept of eie (ours), was perturbed by the policy of anglicisation and concerned that the cost to Afrikaners of conciliation would be too great. Despite their apparent political dominance, the Afrikaners were still a long way away from overcoming their cultural and economic disadvantages. In 1912, Hertzog repeatedly said from public platforms that 'South Africa is to be ruled by Afrikaners'.[7]

Prime Minister Botha could not ignore these inflammatory statements; they flew in the face of his policy of conciliation and challenged his political authority. He knew he had to act, and act decisively, with the authority that he carried if he was to survive as a political leader.

He asked Hertzog to resign, but when Hertzog refused, Botha fired him. At a South African Party congress held in Cape Town in November 1913, Hertzog lost to Botha in a vote that pitted general against general. Announcing that he was quitting the party, Hertzog walked out, taking General Christiaan de Wet with him.

In 1914, Hertzog formed the National Party. It was a watershed step that confirmed the fissures in Afrikanerdom and drastically changed the political landscape. Now there were two official political camps: Botha's Sappe, as members of the South African Party became known, and Hertzog's Nats.

Then, on 4 August 1914, the First World War broke out, further igniting the tensions among Afrikaners. They took up their guns once again, this time against one another over the question of loyalty to the Crown.

The inexperienced Union government had received a request from Great Britain for a military intervention in German South-West Africa. The government had to decide whether to support Britain and risk an Afrikaner revolt, or to remain neutral and risk the empire's displeasure as well as opposition from the English-speaking population.[8] Botha and Smuts resolved that Boer and Brit had made an honourable peace and should stand together, and so were not opposed to sending troops into the neighbouring German colony or wherever else the British military needed to be bolstered.[9] Parliament thus resolved in September 1914 to invade South-West Africa.

The decision by the two war heroes, Botha and Smuts, to side with the power that had so deeply humiliated Afrikaners was for some too bitter a pill to swallow. Memories of the Boer War and the pain and agony of the concentration camps were still fresh; so, too, was the anger at the loss of the two Boer republics. The poison that turns anger and disappointment into hatred and revolt once again seeped into the Afrikaner ranks, and brother turned against brother, comrade against comrade, bittereinder against bittereinder, war hero against war hero.

Generals who had once stood united against Britain were now being divided by their old enemy. With Botha and Smuts resolute in their decision to assist the Crown, four other generals and erstwhile comrades – Christiaan de Wet, Christian Beyers, S.G. 'Manie' Maritz and Jan Kemp – led an armed rebellion with 12 000 men.

The presence in the rebel lines of Maritz, who had served under Smuts in the Boer War, showed the severity of the split in the Afrikaner ranks. But the divisions cut deeper still. General Koos de la Rey, who had promised Botha he would remain neutral, was plotting an insurrection. It was he who had persuaded the commander-in-chief of the Union Defence Force, General Beyers, to resign and join the rebellion. In his letter of resignation, Beyers said that Britain had declared war in her own interests and that, while he was prepared to fight in defence of South Africa, he was sceptical of accusations of German barbarism, given the atrocities perpetrated by Britain during the Boer War.[10]

Smuts rebuffed him, writing simply: 'Botha and I are not men to desert England in this dark hour.'[11]

The 1914 Rebellion divided many Afrikaans families. The Mulder family was one such. Having sat in Paul Kruger's volksraad (people's council), the Mulders naturally took up arms against British imperialism in the Boer War. Freedom Front Plus MP Corné Mulder told me that his paternal grandfather and his grandfather's older brother, both of them bittereinders, had vowed at the end of the Boer War to exact revenge on Britain at the earliest opportunity.

When the opportunity presented itself in 1914, Pieter Mulder went to his older brother Frederik to remind him about their oath. Frederik replied with a short 'No'. The result was that Pieter became a rebel and Frederik fought for the Union government. The brothers spent each day on patrol in their different colours, and at night would meet on the family farm to discuss their opposing views.

Sometime during the rebellion, a government trooper was shot and killed. Pieter was accused, arrested and tried by a military court. He was found guilty and sentenced to death. He had spent six months in a cell at the Johannesburg Fort, waiting to be executed, when the man he had allegedly killed was found alive and well in South-West

Africa. Pieter appealed against his sentence and his alleged victim, an army deserter, was brought back to South Africa and appeared in court to prove that he was indeed alive. A relieved Pieter was released.

Pieter Mulder's son Connie continued the family tradition by becoming an NP cabinet minister. Connie's older son, Pieter, is current leader of the Freedom Front Plus and an MP. Due to parliamentary tradition, he sits next to his younger brother, Corné, in Parliament. They have sat in neighbouring parliamentary seats for twenty-five years.

Like the war before it, the rebellion had its martyrs, men who were eulogised for siding with the volk against the government. One was a young army captain named Joseph 'Jopie' Fourie, who joined the rebels without first resigning his commission. He was taken prisoner on 19 December 1914, charged with treason and court-martialled by a military court. Daniel François Malan, who would become prime minister in 1948, was among several Afrikaner leaders who pleaded with the government to spare Fourie's life, but there was to be no mercy. Attempts to get hold of Smuts, the then minister of defence, to plead for a stay of execution failed (this would be held and used against him for many years to come).

Fourie was executed by firing squad on 20 December 1914.[12] Facing the men who were about to shoot him, he made one final request that demonstrated his commitment to the cause: 'Do not shoot me in the face. I have a large Afrikaner heart.'[13]

The rebellion also claimed Koos de la Rey, a Boer War hero who had often faced death. De la Rey and Beyers encountered a police roadblock on their way to a meeting in Potchefstroom. The police opened fire on their car and De la Rey was killed. To this day no one knows for sure what happened and why, but the rebels believed it was an assassination.

Beyers died some while later. In an attempt to escape a battle near Bloemfontein, he tried to swim across the Vaal River and suffered a heart attack. And General De Wet, who was eventually captured in Kuruman and imprisoned with other ringleaders, lost his son Danie.

The insurrection, which started on 15 September 1914, was finally suppressed on 4 February 1915. With the rebellion put down, Botha travelled to Standerton, the location of his farm and the bedrock of support for his South African Party, to call on another old comrade, General Coen Brits, to be part of the leadership of the South African troops moving into South-West Africa. By the middle of 1915, the forces under the overall command of Botha had defeated the Germans.

Abraham Viljoen's young son Andries was in the army sent to South-West Africa, as were a lot of other men from the district. Their presence was a reflection of their support for the Standerton municipality's decision to pledge its allegiance to the Union government. When General Brits returned to Standerton after fighting in East Africa as part of the Allied forces, the mayor of Standerton and his council were at the train station to welcome him home.[14]

During the Great War, Smuts's star began to rise on the world stage. He became a member of the British War Cabinet and was praised by the leaders of the Empire that had once unleashed its war machine against his people. He was instrumental in the creation of the Royal Air Force and would later play a pivotal role in the formation of the United Nations and wrote the preamble to the UN Charter. Smuts and Botha were also part of the peace negotiations that resulted in the Treaty of Versailles.

For the two Boer generals, the peace process stirred up memories of their own defeat sixteen years earlier. Referring to the Treaty of Vereeniging, Botha wrote in a note on 28 June 1919, 'Today I remember the 31st day of May, 1902.'[15] Two months later, on 27 August 1919, he died of heart failure following an attack of Spanish influenza. Smuts returned to South Africa to bury his comrade and fellow reconciler, saying their friendship was 'as close together as it is ever given to men to become ... the largest, most beautiful, sweetest soul of all my land and days'.[16]

Smuts took over as prime minister of the Union, which put him at odds with Hertzog, who was promoting the growth of Afrikaner nationalism as opposed to the unity that Smuts desired. Hertzog was not impressed by Smuts's international acclaim and was waiting for a chance to kick sand in the new prime minister's face. His chance came when mineworkers went on strike in 1922 over several grievances, the main being that the Chamber of Mines was going to eliminate the colour bar. The Afrikaners were convinced that the capitalist English were using the blacks to get the better of them.[17] Strike leaders saw the industrial action as a clash between black and white, with whites having to defend their privileges. One of their banners read, 'Workers of the world unite and fight for a white South Africa.'[18] But for all the rhetoric, they were not communists or socialists; they were Afrikaners, poor whites really, demanding a better deal for themselves alone.

Aggrieved Afrikaners returned to their old fighting ways and began forming commandos. With most of the Witwatersrand in rebel hands by the first week of March, there were serious talks of forming a republic. But they underestimated the ruthless military figure of General Smuts, who declared martial law and employed the air force, tanks, cannons and machine guns to impose his iron will and secure the future of the Union. Government forces shot and killed at least two hundred rebels within ten days, snuffing out the revolt.

Smuts's triumph, however, was a double-edged sword: it was going to cost him Afrikaner support. 'He was being irrevocably associated with the Empire, but also with the capitalist structure of non-Afrikaner South Africa,' wrote Willem Abraham de Klerk in *The Puritans in Africa*.[19]

Before the 1924 general election and already under fire for being a traitor, Smuts was now accused by Hertzog of having hands dripping with Afrikaner blood.[20] These accusations resonated with Afrikaner voters, who used their ballots to boot Smuts out of power. The National Party formed a coalition with the Labour Party, a socialist party fighting the cause of white workers, and took over from Smuts's government. Hertzog became prime minister.

Smuts not only lost the national election, but his old constituency of Pretoria West turned its back on him as well. Hertzog magnanimously allowed a by-election in Standerton, where Smuts stood unopposed, and he was able to return to Parliament as leader of the opposition.

If Hertzog thought that his being in power would bring an end to the challenges faced by the Afrikaners and unite them, he was wrong. As prime minister he was confronted with a defeated people and a poor-white problem, caused in part by destitute rural Afrikaners moving to the cities. De Klerk wrote that those who made the journey left behind 'a considerable reservoir of rural poor: people who had lost not only the means but also the will to make a decent living, many of whom were, too, on their way to the cities'.[21]

A total of 17.5 per cent of Afrikaans-speakers lived in destitution. To them, the cities represented a new and somewhat frightening world, so different from their traditional society, which in any case had been shattered by the Boer War. According to De Klerk, 'The new immigrant Afrikaners were, in fact, strangers in their own country: hesitant, fearful of using their own language in shops and business, and confined very largely to the humbler areas and jobs.'[22]

While the likes of Smuts and Hertzog had been squabbling for power, a new player had quietly entered the political arena on 5 June 1918, at a meeting of fourteen men in the home of Danie du Plessis in the Johannesburg suburb of Malvern. That day, an organisation called Jong Suid-Afrika (Young South Africa) was born.

From its quiet beginning, Jong Suid-Afrika morphed into what we now know as the Afrikaner Broederbond (Afrikaner Brotherhood). Initially an open organisation, members resolved at a meeting on 26 August 1921 to turn it into a secret society, a decision that would transform the Broederbond into an elite Afrikaner alpha-male group, which would shape South African politics from behind the scenes until the end of apartheid.

A founder and former chairman of the Broederbond's executive committee and a former speaker of the whites-only South African Parliament, Henning Klopper, bragged at the organisation's jubilee festival in 1968: 'The years 1914 to 1917, culminating in the establishment of the Broederbond in 1918, were years of struggle for the Afrikaner, years of dissension, years of scattering (verstrooiing), years of frustration. This was the decade after the English war in which we were destroyed. But we felt that we could not remain lying down: by the grace we had to stand up.'[23]

In 1944, *Die Transvaler* reported: 'The Afrikaner Broederbond was born out of a deep conviction that the Afrikaner volk has been planted in this country by the Hand of God, destined to survive as a separate volk with its own calling.'[24] This was contained in a statement from Broederbond chairman J.C. van Rooy and secretary Ivan Lombard.

The Broederbond began dreaming of ruling South Africa back in 1921. Between 1922 and 1939, the organisation began surreptitiously inserting itself into every sector of Afrikaner society. In 1929, it orchestrated the formation of the Federasie van Afrikaanse Kultuurvereniginge (Federation of Afrikaans Cultural Associations).[25] It was turning into a formidable machine: whoever opposed the Broederbond had to be prepared for a battle. Their path to power involved meeting in secret, devising strategies to put their people in key positions and ruthlessly trampling whoever stood in their way.

By 1934, Hertzog and Smuts were back on speaking terms and merged the National Party and the South African Party to form the United Party, with Hertzog at the helm. Hertzog, however, did not manage to bring all his followers into the merger. In the Cape, D.F. Malan led eighteen other Cape National Party members in a revolt against the new party. These staunch Afrikaner nationalists formed the Gesuiwerde Nasionale Party (Purified National Party) and became the biggest opposition in 1934.[26]

By 1935, Hertzog was again pushing national unity (between whites, naturally) with his slogan 'South Africa First'. This time, the fusion policy of the two generals was proving to be a vibrant force in white South Africa.[27] But the political scene was changing and the Purified National Party, led by a younger generation of Afrikaners who were not committed to the Botha–Hertzog–Smuts vision of the Union of South Africa, began to take hold. This new breed took upon themselves the mantle of leading Afrikaners into a future quite different to the one heralded by Hertzog or Smuts.

Hertzog, who was disinclined to avoid taking on the new group, fired the first shots. Emboldened in his Linksfield constituency, he accused the Broederbond, of which Malan was a member, of Afrikaner jingoism, of believing God had chosen them to rule over others and of abusing their position in the teaching profession, where their members were filling young minds with political propaganda. He also accused the Broederbond and the Purified National Party of being one and the same. As far as he was concerned, the two organisations were bartering away the unity of Afrikanerdom for a Republican-cum-Calvinist union.

'Has the Afrikaner nation sunk to such hopeless depths that it must seek its salvation in secret conspiracy aimed at promoting race hatred, national disunity and civil war?' Hertzog asked. 'Is no higher goal, no nobler task, to be held up to the Afrikaner boy and girl than racial strife and disunity? Can our children attain no higher ideal than that of racial domination – of racial mastery?'[28]

Hertzog pointed his authoritative prime minister's finger at Malan: 'Any doubts that might thus far have lingered concerning the motives that impelled Dr Malan and his "purged" National Party to refuse their co-operation at the inauguration of a United Afrikaner nation are now finally dispelled, with the revelation of this secret association with the Afrikaner Broederbond and the secret conspiracy between the Broederbond and the "purged" National Party. The purged National Party, with its "purged" leaders, now stands forth openly in all its racial nakedness, adorned with only one fig leaf: SECRECY.'[29]

Hertzog's disgust with the National Party (or NP, as the Purified National Party was now known) was an open declaration of war, but he underestimated his opponents and their lust for power. His status as war hero, prime minister and Afrikaner leader was not enough to keep the NP and Broederbond dogs of destruction at bay. In 1938, when the Broederbond used the Afrikaanse Taal en Kultuurbond (Afrikaans Language and Cultural Board) to organise a symbolic ox-wagon trek to commemorate the centenary of the Great Trek, Hertzog was snubbed. His exclusion from the celebrations was a rebuff that laid bare the schism in Afrikanerdom.

The advent of the Second World War a year later strained Afrikaner unity even further, as the age-old question of whether or not to side with Britain reared its head. It was déjà vu as Hertzog and Smuts clashed over the question of South Africa's neutrality. On Monday 4 September 1939, in front of a packed public gallery, Hertzog tabled a motion in Parliament calling for South Africa to remain neutral. Smuts put forward his own motion: to go to war.

A long and heated debate raged until nine o'clock that night, when the bells finally rang and the votes were counted. The atmosphere was tense and heavy with anticipation – the outcome of the ballot would decide not only whether South Africa would go to war, but also the political futures of the two role players. Eventually the result was announced: Hertzog had been defeated, eighty to sixty-seven.

'We had won by a majority of thirteen,' wrote Deneys Reitz, author of *Commando*. 'It is possible that General Hertzog might have secured a small majority had it not been for his blundering tactics in eulogizing Hitler and had it not been for the forceful and powerful speech by General Smuts.'[30]

There was no gloating; Smuts had won, but the significance of what that meant was beginning to sink in. 'We felt it was too grave a crisis for noisy demonstrations and now all the Members filed out, most of them deep in thought, for the full significance of what had taken place had scarcely come home to them as yet,' Reitz recalled. 'Firstly, it meant we were at war with Germany and that we might soon be at war with the Italians.'[31]

It was the end for Hertzog, who resigned as prime minister. After negotiations with other parties, Smuts reported on 6 September that he had formed a government and that he would be prime minister once more. Reitz was made deputy prime minister and minister of native affairs.

Futile attempts were made to reconcile Hertzog with NP leader Malan, and Hertzog eventually resigned as an MP on 11 December 1940. He retired to his farm, where he lived out his life alone, broken, rejected by his people. 'In his woodcutter's jacket he was to be seen at times on horseback riding through the warm veld of his large estate,' wrote De Klerk. 'Then again he would be seen giving instructions to one of his black farm workers. Then one would discover him, a thin and lonely figure, standing among the thorn trees.'[32] He died on 21 November 1942, two years after resigning his parliamentary seat.

3

Early politics of the Viljoen family

Andries Viljoen was no stranger to death. He was familiar with the tears and heart-wrenching sobs of grieving mothers, wives and siblings. By the time he was eight years old he had seen enough death and shared in far too much grief for one so young. He had looked on helplessly as his three siblings died in front of their heartbroken mother in the Standerton concentration camp. He knew about fear, hunger, pain, extreme cold and secrets. Experience had taught him that 'measles' was the name for a disease that killed many. He also knew about responsibility in the absence of a soldier father.

For Andries, freedom did not necessarily bring opportunity: he was still a prisoner of sorts, even after he had been liberated from the camps. The young boy wanted to be a teacher, but in a country slowly recovering from a war, and in a community ruined by extreme poverty, he bottled up his dream, just as his family did with their wartime experiences. His reality was working hard to rebuild a farm and to become a farmer.

After surviving a war and prison camps, Abraham and his family were now free to start a new life. They moved to a new farm, Potfontein, between Standerton and Volksrust in the Standerton district, where they had quite esteemed neighbours. As part of the reprisals, the British had torched Louis Botha's farm in Vryheid, Natal. Instead of returning, he relocated to the Eastern Transvaal, where he bought the farm Rusthof, located some twelve kilometres from the Viljoen homestead. The neighbours became close friends. General Coen Brits was also living nearby.

Post-war Standerton fervently supported the political ideologies of Botha and Jan Smuts, and was a staunch South African Party town. Boer War generals and heroes felt at home there, grateful for the large support base.

Andries received a solid Christian grounding from his parents, who were members of the Dutch Reformed Church. Being deeply spiritual, his father was particularly active in his church. Going to services on weekends was the highlight of Abraham's week. He would diligently clean and polish his cart, brush his two black horses, hitch them to the cart and set off for church. He could often be found there on Saturday afternoons, Saturday nights, Sunday mornings (for Holy Communion) and Sunday afternoons. It was his custom to never miss a Communion service.

Andries's mother, Andriesina, died on 9 September 1924. 'I think she took a knock in the concentration camp,' reasons her grandson Abraham, who never got the chance to meet her. 'It must have been traumatic and heartbreaking for a woman alone in a concentration camp to lose three of her four children. She must have suffered from post-traumatic stress, of which little was known then.'

Abraham never remarried, remaining a widower for thirty-one years until his death on 17 August 1955. Andriesina and Abraham are buried next to each other on their old farm, Potfontein.

In adulthood, Andries married Geesie Maria Kotze. They had three children: a set of twin boys and a daughter, Sannetta. The boys were born on 28 October 1933; Abraham arrived a few minutes before his brother, Constand. To this day Constand calls him Boeta, that warm, endearing Afrikaans term meaning 'older brother'. The younger generations call Abraham 'Oom Boeta' (Uncle Boeta).

The boys were named for their grandfathers: Abraham Carel after the Boer soldier who had been imprisoned in Ceylon, and Constand Laubscher after Geesie's father.

Andries settled the family on the farm Koppie Alleen (Lonely Hill), between Perdekop and Standerton. 'My father called it Toekoms [Future],' Abraham tells me. 'That name must give you an idea of the angst he must have felt in the concentration camps. He was a mere eight-year-old boy when he was imprisoned in a concentration camp. He was surrounded by death, starvation and sickness. My poor father went through a lot in that camp.'

Andries was a successful farmer, according to his son, and he was an avid newspaper reader, philosopher and loyal follower of Botha and Smuts. The Viljoen children grew up in a household steadfast in the politics of the Boer generals. As a sign of his loyalty to Botha, Andries remained for many years the secretary of Standerton's Louis Botha Memorial Committee, formed after the statesman died from a heart attack in Pretoria on 27 August 1919. The committee would meet annually on Botha's birthday to commemorate his life and contribution to South Africa.

Although the Afrikaners were leading the country, they were not doing well economically. These were hard times, marked by severe drought and poverty. While the twins were too young to fully appreciate their surroundings, others, like Marie Barnard, remember all too well the effects of the drought of 1932/33. Marie, now ninety-one years old, still cries when she relives those years. Her father, Petrus Haasbroek, farmed mielies on his farm, Petrusville, near the town of Viljoenskroon in the Orange Free State. She still sees her father looking up at the heavens every morning for just the tiniest sign of rain, only to be greeted by a wide blue sky. Shaking his head, he would return indoors. Marie still pictures him desperately putting poles across the backs of his oxen, tying brown sacks around them and over the cattle's shoulders in a vain bid to keep them upright. It did not help: the animals all died.

Her mother, Saartjie, was tasked with inventing ways to feed the family. When the cattle died, there was no milk. Mielie-meal porridge became a staple food. Saartjie would allow some of it to cool down and harden to use as a substitute for bread. Pork fat was used as a spread.

There were no bed sheets in the Haasbroek home from which to make clothing, and so Saartjie would wash the white mielie sacks in hot water, cut them to different patterns and sew them together as undergarments for her children.

The effects of the drought stayed even when the rains eventually came. 'It gave me an inferiority complex,' Marie admits sadly. 'When you lived on a farm, you had nothing. The children who were living in the town had parents who were working. They could afford to buy fruit. When you're in town and you see these children eating oranges and throwing the orange peels away, you do the simple thing of picking up these peels. It wasn't to smell them: it was to eat them. I still have that inferiority complex. It has stayed with me. I don't mix freely. Once you've been through experiences like that, you're a bit withdrawn.'

By the time the Viljoen twins were of schoolgoing age, the drought had come to an end. 'Every morning when the frost spread itself like a cold white sheet over the veld, we were out long before we had to leave for school and with shouts of "hoi, hoi",' recalls Abraham with a smile. 'Constand and I had to collect our oxen, about fourteen of them. We hitched them to the plough, ready and waiting for my father to put them to work.'

Making the oxen stand in two lines, the boys put the yokes on the animals' necks to ensure that they pulled as a team. Although the oxen were castrated bulls, occasionally one would display some fire. 'Sometimes you'd find a very obstinate animal which would fight, break the yoke and run off. We called these angry oxen jukskeibrekers [yoke-breakers]. In my life I was often called a jukskeibreker,' Abraham adds ruefully.

Both Abraham and Constand found their first day of primary school traumatic: leaving the farm, sitting in a classroom with strangers. But at least they were together, as they would be throughout their school career. After primary school, it was off to Standerton High School as boarders, at a time when the Broederbond was embarking on a campaign of indoctrination in the schools. At Standerton High School there was a history teacher who seldom taught history, but instead preyed on young minds, arousing their fears, stirring racial hatred, planting seeds of Afrikaner racial superiority and warning of the swart gevaar (black peril) on the mineral-rich Witwatersrand.

'Because of the Broederbond we were subjected to a continued and relentless barrage of indoctrination,' remembers Abraham. 'They ensured that the right people, their people, were appointed as principals and teachers. This wasn't to encourage the freedom of being an independent thinker: this was part of a concerted campaign to influence young minds. One of the biggest injustices a child can suffer is not to be taught in the classroom what the freedom to think independently means.'

Although a strict parent who did not take any nonsense, Andries was extremely patient with his children, and left disciplinary measures to his wife. When the Second World War broke out in 1939, he wanted to serve, but his fifty-five years were against him. He became a medic in the South African Medical Service instead, and was stationed in Cullinan, leaving Geesie to keep the farm going.

As with his father, religion played an anchoring role in Andries's life. A deep-thinking Christian, he did not believe in the apartheid ideology that the National Party and the Broederbond were propagating. 'My father was an independent thinker who never accepted the ideology of apartheid,' Abraham says. 'If it weren't for my parents, I would probably have been a nationalist.'

But Andries was not sentimental like his father, and he did not think religious ministers inhabited a higher plane than everyone else. He simply expected ministers to preach and live according to the Word of God, and leave politics to the politicians. One of his relatives, Eric van Heerden, was in the air force and had been called up to fight in Italy in the Second World War. Like all other soldiers, Van Heerden wore a red emblem on his arm to show that he was a serviceman. Before he left for the front, he asked the Dutch Reformed Church, which as a Nazi sympathiser was vehemently against the war, to baptise his infant daughter Cynthia. The minister refused, in accordance with the church's decision not to allow soldiers to attend church services. Cynthia was baptised in the Anglican Church and Andries did not forget the slight to his kinsman.

Years later, in peacetime, the same minister, well known for his nationalist sympathies, was doing huisbesoek (home visits). 'The old minister was a mild-mannered man,' recalls Abraham. 'He took his Bible and read a beautiful piece. He also gave us a good little sermon. When he was finished he said, "Andries, will you please say a prayer for us?" My father was so obstinate. He said, "Dominee, please do your own work."'

The incident stayed with young Abraham: 'I realised that a minister was a human being like me. If he didn't do his work in accordance with God's word, then you must stand up and tell him he's talking nonsense. I remember that in those days he was the all-knowing minister and one didn't dare contradict him. He was the bearer of God's word. That's not how my father saw it. Later, just like I would do in my own life, my father stopped going to church. In the years before his death, I'd sometimes find him in a corner quietly reading his Bible.'

Andries died suddenly in 1947, a year before the NP – on the back of racist election rhetoric warning about the dangers of a black majority – would claim the spoils in a whites-only poll and Standerton would unceremoniously part ways with its parliamentary representative, Jan Smuts.

Abraham, barely a teenager, was working nearby on the day his father died: 'It happened on a Saturday morning. He was busy in the barn looking for nuts and screws. He was sitting down and just keeled over. He had hypertension and suffered a brain haemorrhage. There was no bleeding, he just fell over. I wasn't with him. I was nearby when I heard one of our workers saying, "Hau baas! Hau baas!" I ran over to them and found my dad had collapsed.

'I was in Standard 7 [Grade 9] when my father died. From that moment until her death in 1990, my mother remained a single parent and raised us. I have a lot of respect for her. You know, it was sad, her raising three children on her own.'

But during the war years, when she had kept up the farm and raised the children single-handedly, Geesie had shown that she was a woman with a strong will and character. Like her widowed father-in-law, she never remarried.

A teacher, Geesie was an articulate person. The Kotze family was also firmly in favour of the South African Party and Jan Smuts.

The family had lived in Standerton before Geesie's father, Constand Laubscher Kotze, relocated them to Wonderfontein in the Middelburg region. The move, done by ox-wagon, was a test of character: disaster hit on the trail when a fire destroyed the wagon and everything in it. 'They were wiped out,' says Abraham. But undeterred and unbroken, the Kotzes settled on the farm Nooitgedacht. 'Up to today our family talks with admiration about that disaster and how determined Constand Kotze and his family were to make it.'

While Constand Kotze was not a political person, he dismissed the National Party as humbugs. A self-made man admired for being hard-working, he told his daughter after her husband's death: 'My child, you must teach your children to work hard.' Geesie did just that, instilling her father's work ethic and habit of rising early in his grandchildren.

'Even now, Constand and I follow his philosophy,' says Abraham. 'We're still farming: up early in the morning to do what has to be done.'

In 1951, Geesie moved her children to Pretoria so that Abraham and Constand could attend the military gymnasium there and eventually Pretoria University. 'My mother couldn't afford to pay residence fees,' recalls Abraham. 'We moved and lived at home. We'd kept the farm. Initially I tried to keep a hand on it while studying. It was all too much and this arrangement didn't work well. We sold the farm in the 1960s.'

But like their father and grandfathers, the brothers were born farmers. They loved the land, its smells and sounds, and they enjoyed the feel of approaching rain and working with their hands. It was an occupation to which they would both return in later life. Constand Viljoen recalls a vow he made to himself as his father was being laid to rest: 'I promised myself that some day I would be a farmer like him.'

Abraham still misses Andries: 'You know, in later years when I experienced that narrowness of the National Party way of thinking,

I started to miss him. I remembered what he had taught us and what he had said. There are still so many things I wanted to ask him. One's not very articulate at age fourteen.'

However, he is not certain that his father would have been in favour of his decision to become a man of the cloth: 'I don't think my father would have wanted me to become a minister of religion.' But his grandfather Abraham was overjoyed: 'My grandfather was still alive when I decided to study theology. For him it was the cherry on top that one of his grandsons was planning to become a minister. I can't recall if I told him in person about my plans. News like this travels fast. I know that he was happy with my decision.'

Sometime later, when old Abraham was on his deathbed, the family gathered around him to listen to a church service being aired on state radio, which, like the country, had fallen under the control of the NP and the Broederbond.

'I switched on the radio,' recalls Abraham. 'The oubaas [old man] was lying on his bed. We were sitting on chairs around his bed listening to the service. Now you have to listen carefully if you want to understand the impact of the religious straitjacket put on Afrikaners at the time. The minister, I recall his name was G.J.J. Boshoff, was performing on air. He began pontificating about the white doubting Thomases with black hearts. He was talking nonsense.

'Not one of us got up to turn off the radio. Why not? We were listening to the Word of God being delivered by the minister of God. That's the way in which we were reared then. We didn't challenge.'

Koos Greyling, married to the dying man's daughter, was among those listening to the sermon being given by Boshoff, a Dutch Reformed Church minister notorious for using the pulpit to smear and vilify any political opponents to the current regime. This particular minister usually preached Sunday sermons on air just before an election, in a show of brazen electioneering by the NP and the Broederbond as they sought to monopolise the airwaves and snare listeners with emotional rhetoric that railed against the South African Party and warned about the swart gevaar. They knew that heightened fear was an effective psychological weapon that would trigger thousands of white Afrikaners to vote NP at the polls.

When the sermon was over, young Abraham got up, walked to the radio and switched it off. 'While I was doing this, my uncle Koos Greyling looked at me. He stared at me for a long time. Then he said, "If you ever preach a sermon like that, I'll beat you up."' Oubaas Viljoen died shortly afterwards.

Greyling's blunt warning was an admission that the lines separating church and state had disappeared as far as the NP, the Broederbond and the Dutch Reformed Church were concerned. Nineteen-fifties South Africa was vastly different to the era that he and Abraham senior had been born into. The NP and the Broederbond were now working meticulously with a single-mindedness that would surprise even Smuts.

In the years before he died, the church that Abraham so loved had been seduced and politicised. 'Afrikaner politics was slowly but fatally being theologised,' wrote Willem de Klerk. 'It is not correct to say that the Dutch Reformed Church was (or became) the National Party at prayer. It is more correct to say that the National Party itself was becoming, if not a church, then a party imbued with religion – a secular religion – at its roots.'[1]

This seduction was, of course, a deliberate tactic used by the NP to win over the hearts and minds of Afrikaners to the policy of segregation.

'The fact that the Afrikaans churches were speaking out against integration and the mixing of white and non-white blood proved to be great moral support,' wrote Andries Treurnicht in his *Credo van 'n Afrikaner*. 'By the way, the petition with the most signatures in support of it ever presented to Parliament had a quarter of a million signatures, was delivered in 1939 and called for a separation between whites and non-whites, as well as a ban on mixed marriages. Leading this drive was another kerkman [clergyman], Father Kestell.'[2]

Kestell, a Free State churchman, found his call that ''n volk red homself' (a people saves itself) resonated in the hearts of those Afrikaners targeted by the NP.[3] In 1932 he penned a few newspaper articles, saying that his solution to the poor-white question was 'saamwerk, helpmekaar en redmekaar' (cooperation, helping one another and saving one another).[4]

Plucking emotional chords and exploiting links to the past were things that men of religion such as Dutch Reformed Church minister D.F. Malan well understood. Speaking at the centenary commemoration of the Great Trek on 16 December 1938, Malan touched on the Battle of Blood River and the Afrikaners' glorious victory over the Zulus. The commemoration, which deliberately excluded Louis Botha, was a harbinger signalling that the pungent divisions among Afrikaners could not be wished away. It was also a foretaste of how callously the NP would deal with political opponents, despite their shared language and past.

Under Prime Minister Smuts, segregation was not an official government policy, but the NP was promising to officially introduce it to South Africa when it came to power. It would become known throughout South Africa and the world as apartheid, one of the most reviled policies of racial segregation in the twentieth century.

When Malan began to use the word 'apartheid' in 1943, he was not out of kilter with the rest of his Broederbond cronies. The young Afrikaner rebels were serious about changing the political landscape and shaping it around their own ideology. They had newspapers like *Die Burger* and *Die Transvaler*, staffed by fellow believers, championing and spreading their ideas. Malan and his inner circle were influenced by talk of racial purity and white superiority that had blown over from Nazi Germany, and they had learnt from the Nazis the immense value of first ploughing minds before planting seeds in well-prepared beds.

Religion was just one of the tools of the trade. The volk was being carefully prepared for the new policy, seduced into believing that apartheid was advocated in the Bible and that it was their God-given duty to look after the black races in South Africa. In 1944, a volkskongres (people's congress) resolved that it was in the interests of the white and non-white populations that a policy of apartheid be followed so that each of the non-white groups could develop according to its own characteristics and gain full control over its own affairs in its own areas; that 'it is the Christian duty of the whites to act as guardians over the non-white races until such time as they have reached the level where they can look after their own affairs'.[5]

Later, with the Dutch Reformed Church and the NP now walking hand in hand, another volkskongres on race relations, held in Bloemfontein in July 1947 under the aegis of the church, resolved that should there be sufficient scriptural grounds for the policy of apartheid, there would be no need to concede to any arguments from opponents.

Opposition to Smuts during the Second World War was coming not only from the nationalists and the Dutch Reformed Church, but also from other anti-British, right-wing, racist and violent quarters in the Afrikaner community. The Afrikaner Party, the intensely pro-Nazi Oswald Pirow and his New Order, and the paramilitary Ossewabrandwag were all united in their dislike for the prime minister who was being fêted in Britain.

Dr Hans van Rensburg, leader of the Ossewabrandwag, was posturing as a man of action, one prepared to fight for his ideals, rather than a cultural firebrand (in other words, he was no 'softie'). His message went down well in a community to which war was not alien. With this rabid racist at the helm, spitting fire on receptive minds, the Ossewabrandwag became the most important of the anti-war forces, with an estimated membership of 300 000 by 1941.[6]

Van Rensburg was dismissive of parliamentary politics, outrageously claiming that as the only mass-based organisation representing Afrikaners, the Ossewabrandwag was their legitimate representative. The organisation was agitating for a German victory in the war because it would lead to an Afrikaner republic, loyal to the Nazis. And like the Nazis it so admired and imitated, it had its own stormtroopers, the Stormjaers, an elite paramilitary wing involved in sabotage and assassinations.[7]

Men who would later rise to the apex of Afrikaner politics were to be found in the colours of the Ossewabrandwag, proudly espousing its ideology. Lawyer and future prime minister John Vorster was assistant chief commandant and was among the 723 Afrikaners that Smuts had interned at Koffiefontein in 1942 for their involvement with the group. The organisation and its policies also found traction among Dutch Reformed Church ministers and teachers. Hendrik Verwoerd, the editor of *Die Transvaler* and the architect of apartheid (and another future prime minister), was also a fan.

Ossewabrandwag members trained in secret under cover of darkness, becoming proficient in bombs, sabotage and 'other subversive acts quite foreign to the normal character of our Afrikaans people'.[8] Their intention, wrote Deneys Reitz, 'was to prepare an organization modelled on the Nazi system which would take control the moment the word came that Great Britain was crushed'.[9]

The rage within the Afrikaner community and the growing belief that Smuts had sold them out went unnoticed by the prime minister and his colleagues. High on hubris, they naively believed they were in touch with Afrikaner sentiments and that in the long run (white) Afrikaans-speaking citizens were too level-headed to be permanently led astray by this kind of alien propaganda.

It was not that no one warned Smuts about the Broederbond and the systematic way in which it was spreading its tentacles. His military intelligence advisors had cautioned him in a report that the need for action was urgent because of the organisation's influence on the war effort and on South African public life. 'If we are to dwell together in peace and amity in South Africa, the Broederbond must be destroyed,' the report warned ominously.[10]

But the prime minister procrastinated until, finally, in December 1944, he used the emergency powers embodied in his office to purge the civil service of Broederbond members. Laying down the law, Smuts said that civil servants could remain in the employ of the state and continue to enjoy all the perks that went with it, but not as Broederbond members. Continued loyalty to the Broederbond would invite dismissal. The ultimatum saw 1 094 civil servants resign from the Broederbond, but it was too little too late, a fact that Smuts himself would later admit.[11]

As World War II neared its end and an Allied victory over Germany was imminent, debate about the Broederbond reached Parliament. On 21 March 1945, Smuts felt emboldened to condemn the organisation as dangerous, saying it was built on a foundation in conflict with the interests of South Africa. He accused the Broederbond of being un-Afrikaans (but not of being anti-black) and cautioned that the Union government might have to ban it. Of course, by the 'interests of the country', Smuts was talking about white South Africa only.

Dr Eben Dönges, vice-president of the Broederbond, rose to reply. Somewhat hypocritically, given the NP's subsequent disregard and contempt for the rule of law, he charged that Smuts was in conflict with the fundamental principles of justice, and that his actions against the Broederbond amounted to an offence against racial peace. (Lest there be any confusion, Dönges was talking expressly about peace between Afrikaans- and English-speaking white South Africans, and the principles of justice were those that applied to whites, as there were different principles for blacks.)

Dönges claimed that since 1939 Smuts had acted in the interests of one race only, white English-speakers. He accused the man who had ridden with the commandos against the British during the Anglo-Boer War of being driven by a group in his party to destroy everything that could be construed as being Afrikaans. He charged the statesman who had once held the trust of the last Transvaal Republic president, Paul Kruger, of being a follower of Alfred Milner, that much-despised former British high commissioner to southern Africa.

'Like his spiritual predecessor, Milner, it is apparently his object today to break Afrikanerdom,' announced Dönges. 'I am a young man and I say this with the respect due to the Prime Minister's age and experience, that if he wishes to follow Milner's road ... he is on the road that leads to a dishonourable grave to which he will descend unhonoured and unwept by all Afrikaans-speaking and English-speaking people who perceive in racial peace the only future for South Africa. This injustice to the Afrikaans-speaking people can only make them stronger, the immoral exercise of the authority of the State towards its officials will only be temporary; the crime of the Prime Minister is that he has dealt a blow at the future of South Africa.'[12]

Dönges's forked tongue showed how much he had learnt from the Nazis he so fervently admired. Pushing a lie about Smuts was all part of the nationalists' propaganda war. In 1943 the NP had moved to the top of the leadership pile of formal Afrikaner politics, having overwhelmed the Ossewabrandwag and the New Order at the polls. By 1945 it was the only Afrikaner nationalist party in Parliament, as well as the only party ordained by Afrikaner voters to represent their interests. These developments, coupled with Dönges's threats, were ominous. The warning signs, that Smuts would be involved in a fight to the finish at the polls, were clear.

The National Party used the bitterness and anger at the prime minister that was sweeping through Afrikaner ranks to subvert him. The imprisonment of those opposed to South Africa fighting on Great Britain's side in the war looked much like the concentration-camp measures that Smuts himself had opposed more than three decades before.

Although admired internationally, Smuts somehow failed to see the fundamental remodelling of Afrikanerdom that was happening under his very nose. The Second World War had brought a definitive end to the traditional Afrikaner way of life, as people streamed to the cities in search of jobs. By 1947 the majority of Afrikaners were urbanised, and they held onto their Afrikaner identity, burning with a new nationalism fed by their anger at being in 'foreign areas'. Fear of the unknown and of having to compete for work with a growing black proletariat was another major source of bitter resentment among white Afrikaners, one that made them receptive to the venomous propaganda churned out by the likes of the NP and the Broederbond.

The Broederbond recognised in the mines and trade unions a rich vein that could be exploited for support: here were votes that could propel the National Party to victory in parliamentary seats that had become vacant on the Witwatersrand, an area that was fast becoming the economic centre of the Union.

Die Transvaler published a draft constitution for a future republic, written by a group of young Afrikaner intellectuals who represented the emerging voice of nationalism in Afrikaner politics. This draft constitution was their vision for the utopia that they planned for Afrikaners if the National Party ousted Smuts. 'It enshrined the Afrikaner Dream; a complete restoration of the old Republican Order, but with additions,' wrote De Klerk. 'The world of the city, with its manifold phenomena inimical to the true Afrikaner heritage, would be restructured in terms of the "traditional Calvinistic" world-view of the Afrikaners. The non-whites would firmly but justly be returned to their stations.'[13]

While this vision must have seemed idyllic to white Afrikaners, it was not so for the non-white majority. But Smuts remained preoccupied with happenings abroad and paid little heed to the rumblings in his own backyard. Afrikaner nationalism, a completely different beast from the South African nationalism that he was advocating, was on the rise and marching to the Broederbond tune. It was a song of radical reconstruction to a world that had become alien and intolerable.

As Smuts was to discover, De Klerk wrote, 'Even if the life-style of the platteland had been left behind, there was more than one way of expressing group loyalty, or of expressing group-dread of submersion. Blood still walked where it could not creep.'[14]

'Nationalism,' pontificated Dr Nico Diederichs, professor of political philosophy at the University College of the Orange Free State, 'finds its final justification and anchoring in the religious beliefs that the very ground of the being of a nation is in the will and love of God; that my love for my nation is part of my loving duty towards God.'[15]

And so with God on their side and seemingly in favour of their racial purity, the nationalist behemoth marched on Parliament.

Smuts, meanwhile, strutted on a fawning international stage, appearing in London, the heart of the British Empire, to sit on the War Cabinet and be made a British field marshal. 'Far greater issues claimed his attention,' noted De Klerk. 'What was happening in the laager of nationalist Afrikanerdom had become irrelevant. The world was moving towards a new era and he, Smuts, would play a part in it.'[16] He was a founding member of the League of Nations; Winston Churchill sought his approval on all major decisions; he was internationally respected; he was the most famous and admired South African.

In 1947 Smuts, who had built his policies on the philosophy of holism, was at his zenith. Never in his wildest dreams could he have imagined that the Empire that he had fought against would one day adore him as a respected statesman, soldier, philosopher and intellectual. He dazzled people with his wisdom and ideas. He was a star. White English-speaking South Africans adored him and applauded his self-appointed mission to keep South Africa loyal to the Crown.

His great deeds were rewarded later that year when King George VI, accompanied by Queen Elizabeth and their two daughters, princesses Elizabeth and Margaret, paid a royal visit to South Africa. Smuts proudly showed them around the country that so supported the monarchy. His mind occupied by the royal presence, and driven to dizzy heights by the world's adulation, the prime minister was further blinded to developments at home.

'At the start of the tour, Smuts was formally presented by the King with the Order of Merit. It seems to be the crowning honour in his career,' mused De Klerk. 'When the Royal Family eventually returned to Britain, Smuts and those around him were warmly confident that South Africa had been secured for a larger cause than the parochial politics of the nationalist Afrikaners. This indicated exactly Smuts's loss of contemporary sense.'[17]

Sense would not be all Smuts lost. Standerton had given him another chance in Parliament after his bitter defeat in Pretoria West in 1924. His return had paved the way for his role in the global theatre of war. But Standerton, ancestral home of the Viljoen family, would take it all away.

In 1948, a year after the royal visit and three years after the German surrender, white South Africa went to the polls. Years of fairly unhindered preparation – spent spreading the ideology of Afrikaner supremacy, popularising the policy of apartheid and painting Smuts as a traitor – finally paid off as the National Party roared to power in the election. Incontrovertible proof that the Afrikaner electorate had rejected the general and his United Party came from Standerton: on 26 May 1948, Smuts lost to Wentzel Christoffel du Plessis, once private secretary to General Hertzog.

If Smuts's unseating was good for the Nats, it was honey for Du Plessis, who, as head of the division of diplomatic and consular affairs, had been one of two senior civil servants fired by the government for refusing to resign from the Broederbond in February 1945.

Du Plessis had been tried in a disciplinary hearing held in his old office in the Union Buildings in Pretoria. He admitted to being a Broederbond member, refused to resign from the organisation and was found guilty of the specified offence. Spurned, humiliated and forced out of the civil service, Du Plessis had begun to plot his revenge. The Broederbond gave him the opportunity in 1948, and he needed little encouragement to lead a campaign that would give the colossus Smuts the biggest humiliation of his political career.

Somewhat disbelievingly, Smuts said afterwards, 'to think that I have been beaten by the Broederbond'.[18]

Like the rest of the Boer generals who had been active in politics since the Treaty of Vereeniging, Smuts had failed to heed the prophetic words of General Koos de la Rey, spoken shortly after the Union of South Africa was formed in 1910: 'Noudat ons nie meer teen die Kaffers en die Engelse hoef te veg nie, sal ons sekerlik onder mekaar begin stry.' (Now that we don't have to fight the Kaffirs and the English, we will surely begin to argue among ourselves.)[19]

The internecine conflict – ultimately a clash between the ideology of uniting white South Africa in a common nationhood on the one hand and the nationalists' insistence on a country for Afrikaners governed by Afrikaners on the other – saw D.F. Malan gain seventy seats in Parliament in 1948. Together with Nicolaas Christiaan Havenga's Afrikaner Party, which had nine seats, he formed a government. With only sixty-five seats, the United Party was relegated to the position of the largest opposition and Smuts was replaced as the top dog of South African parliamentary politics for the last time.

It was a significant result: Standerton had bolted and was now a National Party stronghold. The message was clear: Malan's party of Afrikaner baasskap (domination), white superiority and apartheid was now in power and South Africa would change.

'Atlas had stumbled, because he could no longer watch the ground under his feet,' wrote De Klerk of the fallen general. 'What he had been supporting for so long now lay in ruins before him. The country that Smuts had served so long had suddenly, almost without warning, rejected him.'[20]

Smuts rejected a lifeline thrown his way by Havenga, who made it known after the election that he would split from the Nats. Smuts was adamant that he was not prepared to work with a man he called a fascist.

The new political order was harsh on Smuts's followers, cutting them off from power and purging them from the civil service. 'Things were different when the Nats came to power in 1948,' recalls Abraham. 'Those of us who were supporting the South African Party were called jingoes. Smuts stood for reconciliation. Suddenly the ideology over the country was that of glorifying the heroic Afrikaners. They began whipping up emotions as they talked about South Africa becoming a republic. Their ideology needed a symbol. A republic would be that symbol.'

If the new regime was tough on the Sappe, it was brutal towards the non-whites, as it cooked up further ideas on how to strengthen and enforce apartheid.

No doubt aided by the political upheaval, Smuts's health deteriorated. He suffered a slight coronary thrombosis in May 1950, shortly before his eightieth birthday. On 4 September 1950, he retired to the bushveld he so loved. Six days later he played with some of his grandchildren, and the following day he died in the presence of his family. With his death, the age of the Boer generals had come to an end and a new era began.

A group of leaders, made up of Bible-wielding dominees, Afrikaner intellectuals and Broederbond elite, emerged to worship at the apartheid tabernacle and feast on political power. Their feast, however, could not last forever, not if a black nationalism was to rise as Afrikaner nationalism had.

As unthinkable as this was to the rebels who had retired Jan Smuts, if it should happen, would they be able to once again turn to the generals? It was in the Afrikaner character to trust the military generals, those men of war who put the interests of the volk first, when the politicians failed them. And if such generals were to rise once more, they would surely come from the platteland, that hinterland of the Afrikaner.

4

The dissident Afrikaner

ABRAHAM AND CONSTAND VILJOEN enrolled at the army gymnasium in Pretoria in 1951, continuing to learn side by side as they had been since their first day at school. Unbeknown to them, it was to be their last year together as a team.

'In those days the army gymnasium offered a one-year course,' recalls Constand. 'When we had to decide on a future after matric... Let me be honest, I had this problem that my family wasn't financially strong enough to send my brother and me to university. So we went to the gymnasium. Abraham was the top academic student in our year there. The next year he wanted to study theology. My mother was not able to send both of us to university, so I decided to go on in the military.'

The brothers' camaraderie up to this point had been built over almost twenty years, starting in their mother's womb. They shared countless memories, such as searching for stray cattle on misty nights, when visibility was so poor that it was a matter of life and death should they be separated. By blowing their whistles, young Abraham and Constand could check on each other's whereabouts and well-being. Or going to Standerton Station in the afternoons to collect empty aluminium milk containers and return them to the farm. This era was now over. It was time to go their separate ways.

Constand was drawn to the military, with its crisp uniforms, shining medals and regimental parades, to the crack of gunfire and the theatre of war. Abraham, although academically ahead of his brother, was called to the Dutch Reformed Church, the church of his ancestors, to become a religious minister.

'When I faced the ordaining committee of the Dutch Reformed Church,' Abraham recalls, 'old Dominee C. Brink got up and asked his customary question: "Why do you want to be a minister?" When he asked that question, the answer from each student was that we'd come under the conviction that we should become ministers at one or other Christian Student Association camp. I did well in my year at the military academy. On the academic side I was ahead of my brother, who excelled as well and was chosen as candidate of the year. It was recommended that he go ahead and do an officer's course. I'd already told the military selection committee during my interview that I was considering studying theology.

'In other words, I said to them that there was only one study direction for me and that was not the military one. It's interesting to speculate how things would have worked out if both of us had chosen a military career. But that's where our road took different directions. We'd been together since Sub A [Grade 1].'

Both brothers attended classes at Pretoria University, ironically the intellectual home of some of the most faithful servants of apartheid in the Transvaal. It was here that the morality, principles and scriptural foundations of separate development began to gnaw at Abraham. He started to doubt the alleged biblical reasons for supporting racial segregation and found that his own religious beliefs were challenging the political teachings of the National Party.

And he was not alone among Afrikaners in his thoughts; there were others, although few and far between. He identified with one man in particular, the outspoken academic and Dutch Reformed Church minister Professor Ben Marais, who was eventually to become a father figure.

Like an Old Testament prophet, Marais had warned of the folly and the deviation from belief that said apartheid was in accordance with the Bible. In 1948, at the Transvaal Synod of the Dutch Reformed Church, he rose as a lone voice to admonish the church for supporting the policies of the National Party. It was a path, he said, that would lead to isolation. In response, an agitated church elder warned Marais that his opposition to apartheid could cost the NP at the polls in the upcoming election. Undeterred, Marais later warned that apartheid would also be an expensive policy to implement.[1]

More than sixty years after that synod, Marais' daughter Augusta recalls: 'My father was a man who spoke up against the wrongs of apartheid. My father was one of the most honest people I've come across. If he said that something was wrong, then that was so. In 1948 he said apartheid was wrong. He was the youngest person at that synod and he was the only one to speak the truth. When my mother, Sebastiana, arrived at the synod, somebody said to her, "What did your husband do?" She said, "What did he do?" This man said, "He came to mess up the whole election." She said, "Is this synod about the election or the Bible?"'

Professor Marais captivated Abraham, who admired his hero from a distance, until he was one day invited to the investiture of a friend, Piet de Wet. Marais had also been invited, and upon hearing that Abraham would be at the same event in the Western Transvaal, he offered the young man a ride with him and his wife in their Volkswagen Beetle. In the safety of the VW, which took them out of Pretoria, the administrative heart of apartheid, and into the open country, Abraham found the space, security and time to talk.

'In the car I started to share my internal struggles with him,' Abraham recalls. 'How difficult it was for me to accept South Africa's race policies, and how I couldn't understand the church. Suddenly he shared how he himself had been arguing for years that the policy of apartheid was not scriptural. Coming from a house that did not support the National Party and having been raised as a rebel by my father, sharing these intimate thoughts with Ben Marais, and hearing that I had a valid point, was an intense experience. It was extremely liberating.'

Augusta Marais found Abraham's politics very different from that of many young Afrikaners. 'He was an intellectual who didn't allow the dominant political culture to influence him. He rebelled against some of the policies,' she says.

Her father enjoyed mentoring and being in the company of the young man who would become the son he never had. 'My father loved him very much,' says Augusta. 'He spoke about him a lot. They really had a father–son relationship. I know that my father helped him at times and also spoke up for Abraham.'

If Marais was his surrogate father, Sebastiana was his surrogate mother. 'My mother was mad about him,' Augusta recalls. 'We called her Sibs. She always called him "my son". She trusted him. In those days one didn't know who one could trust because there were so many informers. If people asked my father's views I kept quiet because I knew they were looking for something to use against him. We always knew where we stood with Abraham. He could be trusted.'

Like Constand, Abraham values loyalty and friendship, both of which he got from the Marais family. For years he remained a regular visitor to the Marais home, even doing maintenance work for them on occasion. As a trusted part of the family, he was asked to be a pallbearer at Sebastiana's funeral.

In Abraham's final year of studying, Professor Marais gave him the good news that he had secured a bursary from the World Council of Churches that would enable him to visit the United States. 'I had studied for three years and was a candidate minister,' says Abraham. 'Professor Marais urged me to put in leave for my fourth year: "Rather go on this study trip to the US and Europe." Now that intervention changed my life fundamentally.'

In the US, Abraham found his second fatherland. Associated with the national Christian Student Association, he travelled to the Deep South, the Midwest, New Jersey and New York, where he lectured and led discussions. He was met with a storm of questions and condemnations about the apartheid system, which convinced him all the more just how wrong the NP's answer to the race question in South Africa was.

'I was exposed to the question of just treatment and to the belief that people were equals. I was opened to the essential religious differences,' says Abraham, recalling that period when his eyes were opened to another possibility, when he was shown the Bible from another perspective.

While abroad, Abraham missed the World Council of Churches' Cottesloe Consultation held in Johannesburg in December 1960. The conference condemned major aspects of apartheid, and, egged on by Prime Minister Hendrik Verwoerd, the Broederbond began agitating for individual church synods to refuse to ratify the Cottesloe Declaration. As a result, each of the three major Afrikaans churches – the Dutch Reformed Church, the Reformed Church (Doppers) and the Hervormde Kerk – rejected the Cottesloe Declaration and withdrew from the World Council of Churches.[2]

The attack against Cottesloe was also waged in *Die Kerkbode*, the official publication of the Dutch Reformed Church, edited by Andries

Treurnicht, who would become chairman of the Broederbond in 1972. Treurnicht wrote a biting editorial in which he savaged Robert Bilheimer, one of the World Council of Churches' officials who were involved in organising the conference.

Impetuous and free of fear, as only the young can be, Abraham took umbrage and resolved to take Treurnicht to task. 'I was most upset by his scathing attack and immediately wrote a letter to *Die Kerkbode*,' says Abraham. 'I attacked Dr Treurnicht. He didn't publish my letter but sent me a message: "You really don't want *Die Kerkbode* to publish this letter, do you?" I thought that this was the end of the matter, but it wasn't.'

The ramifications of the letter, written with the honesty and seriousness of a young man finding his spiritual bearings, would play out only when he returned to South Africa some months later. In the meantime, however, Abraham was keen to learn and broaden his horizons. In 1961 he was offered the opportunity to extend his stay in the US, but he declined, preferring to travel to the Netherlands to meet a living Dutch hero.

'They offered me a bursary to remain in the US longer but I said no,' says Abraham. 'Before I left South Africa I'd read a thesis by Professor Johannes Hoekendijk, which had influenced me down to the core of my being... As a student I still believed in the reconciliation policies of Botha and Smuts. I was having problems because I refused to swallow the usual arguments [proffered by the National Party] about the race question in South Africa.'

Written in German, Hoekendijk's thesis was about race, church and volk. He saw the church as an instrument and not as the centre of missionary dynamics. To him the church could never become settled in any cultural, social or religious establishment.

It was to see Hoekendijk that Abraham made the journey to the

Netherlands. There the professor told the young theologian about the complex choices Christians were sometimes forced to face, and about how the right decisions could sometimes seem to be in conflict with one's beliefs. As an illustration, he shared one of his experiences of the German occupation of the Netherlands in World War II.

'Hoekendijk was chairman of the Christian Student Association during the Second World War,' explains Abraham. 'He was also an underground resistance movement leader. One of their main tasks was to daily feed a group of Jewish children who were hiding in a house. They wanted to keep these children alive. Keeping their existence a secret was vital if they were to live. The Nazi SS was everywhere. Eventually the SS came to hear that there were Jewish children being hidden in the town. They were out to capture these children and send them to certain death in a concentration camp. They wanted to smoke them out, so they introduced a food-coupon system. Nobody could get food without a German-issued coupon.

'Hoekendijk was in trouble. Should they abandon the children or should they save them? Their decision was to save lives. They asked the most beautiful young woman working for the association to seduce the SS officer in charge of the coupons. She had to do more than that: she had to murder him and steal the coupons. She did it. When I heard this, I was sitting with my system of theology that didn't even allow for this sort of thing. Hoekendijk knew.

'He said, "Remember, we gave orders that the woman should use her body to lure the German into bed. Then she took her weapon and killed him. And she stole the food coupons. In sanctioning this deed, how many of the laws of Moses did we break? Is there hope for us?"

'What Hoekendijk did could never be done in South Africa. Here the Dutch Reformed Church and the Christian Student Association believed and propagated that you should win souls for your country. You must pray that people should convert and that the Holy Spirit should lead them. It wasn't your responsibility to say apartheid is wrong. Your job was to bring people to love gentle Jesus. Then they'll do the right thing.'

The Dutch professor's story left Abraham's head spinning: ordering a murder to save lives, was it right? The emotional storm raging inside him brought up his disquiet over the previous year's Sharpeville massacre. On 21 March 1960, South African police shot and killed at least sixty-nine black Africans protesting against the country's pass laws. Most of those killed were shot in the back. It was a massacre that showed the world the brutality of those charged with enforcing apartheid and of the system itself. A little over a week later, the government had declared a state of emergency and Abraham was called up by the army. He was unwilling to comply with the call-up and sought advice from the theology faculty dean, Professor E.P. Groenewald. Unfortunately Groenewald was one of those conservative Afrikaner theologians who believed the Bible justified apartheid. He rebuffed his student, saying, 'Mr Viljoen, it's time that you did your duty for South Africa.'

Once in the US, Abraham became aware of the international outrage over Sharpeville. At one point he visited the South African embassy in Washington and said to the receptionist, 'The world is upset about Sharpeville.' She in turn told him that an American policeman had been posted at the embassy to protect her and other embassy staff.

Listening to Hoekendijk, Abraham recalled his own abhorrence at what had occurred. He had been asked in the US and the Netherlands to take a stand. 'It was then that I saw that my theology training was bankrupt,' he says.

He was beginning to understand that things had to change – that he himself had to change – and that he could not go on as before.

'A resistance was developing inside me. I didn't know it. I hadn't had it before. Suddenly it was there. This resistance was theology-based. On the day that I left the Netherlands to go home, I went to greet Hendrikus Berkhof, a professor of dogmatics and biblical theology at the Nederlandse Hervormde Kerk [and former secretary of the World Council of Churches]. We talked a bit. Then I told him I had to go. He said: "Young man, life is short. Do what you have to do."'

These were surely prophetic words. Abraham returned home, not knowing what it was that he was supposed to do, but having realised it would not be business as usual. It was time to begin public resistance against the dominant ideology.

He certainly did not suspect what awaited him in Pretoria. While he was conversing with the likes of Hoekendijk and Berkhof abroad, his letter attacking Treurnicht had reached a group of powerful academics, the type of men who decided who became church ministers and who did not. Outraged by the youngster's impertinence and sheer bravado, they had devised to teach him a lesson.

'I came home and met E.P. Groenewald,' recalls Abraham. 'He said I would have to redo the doctoral exams that I'd already done. I sat arguing my case in his office until 5.30 p.m. I fought him. He knew what it was all about. I saw that he was upset. As he told me that I'd not exactly made myself very popular with the Dutch Reformed Church, I knew that Dr Treurnicht had sent my letter to him. Dr Treurnicht had sent me a message saying that my letter had landed in his rubbish bin. But he had clearly shared it with others.'

There was a lot of concern at the time that young Afrikaners were losing their 'innocence' abroad, namely their loyalty to their people.

Many returned home 'changed' by the experience of being in a non-apartheid society.

'They said I had been influenced, that I should never have been allowed to go overseas,' Abraham explains. 'If I hadn't been abroad I would have remained the sheep that I was being trained to be. I suppose I would have been rich today. I would have had a fat pension. I would have been secure. But then I would never have been able to make a contribution to this new society of ours.'

Still determined to become a dominee, Abraham retook his exams, notching up several distinctions in the process. But when it came time for his oral exam, he clashed with yet another Broederbonder, Professor A.B. du Preez.

'He wanted to know if I'd submit myself to the authority of the synod,' Abraham recalls. 'I replied that I'd do this only in so far as the scriptures were respected. The church that didn't obey the scripture could not be respected for it lacked authority. He accused me of avoiding his question.'

Du Preez engaged the young theologian and the oral exam took longer than usual. The more it dragged, however, the more Abraham wondered if his conscience would free him to sheepishly follow the church line. At the end of the day, he passed. But at what cost?

'A.B. du Preez put me through. I asked myself: Is there a place for me in the Dutch Reformed Church? After what I've seen, can I do it?'

Abraham went to his mentor Ben Marais and put his cards on the table.

'I don't see my way clear to be ordained in the Dutch Reformed Church,' Abraham admitted. 'I think I will withdraw my request to be ordained.'

Marais looked at him and was silent for a long time before replying: 'I think it will be right to do so.'

Marais' words were a release, an approval or blessing of sorts. What he said next startled his protégé. The way things were going, said the professor, he may also reach the point at which Abraham had arrived, but only in ten years' time.

'I was at a crossroads,' says Abraham. 'Ben Marais said he'd see what was available at the University of South Africa, which had just opened a new theology faculty, because I had to start earning an income.'

The Broederbond and the Dutch Reformed Church would not forget the slight in a hurry. Abraham was continually reminded of their reach and need for vengeance as they ruthlessly and uncompromisingly sought out enemies in the tribe. When they found them, they made examples of them to discourage other would-be dissidents. Those led by their conscience who dared challenge the system or who tried to escape the one-size-fits-all conformist identity by joining organisations like the Christian Institute of Southern Africa, headed by dissident Dutch Reformed Church cleric Beyers Naudé, felt the wrath of the apartheid disciples. The Broederbond allegiance to the Old Testament dictum of an eye for an eye was unflinching.

Naudé was the son of a founding member of the Afrikaner Broederbond. Given his patrilineage, he was considered a rising star in the apartheid-supporting Dutch Reformed Church and the Afrikaner establishment, and in 1942 accepted an invitation to join the Broederbond to become its youngest member. He was twenty-five. He remained a member for more than two decades, but his association with the secret organisation began to trouble his Christian conscience. The Sharpeville massacre in March 1960 signalled the turning point. Vexed by the oath of secrecy he had sworn to the Broederbond, Naudé handed over documents to a close friend, Professor Albert Geyser, to get his opinion on the Broederbond's hold over the church. He was also driven by another, more personal, ulterior motive: he wanted to know if he should resign from the organisation.[3]

Geyser leaked the secret documents to the *Sunday Times*, which began publishing a series of exposés that rocked the Broederbond and gave the country an insight into its machinations. Incensed by this betrayal, the Broederbond went hunting for the traitor in their midst. On 1 October 1963, a police squad under the command of Captain Van der Westhuizen of the Hospital Hill police station raided the *Sunday Times*'s Johannesburg offices.[4]

The following month, the Broederbond announced that the source of the leaks was none other than Reverend Beyers Naudé. He was summoned to appear before the executive committee on Tuesday 12 November 1963. Among those present was security police head Hendrik van den Bergh, a fellow Broederbonder.

That same month, Naudé did what he had been contemplating for some time and quit the Broederbond. He sent a letter to Afrikaans newspapers to explain his position, but those who supported the government refused to publish it. Only the liberal *Cape Times* did, on 20 November.

'During March this year I submitted certain AB [Afrikaner Broederbond] documents to a fellow theologian who is not a member of the organization,' Naudé wrote in his letter. 'The documents in my opinion, confirmed my personal deep concerns that the AB, contrary to the Scriptures, wants to use the Church of Christ to further its own interests. I showed the documents to my colleague because I wanted his advice in choosing between two loyalties, and about which I could not think clearly at the time. Because you have the right to know why I broke my oath about discussing the documents with a non-member, I now give my reasons.

'My division [of the Broederbond] was for some considerable time aware of the misgivings, I, as a Christian and clergyman, had about the principles and methods of the organization where the Christian church was concerned. I failed to find satisfactory assurance that my objections were unfounded when I discussed my misgivings with fellow-clergymen, who are members of the Afrikaner Broederbond. And my concern increased as a result of further circulars and study documents issued by the executive council from August 1962.'[5]

Now considered the prime traitor of Afrikanerdom and cast out of the comfort, protection and camaraderie of the Afrikaner elite, Naudé completed his break by refusing to give up directorship of the non-denominational ecumenical institute of Christian research and study, the Christian Institute of Southern Africa, of which he was a founder member. Soon after, he took the radical step of condemning apartheid from the pulpit and walked out of his church. He joined a Dutch Reformed congregation in the black community of Alexandra and was forced to resign as a minister.[6]

The apartheid state turned its vengeance on Naudé. In 1973 his passport was withdrawn, and in 1975 he was imprisoned for a night for refusing to give evidence to the Schlebusch Commission, a parliamentary commission which had been established to investigate the Christian Institute, the University Christian Movement, the National Union of South African Students and the Institute of Race Relations. On 19 October 1977 the government struck against individuals, organisations and newspapers that it deemed enemies of the state. Naudé and the Christian Institute were banned, and the institute's publication, *Pro Veritate*, was closed. Severe restrictions were placed on Naudé's and his colleagues' movements, and they were legally prevented from being with more than one person in a room at any one time.

Shortly after his brush with Du Preez, when Abraham was a member of the Dutch Reformed Church in Kameeldrift, near Pretoria, he was approached to be an elder, a position offered only to those Afrikaners with high morals who enjoyed the respect and acknowledgement of the gemeente (congregation). In a mainly rural community where the Broederbond wielded much influence, the offer could have been construed as a sign that Abraham was marked for success in Afrikanerdom. But he knew the truth. Du Preez, as a theologian with considerable influence and a member of the congregation, had orchestrated the nomination so that Abraham would be forced to reveal his political views to the dominee.

'I thought I should meet the minister, Eric Harrington. I said: "Eric, you've called me to be an elder. I have to be honest with you. If I come on board I want to work, but I want to follow my conscience. Do you know where I stand with the Christian Institute? Do you know that I support Beyers Naudé? Do you know that I'm fighting and resisting the scriptural rationalisation for apartheid? I will serve if you're okay with this."' Abraham breaks into a hearty laugh as he relives the conversation.

'Eric looked at me. He said: "You know, I knew about your leanings. Until now I didn't know where you really stand. Do me a favour and give me a week to think and to consult with the brothers." I didn't know who these brothers were, but I assumed that they were the Broederbond. Maybe he also had to talk to his church council.'

A week passed. As the Sunday approached on which he was to publicly announce whether he would heed the call of the gemeente, Abraham waited to hear from Harrington. Eventually the call came. They met at the church on the Friday. Harrington began with a preamble: 'You know I like you. Personally I have nothing against you and I hope that our relationship will always be a good one.' Abraham knew what was coming next. Harrington confirmed his expectations: 'I don't want to have a fight in the congregation, so I'm asking you to decline the nomination.'

As Abraham tells me about this, he observes in his dry manner: 'You know, calls to serve on a church council are usually made after deep prayers. They must have prayed and got a word from God to call on me. So I assume they prayed again and got direction on how to resolve my situation.'

But as one door closed, another was opening. True to his word, the compassionate and fatherly Marais did what he could to help and spoke to Professor Johannes Antonie 'Dotjie' Lombard, the first theology lecturer appointed at UNISA. 'Abraham has reached a stalemate,' Marais told Lombard. 'He has studied, did well, and went abroad.'

Lombard asked Abraham to come and see him at his office. He asked the young man about his theological beliefs and background, and then asked him when he could start. 'I told him I was bankrupt and was keen to get going as soon as possible,' recalls Abraham. With few other prospects, he had been doing some relief ministry work in Rhodesia.

Thanks to Lombard's intervention, Abraham was offered a position at UNISA as a lecturer of mission history and mission science (sendingsgeskiedenis and sendingswetenskap). In those days UNISA was a fledgling institution located in Pretoria, not the giant of distance learning that is today housed in the imposing set of buildings dominating the skyline as one enters Pretoria from Johannesburg. But there was a slight wrinkle that had to be ironed out before he could begin work. He had to meet the rector, who, much to Lombard's surprise, told Abraham that his appointment still had to be finalised.

Abraham, unsure whether or not he had a job, left the rector's office with Lombard. But the professor was principled, a man of his word. As they were walking, he stopped, asked Abraham to wait for him, turned around and headed back to the rector's office, determined to tell the senior academic of the unfairness of it all. He suspected the

Broederbond was somehow involved. In the end, Lombard resolved the matter and Abraham was appointed.

There was one more loose end to tie up, however. Abraham sought out Professor Groenewald to inform him that he had reassessed his position and was considering a job offer from UNISA. He got an honest reply: the dean agreed with him. With that, Abraham withdrew his application for ordination, simultaneously dousing the fire that had been calling him to the missionary field.

Abraham was not yet out of the woods, though. He had to have one more conversation. This one was going to be more personal and painful, and would stay with him for the rest of his life. 'My wife, Marietjie, and I met one another while on a mission trip in Central Africa,' he recalls. 'We didn't click immediately. I was hooked on her. She was a medical student and wasn't ready for the kind of relationship I was seeking. Later we started dating. She also thought of being a missionary. I think she thought we could be a missionary pair: she as the doctor and me being the missionary. We'd decided we'd go into the missionary field after she had completed her studies.'

Now those plans were dashed, and Abraham had to tell the woman he loved that he had taken steps that irrevocably changed their vision of a joint future as Christian missionaries.

'I was walking with my head bowed down. We weren't married yet. I arrived at her work and said, "Something went wrong with my exams. The meeting with the commission didn't work out. I don't see my way clear to enter the ministry as a Dutch Reformed Church minister. I will not be ordained."'

Marietjie was surprised and clearly hurt by the news. The strength and depth of her commitment to Abraham was being severely tested. As he relives the poignant moment, the air throbs with emotion, pain and regret: 'You can't begin to imagine how my news shocked her. The first thing she asked me was, "What about the mission then?" Over the years people have asked me about the road that I have travelled. Like Beyers Naudé, I had to walk this road. It cost me. I don't know if people know how much it wrenched from me, about the angst, or when the young woman you want to marry says, "What about the mission then?" My life's journey brought its own kind of loneliness that scalded me.'

But the young woman loved him deeply, this rebel for change who was seemingly against his own people, who would be called a traitor, who would be battered – but not flattened – by the strong winds he was sailing into. Today, Abraham and Marietjie are still together, having weathered severe storms and whatever other disasters life has thrown at them. She now understands what drove him, that he had no choice. She loves him.

Shunned by his church, but with Marietjie by his side, Abraham had to contend with the next onslaught. Whispered rumours that he was a communist began to gain traction, as the Broederbond employed their tactic of using the tongue to ostracise opponents and oust them from the laager. Anyone branded a communist was on par with the antichrist, a Soviet apparatchik, a Stalinist. They were to be avoided because they contaminated and sought the destruction of the volk. Abraham quickly became persona non grata, a pariah and an outcast like Naudé and others who disbelieved the biblical arguments used for apartheid.

With his skills, intellect and work ethic in danger of going to waste, Abraham found an outlet for his energy and commitment to change at the South African Council of Churches (SACC), an interdenominational forum that had stepped into the vacuum created in black politics and maintained by the NP following its outlawing of the ANC, the Pan Africanist Congress (PAC) and other political organisations.

As the NP had labelled the SACC a communist organisation, by throwing in his lot with them Abraham was confirming, as far as his opponents were concerned, that he, too, was a communist.

Strong on justice and reconciliation, Abraham became a committed member of the SACC's division for justice and reconciliation, faith and ideologies commission and study project for Christianity in an apartheid society. As far as Afrikanerdom was concerned, he was lost to the cause: he was a traitor and a turncoat who had to be crushed.

Then one day, the Dutch Reformed Church dispatched an elder to Abraham's smallholding in Kameeldrift. He carried a message: the Ring of the Pretoria North church had resolved that those congregants who remained members of the Christian Institute were guilty of mutiny and involved with a sect, and could therefore not attend the Lord's table and partake in Holy Communion. Abraham was being given a choice that would test his resolve. He knew it was an attempt to further marginalise and demonise him, and that, if he listened to his conscience, his decision would be used to brand him unchristian.

'That message was unambiguous: if I didn't resign from the Christian Institute then I was against the church,' he says. 'I would also be against a decision taken by the synod. The fight that I had had with A.B. du Preez was precisely about this. When is authority binding and when is it not? When I got that letter saying that I was rebelling against the authority of the church and busy with a sect, I thought that they would discipline me. In the Protestant Church there are two important things: the Word and the Communion. They were going to prohibit me from taking Communion. That's when I decided not to go to church any more. Why should I go and listen to the Word if they weren't going to serve me Communion?'

He did not arrive at his decision overnight. Deep reasoning went into its making. All the consequences were carefully examined and weighed because, make no mistake, there would be consequences for him and his family.

'My staying away from church hurt my wife intensely. When she arrived on her own, people who knew what was taking place would ask, "Where's Abraham?"' He sobs in pain as he tells me this, recollecting the agony of it all. An invisible cord still binds him to the Dutch Reformed Church. It is the church of his forefathers, the only one he has ever known, the place in which he was baptised and confirmed, and which served as his spiritual home for most of his early life. He has never resigned from the Dutch Reformed Church, but does not regard himself as a member. He could possibly be termed a 'lapsed member'.

His new status as an outcast surfaced in a talk with Naudé. 'All that he asked me,' Abraham says, 'was did it bother me. I said no. I'm almost afraid to say that it was liberating for me. It's a terrible thing for someone like me to say. I was a theology student for seven years and wanted to be a minister or a missionary. But it was liberating for me not to go to church any more.'

Like Naudé, Abraham realised that he had to leave the laager if he was to be at peace with himself. But that peace would come at a personal cost. He was now on the lonely road of the dissident Afrikaner.

5

Military in the blood

'Why can't we agree that we all have dirty hands? We fought a war that should have been avoided from the start or even been abandoned earlier. We fought a dirty war.'

~ Constand Viljoen to the Truth and
Reconciliation Commission

AFTER THE VILJOEN BROTHERS' year together at the army gymnasium in 1951, when Abraham decided to study theology, Constand opted for a career in the army. In fact, the selection committee had recommended him and not Abraham for a military career. The military afforded him the chance to attend university, and so he and his brother both enrolled at the University of Pretoria the following year. Then a whites-only, Afrikaans-language institution, it stood in what was once the capital of the Transvaal Republic. Constand completed his BSc Mil degree in 1955. 'I was interested in a science and military direction,' he says. 'Then it was the defence force for me.'

But the recently graduated Afrikaans-speaker was in for a culture shock: 'The defence force was overwhelmingly English. Everything was English. I was overwhelmingly a Boer. I made no secret of my feelings, which were that I was unhappy with the situation.'

His heart revolted at the historical injustices carried out by the English on his people. Being compelled to attend a Union Day celebration offended his Afrikaner nationalism, and fed his inner rebel. By now Constand was in the artillery and driving a second-hand Nash motor car, a snazzy, eye-catching vehicle. 'On that day a group of us, all Afrikaners, were in my car, a Nash. We were on our way to Union Day celebrations. In those days, Pretoria was alive with politics. The whole army was English-orientated. I don't know where I got the courage from, but I tied a Vierkleur [the flag of the Transvaal Republic] to the front of my car before we arrived at the Army College.'

Constand's act of defiance showed what was in his heart and publicly exposed the divide between Afrikaans- and English-speaking South Africans serving in the military. Afrikaner resentment, born when the British first arrived in South Africa centuries ago, bristled at the slightest provocation. Language and cultural differences combined with memories of past hurts and bitter wars to drive a wedge between the two groups. The Afrikaners keenly felt their alienation from some of the very English traditions prevalent in the military, and many declined to join the Gunners Artillery Association of South Africa.

'In Ronnie McWilliams I had a good commanding officer,' Constand tells me. 'He was an English-speaker and I thought very highly of him. One day he called me to his office. He said the Association was dying. I said, "Sir, do you have a programme?" He gave me one. It had the artillery memorial badge underneath a crown. Pointing to the crown on the programme, I said, "Whose crown is that?" He replied, "It's the crown of England." I answered, "What do we still have to do with England?" You see, the Anglo-Boer War and South Africa's taking part in England's wars were still affecting me.'

More than fifty years after the end of a war that they were not even around to experience, Constand and many other young Afrikaners were looking over their shoulders, imagining the thunder of approaching horses and the shouts of their riders as they charged Boer lines, and the death rattles of women and children dying in concentration camps. They were captives of a shared past, held there by the National Party and the Broederbond.

But despite their simmering resentment, Constand and his peers were, after all, hot-blooded youths in a military outfit. Constand himself was a serious young officer who impressed those who met him. A captain at the time remembers Lieutenant Viljoen as a confident officer who saluted as if he were a general.

According to one of his former lecturers from the military academy, 'He was a model of an Afrikaner officer, emerging from a community which had its own language, history, background and characteristics that set it apart from other groups in South Africa.'

Furthermore, Constand loved the thrill of action, the whistle of bullets, the sight of helicopters on a mission, the sheer camaraderie of soldiering. He relished sitting in front of a Ratel pugnaciously entering enemy territory. His stock weapon on the front line was a 5.56-millimetre R4, an adaptation of the Israeli Galil assault rifle, which later became the standard South African Army rifle. And as testament to his dedication, he got his wings as a paratrooper. 'I was interested in war. It was in my blood.'

Constand spent the late fifties, sixties and early seventies diligently rising through the ranks of first the Union Defence Force and then the SADF. By 1974 he was named the South African Army's director of general operations, and subsequently served as the principal staff officer to the chief of the SADF, General Magnus Malan.

Constand's position made him an ideal candidate for the Afrikaner Broederbond. When he was eventually recruited, he joined the crème de la crème of Afrikaner society. It was an accomplishment that proved he was an insider; an upright Afrikaner comrade who had the telephone numbers, respect and acceptance of his fellow Broederbonders; a defender of the Christian faith as defined by Afrikaners; and an enemy of communism.

When joining the Broederbond, recruits took an oath of secrecy, and even today many are unwilling to discuss their membership. 'Yes, I was a member,' he says. 'The Afrikaner Broederbond was a better think tank than the National Party had been. The day I joined I said: "Look, I'm here to serve my people. I don't want any perks just because I'm now a member of the Afrikaner Broederbond." I was adamant that I didn't want to benefit from being a member. That story that the Broederbond manipulated situations to have its members appointed to key positions is true.'

As a Broederbonder, Constand was, as they say in the Mafia, a made man. Members were carefully vetted before they were asked to join, and once they did, their careers and opportunities generally flourished and increased. These were the men who could make or break the careers and lives of others, men to be feared. Endowed with the trust of his government ministers, most of whom were fellow Broederbonders, the general undertook several clandestine missions of a political/military nature. One of his tasks was to bring together the South African government then under Vorster, defence minister P.W. Botha, the SADF and Jonas Savimbi, the leader of the National Union for the Total Independence of Angola (UNITA).

As South Africa was being sucked into Angola, Vorster was keen to step up aid. On his orders, Constand and Gert Rothman of the Bureau of State Security (BOSS) went to Zaire in July 1975. They met Zaire's Mobutu Sese Seko and two Angolan freedom fighters considered to be friends of the West: Holden Roberto of the National Front for the Liberation of Angola (FNLA), who happened to be Sese

Seko's brother-in-law, and Jonas Savimbi. Part of the South African mission was to execute Vorster's order that a proper study be made of the requirements of the pro-West Angolan movements. Between them, UNITA and the FNLA, among others, asked for two-way radios, missiles, landmines, ammunition, armoured cars, rifles and uniforms.

On his return to South Africa, Constand recommended that weapons and equipment be supplied. Costs were to be capped at R20 million. To maintain secrecy, it was stipulated that the weapons could not be purchased in South Africa. Vorster approved the budget, and within a month arms were on their way to Zaire on board Central Intelligence Agency C-5A and C-141 planes. From there the weapons were transferred to South African military transport aircraft and flown to Angola.[1]

Angola was due to become independent on 11 November 1975. The pro–Soviet Union MPLA (People's Movement for the Liberation of Angola) was in control of most of the strategic parts of the country. Rumours that the MPLA was not going to wait until November but instead declare independence from Portugal at the end of October lured South Africa into Angola. By November 1975, South Africa was deeply embroiled in the country, albeit secretly, a pawn in the Cold War between the United States and the Soviet Union. As always with the apartheid advocates, there was an ulterior motive for South Africa's secret presence. The politicians believed South Africa should assist Angola in such a way that the concept of individual ethnic groupings in specific areas in a country could be established. It was a blatant attempt to sow apartheid policy and the concept of homelands on the African continent.

But by December, South Africa's military intervention in Angola was being condemned internationally. Thousands of Cuban soldiers were fighting alongside the MPLA, while the Soviet Union was pouring millions of US dollars in aid into it. In Washington, the political tide was turning against South Africa.

On 19 December, the US senate voted by a margin of fifty-four votes to twelve to cease American involvement in Angola. The South African ambassador in Washington, Roelof 'Pik' Botha, phoned Vorster a day later to give him the bad news. Under pressure and fearing that South Africa would get bogged down in Angola for years, Vorster convened an urgent meeting at his holiday home, Oubos. The only item on the agenda was Angola. Pik Botha flew in from Washington, while Constand, defence force chief Magnus Malan and Gert Rothman arrived from Air Force Base Waterkloof in Pretoria.

Afterwards, Constand was sent to Angola, carrying a secret message for Savimbi. The secretary for foreign affairs, Brand Fourie, was sent as an emissary to Lusaka to see Zambian president Kenneth Kaunda. The secret message was simple: South African troops would be withdrawn from Angola.

On 14 January 1976 the South African cabinet resolved to end the campaign in Angola. Constand was ordered to write the message to withdraw, and a day later, all sections of the SADF were informed. Finally, days before the end of January 1976, defence minister P.W. Botha shared the by now old news with the public that South African troops had fought in Angola. Constand was then appointed head of the South African Army College in Oudtshoorn.

Like the government of the Republic of South Africa, Constand could not have known what a seminal year 1976 would turn out to be for the country. The Soweto pupils' protest in June against the introduction of Afrikaans as the medium of instruction in schools was the spark that simmering black anger and hatred of the apartheid system needed to ignite. State-sponsored violence began to be met with violence. From the streets of Soweto, the protest spread to other parts of South Africa. Burning tyres that sent up columns of black smoke became popular barricades to keep out security forces or to retard the progress of their vehicles as the government responded with predictable brutality.

It was the beginning of the end of apartheid, but white South Africa was by and large blind to the signs. As for Constand Viljoen, he was preoccupied with finding ways and means to fulfil a vow he had made to his dead father a decade earlier.

'I have to tell the story of my promotion in conjunction with my quest to be a farmer,' Constand says. 'At my father's funeral I told myself, "I'm going to be a farmer. I don't know where I'll get the money to buy a farm, but I will retire one day to be a farmer." I was commanding officer of an army base in Bethlehem in the Free State province. I was walking around the base when an oubaas who was in charge of a group of prisoners working on the base stopped me. We talked a bit about the garden, what he was doing and if he was happy.

'Then he said, "General, I hear you want to buy a farm?"

'I said, "Yes, I'm going to buy a farm one day, but I don't have the money to pay for one. I have a problem because the Land Bank tells me I'm not a bona fide farmer, therefore they can't give me a loan. Companies like Sanlam and Mutual will give me financial aid, but the interest they're charging will kill me."

'He said to me, "General, I'm an alcoholic. My biggest fear is that I will lose all my money and become dependent on the government for assistance. I still have enough self-respect left in me to say that I don't want this to happen to me. I will give you a loan to cover a mortgage, but on condition that you must only repay this loan after I've died. I also want you to pay the monthly interest to me every month."

'That's how I got to buy a farm in 1965.'

Constand named the farm in the Ohrigstad district of what is now

Mpumalanga 'Betel', meaning 'House of God', a name that speaks to his Christianity.

The kind oubaas, Dolf Cronje, died in 1976.

Constand's focus in the 1970s was thus firmly on the dearth of funds needed to keep his word to his benefactor. Luckily, he and his wife Ristie had bought and renovated a house in the upmarket Pretoria suburb of Brooklyn. It was an investment that would help them out of their dilemma.

'We had turned our Brooklyn house into a beautiful dwelling,' recalls Constand. 'I suggested to my wife that we put our house on the market because we would have to move to the Army College. She agreed. We sold the house and paid off our debts.'

In 1976 he was appointed chief of the South African Army. Prior to this promotion, Constand crossed paths with senior officers in the Israel Defense Forces. He admired and respected them, and appreciated their ethos and policy of keeping leadership at the top as fresh and abreast of modern ideas as possible. Once an Israeli officer shared with him his philosophy of appointing generals and reserving the right to place them on pension within two years if their performance was unsatisfactory.

It was a philosophy to which Constand had warmed, and which he now proffered to Magnus Malan when he took over as army chief: 'I told him I would serve for five years, after which I would follow the Israeli example and move on. He said, "That's fine with me."'

As chief of the army, Constand presided over covert and controversial operations, but he also enforced discipline in a highly orthodox way, something that did not endear him to everyone.

In 1977, in the aftermath of Operation Savannah, the SADF's covert intervention in the Angolan civil war, SWAPO guerrillas were still infiltrating South West Africa in an attempt to end the

South African occupation there. At the same time, South Africa was assembling a highly secretive killing machine, 32 Battalion, under the command of Colonel Jan Breytenbach. This band of mainly FNLA refugees – trained killers who spoke Portuguese and indigenous Angolan languages – provided a useful surrogate force that could hustle, forage and raid in Angola. Breytenbach was larger than life and admired by his troops. The 32 Battalion's attritional cross-border raids gave substance to Breytenbach's credo to 'turn the southern Angola bush into a menacing, hostile environment for SWAPO' and to 'out-guerrilla the guerrillas'.[2]

However, once the soldiers of 32 Battalion were assembled, their commanders found themselves in an ethical, moral, cultural and military nightmare. With 1400 troops, and 206 women, the majority married, under their command, camp commanders had to tread a fine line. The situation was not made any easier by the fact that their base was a secret, cut off from the rest of the world and accessible only to those with special clearance.

Tensions in the camp had to be managed carefully, given that testosterone was rampant among some of the young and virile men. It would require some unorthodox methods. One such was the decision to build a brothel on the base. Given that the proposed bordello was in total conflict with military prescripts, the establishment had to remain a secret, especially from the SADF high command. 'We were an isolated base and we had a problem,' one senior officer involved tells me. 'So after talking to Jan Breytenbach I went to work. I must say that I wasn't innocent and I don't want to claim that I was following orders. We had a dilemma and had a crisis on our hands. We tried to be practical.'

My source sought out some female Angolan refugees and explained the nature of his visit, the problem and the solution that he had come up with. 'I found a madam and some women who were willing to do what I had proposed,' he says. 'They came out of their own free will. They knew what they were letting themselves in for.'

The brothel consisted of six bedrooms, one for each of the five women and the madam, and a communal kitchen. Each bedroom had a bed and a wardrobe for personal items. The arrangement was such that men wanting to use the women's services would pay for the privilege; the madam kept a portion of this money and the rest went to the women.

An army doctor, much to his disgust, was instructed to regularly examine the women to ensure that they were healthy and not carrying sexually transmitted diseases.

The unorthodox solution seemed to work until the day the camp received a communiqué that army chief General Constand Viljoen was planning a visit. His instructions were simple: no fanfare, no special foods, no fuss. The general would be quite happy with a cup of tea before performing an inspection of the base.

That was all well and good, but camp commanders were pretty certain their general would also like his favourite soft drink, Lemon Twist. As it was unpopular with the troops, supplies had to be procured from Grootfontein in South West Africa.

The order to keep things simple did not go down well with the camp's Angolan chef, who wanted to go all the way and show off his culinary skills to the general. He also had a new oven of which he was incredibly proud; it would be a shame not to make use of it.

On the appointed date, the base was ready for inspection. Everyone knew they had to be on their best behaviour because the big boss would be watching them closely. When Constand and his entourage walked into the mess for tea, tables creaking under the weight of freshly baked cakes and pastries greeted them. It was an inauspicious start and things were not about to improve.

After tea, the general inspected the operations tent, which was usually a rather dull place to work. In this tent, however, young men being young men, the troops had added some colour by pasting photographs of bikini-clad women cut out of the controversial and provocative *Scope* magazine all over the place. The photographs upset Constand and he ordered that they be removed.

Obviously, before the general arrived, the men had implored Breytenbach not to take him near the brothel. The officer responsible for this adult entertainment reasonably assumed the colonel would remember his promise to steer clear of the establishment. But, for some inexplicable reason, Breytenbach took the army chief directly to the brothel, pointed to the officer responsible and asked him to tell the good general what he had been up to. The officer scrambled to explain the motivation behind the rather unmilitary situation, but Constand nevertheless exploded. The brothel had to go. Immediately.

After its removal, the atmosphere in the camp changed almost overnight: fights became common, homosexuality emerged, and some of the married men took to placing explosives around their tents when they went out on patrol in a brazen attempt to keep other men away from their wives.

The disgruntled officer who started the brothel says, 'I really didn't know General Viljoen very well. As a soldier I submitted myself to the army's command structure and went along with orders. But I did not receive his orders in a very positive light. I would imagine that a man at his level would be sensitive enough to look the other way at times and to think outside the box.'

General Gerhard Beukes has another amusing tale to tell that paints the chief in a not-too-favourable light.

'We held a medal parade for Group 36 in Ladybrand in the Free State,' he says. 'General Viljoen was there to hand out medals. Group 36 consisted of commandos from Senekal, Winburg, Ladybrand, Ficksburg and Fouriesburg. I was commander of Winburg commando. It was one of those hot summer days. Usually in the rural areas, a rugby field and an athletics track are part of the same sports complex. The athletics track is slightly lower than the rugby field. On this day the important guests sat on the athletics track, separated from others who were in the small pavilion. I was on the podium with General Viljoen. The troops were facing us.

'While the general was speaking to the troops, one of them fainted. Two medics ran to his assistance. They came from the pavilion side. One of them was tall and the other was a bit shorter. They had to cross the athletics track. The one in front saw that the sports field was a little bit higher than the track and adjusted his stride. The one behind didn't see it, stumbled and fell. He got up and went to get the troop. They put him on the stretcher and ran off to the pavilion. Again the one in front saw the danger and made adjustments and didn't fall. Again the one behind didn't spot it: he fell, dropping the stretcher with the troop rolling off the stretcher. The stretcher-bearers picked up the troop and put him back on the stretcher. They picked up the stretcher, ready to start running again. The stretcher broke. The crowd laughed. The patient got up, dusted himself off and returned to his place in the parade. The stretcher-bearers stood there with the broken stretcher in their hands. By now the crowd was roaring with laughter.'

General Viljoen, however, was not amused. After the parade, he called the senior officers together and gave them a lecture about how soldiers on parade should breathe, presumably to avoid fainting. 'It was interesting to me,' observes Beukes. 'Here was the chief of the army lecturing his officers on parade issues. But these troops were commandos, they weren't full-time soldiers. I don't think the lecture was necessary.'

More than anything else, these stories are illustrative of Constand's conservatism. Everything had to be done by the book. Known to be an avid jogger and fitness enthusiast, he once visited Free State Command. The base knew all about his dictum that soldiers must be fit, as well as his love of running. 'Well, one morning he went out on his normal run,' remembers Beukes. 'Over coffee, or it could have been tea, he told us that he had been out on his early-morning run and had not seen any troops exercising. General Pine Pienaar, who was a heavy man, said, "Yes, General. You must remember that you get two kinds of fitness levels: physically and mentally fit." I don't know how Pine had reached the rank of general or why he had to say it, but I know that General Viljoen didn't think it was funny. I know Pine meant it in a good way, though.

'We all knew that the general was conservative and had a conservative outlook on life. One does need conservative people to bring balance because we can't all be liberals. We respected his conservative views but ... I think that these views came from his childhood and helped to shape his character.'

Constand loved warfare and the energy of battle, and sometimes he participated in operations, much to the consternation of the officers on the ground. One example was the Battle of Cassinga, an airborne assault on a SWAPO camp in May 1978. 'Jan Breytenbach was in command on the ground. In the heat of the battle, he called me: "General, come here. These bastards are going to kill you,"' Constand recalls, his blue eyes twinkling with laughter.

'I must say it was close. Firstly, the Cubans had some tanks in the vicinity, and, secondly, the whole operation was taking too long. On that day we expected to be out of there by 10 a.m. Yet 2 p.m. found us still fighting. Then the Cuban tanks began to approach. I watched as our air force attacked them. Some tanks broke through. One went up a hill, but it couldn't come down. If it did it would have shot my helicopter to pieces.'

The South African forces realised it would be too dangerous for their evacuation craft to land and remove them from the battlefield, so plans had to be quickly altered. 'We decided to walk back to our base some 250 kilometres away,' continues Constand. 'I removed everything that could make it easy to identify me if we were caught, my epaulettes and cap, and buried them. We'd walked one kilometre when the air force came to the rescue. Their helicopters came in like a group of butterflies. Not everything went according to plan. I knew which helicopter I was supposed to board, but when these craft landed, our men stormed into the first available ones. Some of the helicopters were overloaded.'

Breytenbach saw General Viljoen's arrival on the battlefield quite differently. Even by 2013 he was still not amused. 'Cassinga was a major parachute operation,' he tells me. 'General Viljoen was with me when I was wounded. He didn't jump with us. He flew in by helicopter. We were being attacked by tanks. We were about 250 kilometres behind enemy lines at Cassinga. We had to jump in and be choppered out. But we had an idiot brigadier who didn't need to interfere with our plans. He did. He buggered it up. General Viljoen was head of the army. It was a hell of a surprise to me when he arrived. I was busy fighting. I saw this little guy. I said, "What the hell are you doing here?" Later I climbed into a chopper as some troepie was being extricated. He said, "Generaal, wat die fok maak jy hier?" (General, what the fuck are you doing here?) and Viljoen replied, "Dis my army en ek kan maak wat ek wil." (It's my army and I can do what I want.)

'He shouldn't have been there. But he was. I had an added responsibility: I was responsible for this man's life. He was head of the army. We were being attacked from the south and the north and I thought,

"Jan Breytenbach, today they're going to capture you and march you through the streets of Luanda." That's when he took off his identification. It would have been a tremendous victory for the MPLA if they could boast that they've captured the chief of the South African Army and Jan Breytenbach. They would have displayed us as captives. They would have displayed us. Can you imagine the enemy's reaction if this had happened? I told him, "We are going to walk back." I said, "Take off your epaulettes because if they capture you ..." Later the choppers came.'

It was a close call, but, with the gift of hindsight, Breytenbach admits that Constand's presence was good for troop morale in Cassinga, just not for his. 'They were glad to see him. They thought, "If a general is here with us it can't be so terrible." His action was unusual.'

Was it necessary for the chief to become involved in fighting on the ground?

'Let me tell you why I took part in battles,' Constand says. 'My father was a soldier. I'd read about the Anglo-Boer War, yet I felt as head of the army I didn't have enough experience of being in a war. Because I wanted our senior staff who had not been in a war situation to experience one, I initiated a policy that said that these officers should accompany our conscripted troops on the battlefield as observers. I was convinced that I wouldn't know how I'd react if I actually hadn't experienced being under attack. I also wouldn't know whether we had the appropriate weapons for the warfare we were waging. Yes, we got reports, but I was after first-hand experience. I didn't want to rely on reports that might have been cooked. So I was on many operations. I came close to being part of an air assault in Zambia. We were on our way when the mission was called off.

'I was interested in the art of war. I wanted to be there, to test myself. In 1980 we launched Operation Smokehill. I was head of the army then and was on board a Ratel armoured vehicle. We advanced 250 kilometres into Angola as we attacked enemy bases. We encountered stiff resistance. Thirteen of our men were killed. This party entered an enemy camp too quickly. Anti-aircraft guns were fired at their vehicle. Ammunition inside the Ratel exploded and our men died. My vehicle detonated a landmine. I was thrown out of the vehicle. Nobody can tell me what it's like. I've been there and I've experienced it for myself.'

All well and good if you are General Viljoen, but the boss's quest to test himself under fire left many of his senior staff jittery. General Jannie Geldenhuys, who visited operational areas with Constand and who would succeed him as SADF chief, knew that warfare did not discriminate on the grounds of rank or station, and that death was ever present when bullets were flying. He was at tactical headquarters on 10 June 1980 when he heard about the Ratel's encounter with the landmine on his radio.

'It was here [at tactical headquarters] that I experienced some of the most anxious moments of my life, all because of General Viljoen,' wrote Geldenhuys in his memoir, *At the Front*. 'I heard his radio going off air and from the rest of the signals on the net I gathered that something had happened to his Ratel. The seconds and minutes dragged by, and I was eventually told that his Ratel had detonated two anti-tank mines, which had been set to explode simultaneously, the resulting explosion tossing him right out of his hatch.'[3]

Major General Chris Thirion, the former deputy chief of staff of Military Intelligence, recalls stories about Constand over several cups of strong coffee at Die Werf, his popular Pretoria restaurant that serves traditional Afrikaner cuisine. Their paths first crossed in Pretoria, just as Colonel Viljoen was promoted to the rank of brigadier. 'My first impressions were: this man is a soldier, a fighting man,' Thirion tells me. 'To say that we became friends would be wrong. We walked a road together in the hierarchy of the army's ranks. Our relationship then was one of respect from my side for him. Later we became friends. Maybe I should say that we moved closer to one another. Even if we were friends, I never lost my respect for him as my senior officer.'

It was as a friend and subordinate that Thirion saw another side of the general and came to appreciate him as a principled, upright and fair human being. 'He treated everyone, irrespective of colour or race, with the utmost respect. He was a high-level leader. For me, General Constand Viljoen was the last of the great Boer generals. With this I mean he belongs with those who understood the ethics of warfare. There are ethics involved in war. He understood it. He lived by it. According to the ethics I'm talking about, one must be honest and treat people with dignity even if they're prisoners of war.'

Thirion witnessed this side of Constand more than once, and was present on numerous occasions when he forbade operations that he felt crossed a moral line.

On one such occasion, during the Battle of Cassinga, a group of guerrillas had been captured. 'We had identified a few whom we planned to take to South West Africa to be interrogated,' recalls Thirion. 'When it became obvious that we had to evacuate sooner than we had planned, he ordered the release of those prisoners who weren't going to be taken to South West Africa. He surprised our medics by commanding them to treat their wounds. Then they were freed. The prisoners couldn't believe that they were being released. They had expected something far worse than that.'

On another occasion, Constand surprised Thirion with his philosophy about the difference between terrorists and the SADF. While at Katutura, a black township in Windhoek in what was then South

West Africa, Thirion went to the general 'to suggest how we could strike a blow against SWAPO. We'd found a drum packed with explosives in the single quarters of a hostel. I told him we could booby-trap the drum so that it could explode at a time when the place was full of people and cause huge damage. He listened to me. Then he said: "You'll be disappointed in me but my answer is no. If we do this we'll stoop to the level of being terrorists." He said it was a matter for the police. He advised me that we could be part of police action by surrounding the hostel and seeing arrests being made.'

Constand had planned to resign as chief of the army after five years, and knowing that he was close to his farm and the life he truly wanted, he was considering acquiring another property. But his plans changed after the former defence minister, P.W. Botha, replaced Vorster as prime minister in 1978 and began putting his mark on government. On 7 October 1980, Magnus Malan became the new minister of defence and, in November, Constand stepped into his shoes as head of the South African Defence Force. General Jannie Geldenhuys succeeded Constand as chief of the army.

Constand recalls that Botha and Malan called him in to tell him about his appointment. 'I tried to tell them about my farm. In the end I said, "I will make another deal with you: I will serve for five years, then I will retire." They agreed. Many people speculated that I quit because I had had some trouble with P.W. Botha. That's not true. I said I would leave after five years as SADF head and I did.'

Constand was in the vanguard of radical change in the way South Africa conducted its wars. Up until 1968 the SADF was still following the conventional way of fighting, with armies meeting one another head-on on the battlefield. This was referred to as the 'World War II approach'. But in the early seventies a new philosophy of mobile warfare began to surface. This approach included the use of tactical surprises, commando attacks, infiltration, raids and mobile defence techniques; all strategies suited to fighting guerrillas in Africa. Instead of gaining ground, the idea was to design the battle in such a way that you could lure the enemy into a 'killing ground' and then utilise your superior firepower and movement to destroy him.[4]

In his time as SADF chief, Constand was relentless about taking the war to South Africa's enemies, as long as the strikes were executed outside the country's borders. In 1981, concerned about the possible introduction of chemical and biological weapons into the Angolan theatre of war, Constand agreed at a meeting that one of Lieutenant Colonel Wouter Basson's first tasks would be to gather as much information as possible about such weapons in the international arena.[5] The so-called death squads operating under the aegis of the SADF only started after his retirement. 'Hit squads were used in South Africa after my time,' he says. 'I was blessed that I didn't have anything to do with hit squads killing people inside South Africa.'

Constand remained opposed to indiscriminate killing, a conviction clearly demonstrated by another story that Thirion tells me. In the early 1980s, Constand was briefed by Military Intelligence on a plan to kill Chris Hani in Maseru. The men giving the update in Pretoria were in the business of killing; hard men who were part of an elite force trained to quietly infiltrate neighbouring countries on government-sanctioned missions to assassinate identified targets; men who carefully planned their missions and who could strike at any time to kill South Africans damned as enemies of the state before disappearing back into the shadows. Each mission further honed their skills and added to their professionalism and fearsome reputation as state-sanctioned executioners. Although other liberation movements were targeted, the focus was mainly on members of Umkhonto we Sizwe (MK), the military wing of the African National Congress. While

MK soldiers called themselves guerrillas or freedom fighters, to the government they were simply terrorists.

In the eighties, Constand was a rugged blond officer, the most powerful military man in South Africa. His soft, some say gentle, blue eyes quietly absorbed and analysed everything that was presented to him. As a member of the Afrikaner Broederbond, and thus a representative of the ruling elite, he had Prime Minister Botha's trust, respect and confidence.

At the end of the briefing on this particular afternoon in Pretoria, the general gathered his documents, his movements focused and deliberate, and returned them to his briefcase. Several pairs of eyes were fixed on him, waiting for him to formally sanction Hani's elimination. Instead, he surprised them with an unexpected question: 'Will Mrs Hani and her children be in the house?'

The military briefers were clearly unprepared, having never even considered Mrs Hani or her children. They were simply there to get General Viljoen's go-ahead to kill one of the most wanted men in South Africa. By 1974 Hani had established himself as a fearless fighter and a rising star in the South African Communist Party (SACP).[6]

Hani was yet to become MK's chief of staff, but in the eyes of Military Intelligence he was already a legitimate target. Killing him outside South Africa's borders fell well within the general's doctrine of battling and visiting damage on the enemy outside the country. What was this now about his wife and two daughters? Who cared about a terrorist's family? Had the State Security Council (SSC), the shadowy body chaired by Botha and which included key cabinet members, not already sanctioned the killing? If the SSC was happy with the plan, why should General Viljoen demur?

Of course, these thoughts could not be spoken aloud. This was a disciplined army where orders were followed, especially if they came from its most senior officer. And this was a general who had fought alongside his troops, who had jumped from aeroplanes as a paratrooper and who had faced death in cross-border raids. He was a hero of South Africa's war in Angola; an officer who, more than anyone else in the period between 1980 and 1985, could be hailed as a true soldier's soldier. He was an alpha male in Afrikaner circles where military men were admired and treated as heroic defenders of the volk in the tradition of the Boer War generals. General Viljoen was the most admired and respected officer in what was regarded as the most fearsome defence force in Africa.

And when the general asked a question, he expected an answer. On this day, the answer was 'We don't know'. There was also the suggestion that it really did not matter if Mrs Hani and the children were to die during the assassination. The target would be taken out, the mission would be successful and that was all that mattered.

They had underestimated the soft, compassionate side of their general; the side that remembered the Anglo-Boer War and the price exacted from his people by the British. 'We don't make war against women and children,' he said firmly. As his words hung in the air, and the group digested their impact, the chief shocked them further by calling off the operation. The men were stunned and disappointed: intelligence sources and careful planning had brought them so close to eliminating Hani; it was a coup, and now this. The target would escape and plan more sorties against South Africa, all because of General Viljoen's philosophy of warfare.

In his role as chief of the defence force, Constand nailed down a policy stating that the SADF was not to be involved in politics. 'He was uncompromising about this,' says Thirion. 'The defence force was apolitical. He was a professional soldier who was loyal to the constitution of the country. For professional soldiers such as

General Viljoen, Colonel Jan Breytenbach and me, it wasn't about the National Party. General Viljoen often said, "We don't support a political philosophy or policy, we serve the government of the day." The ethical code of a soldier demands that we serve the legal government of the day. We still hold that view. Let's say that there were to be an insurgency war against the legally elected ANC government; then they can call on people like Constand Viljoen, Jan Breytenbach and Chris Thirion to oppose this with all our might.' Thirion says all of this with a steely determination that shows just how serious he is.

Thirion is not alone in his appreciation for the former chief. Many of the men who were under his command have fond memories of Constand, who was affectionately called Stofstrepie due to the speed at which he moved and got things done. They loved his enthusiasm, energy and can-do attitude. Former spy Maritz Spaarwater treasured the general's willingness to listen and take advice, even from subordinates, a quality that sometimes led to innovative changes in the SADF. Once, on the Border, they were shaving and shooting the breeze, sharing their frustrations over the SADF's failure to follow the tracks left by infiltrators. The horses and dogs being used were not ideal for follow-up operations, and the infiltrators stood a good chance of disappearing before they could be engaged.

In his autobiography, Spaarwater wrote: 'Horses required large and cumbersome logistics, and even the best of dogs had problems of stamina in that environment. Also their paws, even in leather bootees, succumbed very quickly to the extremely hot sand of Ovamboland. I was then in my bike phase and suggested to the general that we try off-road motorcycles, or scramblers – quads were not yet around. The general objected that they would be too noisy for the purpose. I disagreed, pointing out that they could be very effectively silenced and would also give a psychological advantage to the rider, given the speeds of which they were capable and their height, which would provide better observation.'[7]

Constand took heed of what Spaarwater said and, after he had shaved and given the matter some more thought, decided he liked what he had heard and instructed his operational staff to do an assessment and make submissions 'to higher authority requesting that such a unit be established, including calling up a contingent of biking national servicemen. These units were deployed with little delay although I didn't know from which regiment and, after devising and practising the necessary tactics for employing the new weapon, I was later told that they had proven to be effective.'[8] Thus the nugget of an idea that Spaarwater had dropped in a rudimentary block while shaving next to the general brought about a major operational change.

Fiercely loyal, Constand remembers friends, such as his old lecturer Cas Bakkes. When Bakkes moved to Paarl from Gauteng, he left many friends behind and Constand planned to visit him. So, too, with former president P.W. Botha, after he was forced out in an internal National Party rebellion. 'We weren't friends,' says Constand of Botha. 'After he'd retired to Wilderness many of his colleagues turned against him. Ristie and I used to visit him when we were in the Cape. I realised he was lonely. He wasn't my friend but I respected him. We didn't always see eye to eye, you know.'

General James Kriel, now farming in the beautiful Baardskeerdersbos area near Gansbaai, that infamous abalone-poaching hot spot in the Western Cape, remembers Constand as a hard-working teetotaller with whom he often shared a tent in the operational area. Once head of the South African Air Force, Kriel had shared in the dangers of Border warfare with the general, and had also seen his sense of humour at play.

'We were on the road between Grootfontein and Ondangwa,'

Kriel recalls. 'For safety reasons we wore khaki clothes without any insignia. We saw a young national serviceman. He lifted up his hand to hitch a ride, something he wasn't supposed to do. We stopped. The young man didn't recognise General Viljoen. "Where are you off to?" the young man asked. General Viljoen laughed. The young man said he'd missed his lift. Constand said, "Get in." They continued talking. Constand never told him he was head of the defence force.'

Being something of a maverick in the SADF, Constand identified strongly with the Afrikaners' struggle against British imperialism. As chief of the army, perhaps remembering those days when he was a whippersnapper showing his contempt for the defence force's Englishness, he ordered that the memory of Boer general and 1914 Rebellion leader Christian Frederick Beyers not be forgotten. 'He drowned in the Vaal River while trying to escape from men who had been his own troops. Can you believe it?' asks Constand incredulously. 'He was the first head of the first defence force of the Union of South Africa. When I was still the chief of the army I unveiled a monument in his honour.'

When he ended his career as a professional soldier in 1985, Constand was earning a monthly salary of R6 000, or R72 000 annually. He also got a lump sum of R240 000. 'That was enough to sink a few boreholes on the farm,' he reminisces. 'I started farming the land. Remember that I'm from Standerton and in Standerton they plant mielies. I became a mielie farmer. But I'd also promised myself that I would progress to cattle farming, which I did. Now I'm also into game farming. As a game farmer I can continue farming until I turn ninety.'

In 2013, Constand was nearing his eightieth birthday and still carrying himself like a professional soldier, his once blond hair now silvery grey, his face clean-shaven like that of a troop on parade, his words measured, his eyes still as blue as ever. His ways are those of a gentleman of another age, a man who still opens the door for his wife and who pulls out a chair for her as she takes her place at the table. He has a presence: he does not need to draw attention to himself, people just naturally look at him. He is a teetotaller, and has been all his life.

Constand and Christina Sussanna Viljoen form a redoubtable pair: Afrikaners, Christians, friends, lovers, comrades, fellow travellers on the military path of his career, and trusted, reliable shoulders to lean on. Christina, affectionately known as Ristie, describes their marriage and the defence force as interlinked. 'When you're married to a soldier, you know that you're on full-time duty but without any pay,' she explains. 'That's the first thing. You don't even ask questions. If you're expected to be somewhere, you see that you're there. They don't ask you if you have the necessary experience to do anything, they expect you to do it. Look, I went up in the ranks of military wives. I got more senior with each promotion that my husband got.'

As an army wife, she had to be independent and manage the farm on her own. She learnt to cope with each situation that came her way. 'I think I drove my children crazy. You know that your husband isn't dead. The children have a father, but the father isn't there. Then they tell you that he would have done things this way or that way,' she says with a sigh.

The defence force placed huge demands on their marriage. 'I think you have your ups and downs,' Ristie says. 'I don't think we ever wanted to go our separate ways or something like that. We did things together. We had quite a few children. From the time that we bought the farm in 1965, we lived a sort of double life. In all those years, we kept the farm going. The farm grew on us. At one stage I had to live on the farm with the children.'

Proud of his life partner's grit and courage to stick by him, which often meant temporary separation and added responsibility on the farm, Constand tells me how his wife farmed tobacco and cattle, and grew parsley and paprika for the export market. His march to the number-one position in the SADF would probably not have been possible without Ristie at his side, and he knows and appreciates this.

Constand kept his personal life separate from his army career. His ring-fencing ensured few of his colleagues knew that he had an identical twin brother, for example. James Kriel was surprised when I asked him if he knew about Abraham's existence. And Jan Breytenbach recalled an incident in the centre of Pretoria one day. 'I saw the general and said, "Dag, Generaal." (Good day, General). He said he wasn't the general, but his brother. I thought he was having me on. I never saw that man again.'

6

In enemy colours

IN 1987, TWO YEARS after Constand retired from the SADF, Abraham heard the call of politics. Not the politics of the National Party, but that of the English-speaking opposition: the Progressive Federal Party (PFP). A white liberal party, the PFP was viewed as being in the same league as the communists. The NP nicknamed it 'Packing For Perth', after the Western Australian city to which large numbers of English-speaking South Africans had emigrated. In a not-so-subtle bid to capitalise on his surname, the PFP approached Abraham and asked him to stand as a parliamentary candidate in the Waterkloof constituency.

He did not bite, saying that active party politics was not for him and suggesting that his bosom friend and colleague Professor Johan Wolfaardt, dean of the theology faculty at UNISA, would make a better candidate.

Now retired, Wolfaardt lives in a flat overlooking Hartbeespoort Dam in North West province. Endearingly known as Harties and named after the antelope that once roamed the region, this dam lies between the Magaliesberg and Witwatersberg mountain ranges. The view from Wolfaardt's home is stunning: one can see straight through the poort and marvel at the engineering skills that built the dam. Abraham and his friend have found peace in this view over many shared cups of coffee.

Wolfaardt laughingly recalls meeting Abraham in 1975, an occasion made memorable by his own taste in clothing. 'I had on a multi-coloured shirt, which Abraham associated with the security police,' he says. The man in the garish shirt, however, was far from a spy. An ordinary academic, Wolfaardt was in fact hostile towards the Broederbond and the NP. Despite these suspicious beginnings, the two men developed a bond, a friendship that would strengthen through shared experiences and their mutual distaste for apartheid. Both had been awarded a World Council of Churches bursary, both had had a run-in with Professor Groenewald and experienced first hand his vindictiveness, both were ordered to redo their studies, and both had endured the chagrin of the Broederbond and the NP. They were fellow rebels. 'Well, I wouldn't say Abraham and I are twins,' says Wolfaardt, 'but I would say that we trust each other, and respect the other's integrity, uprightness and judgement.'

What drives Abraham? 'I think he has a strong philosophical drive for the truth. He can be very cautious at times, but that's because he qualifies his own decisions by stating that he doesn't have all of the truth. Abraham has been hurt by the church, politics and people. You'd have to walk a long road with him before he'll call you a friend.' Wolfaardt's theory as to why Abraham did not formally terminate his Dutch Reformed Church membership has much to do with one's church being like 'part of a family in which you've grown up. You've invested a lot of your life in your family and you just don't leave. Even if you have a stepmother, you don't have any other mother except your stepmother. I left the Dutch Reformed Church. I couldn't stomach the teaching of Professor A.B. du Preez, who claimed that only we in South Africa knew the truth about apartheid. According to him the rest of the world was wrong.'

Wolfaardt was enjoying his job at UNISA and living in Nieuw Muckleneuk, a Pretoria suburb known for its diplomats' houses and quiet tree-lined streets, when Abraham arrived at his home with PFP politician Robin Carlisle to talk about politics. 'Abraham said that I lived in the Waterkloof constituency and tried to persuade me to make myself available as a candidate for the Progressive Federal Party,' Wolfaardt recalls. 'I declined. I said, "Abraham, I'm not a politician. I believe that with your background and connections you'll make a much better candidate."'

Cornered and with no counter-arguments, Abraham agreed to contest the seat, a decision that would prove unpopular. Professor Theo van Wyk for one, then rector at UNISA and Abraham's personal friend, was unhappy with his plans and sought to dissuade him by warning of the risks, the first being that he would have to resign once his nomination became official. Van Wyk implored Abraham to consider his wife and children, who would forfeit their medical cover if he failed to win the seat. He would also lose his pension. Abraham listened, but he was acutely aware of the dilemma he faced: he was a man of principle and he had given his word.

'Theo said, "Think about your family. You won't win. You know that nomination day is also resignation day. You won't return to UNISA." To which I replied, "Theo, I would have followed your advice but I've given my word to them. I can't go back on it now."'

Today, more than three decades later, an older, wiser and more experienced Abraham says, 'Now I know what Theo meant. My family has battled over the years. It's been hard at times. I still remember how Professor Nic Olivier, an Afrikaner and a PFP MP, warned me before that election. He took me aside and said, "I'm glad that you're here. I want to warn you that there are people who'll promise you a directorship in this or that company if you lose. Don't believe them. They won't keep their promise."'

Abraham's opponent was a UNISA colleague, Org Marais, who

had the formidable National Party political machine, as well as the Broederbond, behind him. In the end, it was Marais who won the Waterkloof seat in 1987.

That election was characterised by two things. First, Abraham started to assert himself and claim an identity distinct from that of his twin brother Constand. It was now that people began calling him Braam, a new name marking a new identity. 'I only became aware that he was also known as Braam during his foray into the political world,' observes Wolfaardt. It was a signifier that he had formally entered politics.

Second, Abraham's ability to reach out to different groups was apparent. In those pre-SUV days, one particularly memorable sight was of farmers, known to hold strong right-wing views, arriving in Waterkloof in their bakkies to put up Abraham's election posters. They were not helping his party; they were helping the man whom they trusted and respected.

'I don't think that Abraham did too badly,' says Wolfaardt. 'He fought a seat in the heartland of Pretoria. I was one of his colleagues who canvassed for him.'

Still, Abraham had lost and was now effectively unemployed, a man without a salary and all the other perks that a lecturer at UNISA enjoyed. His stand, which was a shot across the bows of government, had also stirred up tensions in his family. He was not a good topic for dinner-table discussion.

Abraham would have remain unemployed, and unemployable in areas where the NP and the Broederbond exerted their influence, but his friend Frederik van Zyl Slabbert came to his rescue with an offer of a job. Brilliant, articulate and charming, Van Zyl Slabbert went to Parliament in 1974 as a member of the PFP. By 1979 he was the party leader and admired as one of the golden sons of Afrikaner politics.[1]

A former provincial rugby player, he brought a new dimension to white opposition politics in Parliament. Being Afrikaans and able to think on his feet minimised the opportunities for ridicule by the ruling party: he not only responded in their language, he did so without tripping over his own words or pronunciation. Moreover, the youthful Van Zyl Slabbert was fearless, far-sighted and confident that ultimately the future of South Africa would have to be negotiated between those in Parliament and those fighting a liberation war.

On 11 February 1986, Van Zyl Slabbert resigned as an MP and as a member of the PFP. His friend and fellow MP Alex Boraine followed him out of Parliament a week later. Neither had any plans for the future. The former PFP leader had R2 500 in his bank account after using his R120 000 gratification from Parliament to repay his home loan.[2]

Comrades in the cause for political change, Van Zyl Slabbert and Boraine launched the Institute for a Democratic Alternative for South Africa (IDASA), an independent organisation that they were adamant would not be part of the 'struggle' or 'system', but which would endeavour to encourage dialogue between people on both sides.[3]

It was easier for the National Party to vilify the two men than to engage with them. Instead of taking a hard and honest look at the frustrations that led them to leave the comfort of Parliament – where they could have remained for years debating in a process that was not bringing the black majority any closer to the franchise – the NP lashed out at them and IDASA, branding them white communists. The government failed to see what Van Zyl Slabbert and Boraine had recognised in 1985 when President Botha had to declare a state of emergency to quell black anger in many South African townships: the time for change was now.

As any association with the men or their organisation could be a debilitating move both politically and socially, it was perhaps inevitable that Abraham would one day join them.

It was Van Zyl Slabbert who recruited him into IDASA, honouring a promise he had made to Abraham when the latter was searching for advice on standing for the PFP in Waterkloof. When Abraham sought his counsel, Van Zyl Slabbert was blunt: he thought Parliament had become irrelevant and that the future of politics lay outside and not inside Parliament. It was one of the reasons why he had relinquished his own seat. But he was adamant that Abraham would have to decide for himself. Van Zyl Slabbert did, however, promise Abraham a job if he failed to make it to Parliament.

The IDASA job drove a further wedge between Abraham and members of the Viljoen clan. Standing for the PFP was bad enough, but to associate with Van Zyl Slabbert and Boraine was begging excommunication from the family. In July 1987, IDASA took a group of Afrikaners to Senegal to meet the exiled leadership of the ANC in Dakar. Abraham was among them, unashamedly flying his colours for all to see and embarrassing his extended family in the process. The chill caused by his Senegal adventure was to affect the Viljoen family for many years, but not all members saw him as a traitor.

'An uncle of mine, Adriaan Strydom, who was farming in Northern Transvaal, was gravely ill when I returned from Dakar,' remembers Abraham. 'Members of the family were visiting him. Some of those on his farm were fuming over my indiscretion in meeting the ANC in exile. There was talk that I had brought shame on the family. It was said that I didn't care about their future or feelings. That uncle of mine stood up for me. He said they should leave me alone because he knew I knew what I was doing.'

Adriaan Strydom was a Nat, but he believed in facing the truth and standing up for it. 'I appreciated his support,' says his nephew today.

'I walked a lonely road. I got used to the loneliness. But I never got used to being alienated from so many things in my life. Every person is a member of a community, culture and family. I was alienated. I was alone.'

The vitriol that greeted the news of the Dakar meeting also came from an apoplectic President Botha. Hot with anger, he condemned it, as did the right wing, which took its wrath to Jan Smuts International Airport. On their arrival in Johannesburg from Dakar, IDASA received a hostile reception and Abraham was once again sharply reminded that he had an identical twin brother. 'A few police officers thought I was General Constand Viljoen and saluted me,' he says. 'I wasn't in uniform. I don't know what they thought of the general returning from Dakar. Usually I correct people when they mistake me for Constand. This time I wasn't going to tell them I wasn't the man they thought I was.'

Abraham's political profile was putting him on the radar and he began to warrant more than a passing interest from those who were eliminating so-called enemies of the state. Unaware of it at the time, state-hired killers were watching him, planning to send him to his grave. On 1 May 1989, one of a number of annually significant days for workers and their trade unions to symbolise and mobilise resistance to the apartheid government, social anthropologist David Webster was gunned down outside his home in Troyeville, Johannesburg. The murder was organised by the Civil Cooperation Bureau, a government-sponsored hit squad, and carried out by Ferdi Barnard, one of its operatives. Abraham, who was close to Webster, found out years later that he, too, was on Barnard's hit list.

Abraham was also attracting the state's attention in the so-called independent homeland of KwaNdebele. Abraham was farming in Kwa-Ndebele and had access to the royal family. He gathered information about police atrocities, which were largely unreported, and used his contacts in the PFP to raise questions in Parliament about the havoc being caused there. The authorities were sharpening their knives, preparing to retaliate against him, when his friends in the homeland got wind of their plans and urged Abraham to stay away from KwaNdebele. He listened and lived.

By now Abraham and Constand were politically estranged, but were on speaking terms, at least. Afrikaners have a word to describe conflict in their ranks: broedertwis, meaning disagreement among brothers, mainly about politics.

But this was more than a simple disagreement between siblings: this was a separation along political lines that was dividing an entire family. Constand had distinguished himself as a fighting man in his country's army, while his twin brother was aligned with forces working for change. It was a crisis, and a painful period in their relationship. But, as they say, blood is thicker than water, and can compel people to reach across the divide. From Betel, Constand reached out to his Boeta. 'He got a message to me via our mother, warning me that if "I knew what was good for me" I would quit the committees of the South African Council of Churches,' recalls Abraham.

Speaking about the relationship between the Viljoen brothers in the eighties, Johan Wolfaardt says he sees no reason why Constand would have approved of Abraham's politics: 'Why should he? He was a member of the powerful Broederbond: he had to be if he wanted to be head of the South African Defence Force. I knew that they seldom discussed politics because they accepted that they'd never agree. I think Abraham took a position that was never judgemental towards his brother. He didn't agree with him.'

Of the nature of their estrangement, Wolfaardt says: 'There were times when they didn't have any contact. But there was this bond between them. It would have been interesting if the National Party government had detained Abraham or even placed him under house arrest. I wonder what Constand's response would have been then?'

Despite being left of his family, Abraham is respected and the younger generation often seeks his advice. 'I think he has authority in his family because of his kindness and humanity,' explains Wolfaardt. 'He listens to them without judging them. He's open and has a capacity to give people room – yes, even for their weaknesses – because he doesn't criticise them easily.'

In his memoir, former president F.W. de Klerk, who played a key role in ending white rule in South Africa, described the Viljoen twins as opposites, saying, 'Braam was a softer version of his brother.'[4]

It was this softness that appealed to those in his family who stood by him, as well as made an impression on Peter Storey, a former bishop and president of the Methodist Church of Southern Africa. Storey remembers Constand as being direct, honest and straightforward. 'What you saw is what you got,' he says. 'I suggested to [Constand] once it would have been fun to borrow [his] uniform, dress his twin brother up in it, and send him to Angola to declare the war over and order the SADF home. Humour was not one of the general's strong points.'

7

Riven by politics

THE CONTRAST BETWEEN the Viljoen brothers – between the conservative and the liberal, the Broederbonder and the dissident – was not the only division within Afrikanerdom. Even within the ruling National Party itself, there were deep divisions that had a profound impact on the politics of the country.

Like the Viljoen clan, the Mulder family has deep roots in Afrikanerdom, and has tasted the bitter medicine of broedertwis and lived with its painful results. The brothers Corné and Pieter Mulder followed their father Dr Connie Mulder into politics, and moved from the old South Africa into the new with Constand Viljoen.

Connie Mulder was a true-blue National Party member, reared in a household that did not view Jan Smuts as a hero of the volk. But, as with so many other families, the Mulders did not all see eye to eye. Connie's brother Frederik angered their mother when he joined the Union Defence Force to fight in World War II. When he was due to leave for the front line, she locked herself in her bedroom, angry at his betrayal, and refused to see him off.

'This is part of our history,' says Corné. 'It shows how politics was influencing Afrikaner families. In our house we talked politics in the morning, afternoon and at night.'

That politics was the main talking point in the Mulder home is understandable, as Connie Mulder filled various positions in his career, from leader of the Transvaal branch of the National Party, cabinet minister and contender for prime minister, to right-wing campaigner and co-founder of the Conservative Party (CP).

Mulder, appointed information minister by Prime Minister John Vorster in 1968, was once considered a crown prince in the National Party. The Great Hope from the Transvaal, supported by the Transvaal-based Afrikaans media group Perskor and the ever-faithful Nasionale Pers, he was set to take on the Cape wing of the party. However, his political career was effectively destroyed in 1977 when he was implicated in the Information Scandal, dubbed Muldergate, in which he, Vorster and secretary for information Eschel Rhoodie were accused of using government money to finance the newspaper *The Citizen*, a pro-NP publication that would compete with the liberal morning newspaper *Rand Daily Mail*.

Denial after denial could not calm the storm, and Mulder made one too many when asked outright by the PFP's Japie Basson in Parliament if the government was bankrolling *The Citizen*. Vorster did not repudiate the allegation and retired as prime minister in October 1978 to take up the largely honorary position of state president.[1]

In late 1978, with Vorster out of the way, Mulder put up his hand as a candidate to replace the disgraced prime minister. So did defence minister P.W. Botha. Mulder stood a good chance in the bruising head-to-head melee, but on 28 September 1978 he felt the cold winds of betrayal as his colleagues in the Transvaal turned against him. Botha's subsequent victory ushered in an era of arrogant, uncompromising, us-against-the-world politics. The police, who had been Vorster's private army under Van den Bergh, had lost out to the military, and Botha trusted his generals implicitly.

Although Botha retained Mulder in his cabinet reshuffle, when a clearer picture of his role in the Info Scandal emerged in news reports, he was forced to resign as minister. By the second week of November 1978, Connie Mulder was gone.

In mid-1979, a commission of inquiry concluded that Vorster 'knew everything' about the corruption and had tolerated it. He resigned from the presidency in disgrace. The following year, his fellow Koffiefontein internee and the man who did his dirty operations, the notorious Lang Hendrik van den Bergh, was kicked out as head of BOSS and the agency was replaced with the National Intelligence Service under Niel Barnard.

Corné Mulder believes that his father's downfall was detrimental for the government. 'He held that the ANC could not only be defeated internally. The ANC also went about isolating South Africa globally. My father's operation was a propaganda war to put South Africa's case. When they destroyed my father, he warned them that they did not understand what they were doing. He said: "You can destroy me but you'll also wreck South Africa's propaganda offensive, and if this happens you'll lose the war militarily." Subsequent events showed that my father was right. P.W. Botha militarised South Africa and introduced the total-onslaught concept. When we reached a dead end he was forced out. All of this had an effect on Afrikaners, especially those labelled right wing.'

Because of his background as minister of defence, Botha had an affinity for the military, and he used the military as his own personal iron fist to smash his enemies whenever the opportunity presented itself. When it became clear that state violence was not going to be enough to intimidate white South Africa's enemies, the government resorted to demonising its opponents by hanging the placard of communism around their necks. When this, too, failed to quench the flames, Botha and his cronies began to ramp up the fear among white

South Africans, fanning a siege mentality that would push them further into state-created political paranoia. 'Total onslaught' became a popular government catchphrase used to define what South Africa was up against. But what exactly did it mean?

Magnus Malan, the former defence minister and Constand Viljoen's predecessor as SADF chief, said years later that the 'intended victim of communist aggression was deprived of the luxury of preparing for the conflict, right from the stage of mobilization up to the declaration of a formal state of war. The strategic goal was to make the country under attack ungovernable and to rob the population of its will to resist.'[2]

So a total onslaught, according to Malan, was an attempt to make a country ungovernable, which is what the ANC was essentially trying to do in South Africa. To respond effectively, Malan continued, the target country would have to initiate measures at the highest level that were managed in accordance with that country's total national strategy. In other words, give your enemies no foothold in your country, destroy them where you find them, and use every means at your disposal to do so, even if it requires stepping outside of the law. For enemy collaborators inside South Africa in the 1970s and 1980s, it meant detention without trial, banning, state harassment and death.

At the same time, Botha began a process of reform, repealing some of apartheid's petty laws. But the fundamentals – the classification of people according to race and the denial of the franchise to non-whites – remained firmly intact.

Because of his reforms, however superficial, Botha faced discontent within the National Party. The broedertwis intensified and Botha could not quell the dissent. One of the unhappier voices that rose against him belonged to Andries Treurnicht, the former dominee who had succeeded Mulder as Transvaal leader of the party. By 1982

Treurnicht had had enough. Opposed to Botha's reforms, which he saw as a threat to white minority rule, Treurnicht left the party, taking seventeen MPs with him. The rebels formed the Conservative Party, which would become the largest opposition in the whites-only Parliament after the May 1987 elections.

'The NP was in the process of being split on ideological grounds around the question of power-sharing,' says Corné. 'That's why the Conservative Party was formed. The effect of this break was felt by Afrikaners up to the period of constitutional negotiations and beyond. Afrikaners started to fight and wrestle among each other. They were out of breath when they had to stand against the ANC.'

The white right was now a competing force, trawling the same waters that the NP exclusively had once fished for voters. Public servants, middle-class Afrikaners, farmers and even some English-speaking South Africans now had an alternative.

In 1987 Connie and his two sons stood for Parliament for the Conservative Party. While the brothers lost, Pieter in Potchefstroom and Corné in Gezina, Pretoria, Connie was elected MP for Randfontein. By then he was a sick man, and in January 1988 he succumbed to terminal cancer before he could take up his seat. On 29 March, Corné was elected to fill his father's now vacant position, keeping the seat in the CP and in the Mulder family. And in a by-election three weeks earlier, voters had endorsed Pieter as a Conservative Party MP in the Schweizer-Reneke constituency.

With the 1987 election, the CP took over from the PFP as the largest opposition in the white Parliament. The CP and the National Party were now the two major groups claiming to represent Afrikaner interests. On the fringes, on the far right, were Jaap Marais and his Herstigte Nasionale Party (HNP, Reconstituted National Party).

Marais and Albert Hertzog (son of former prime minister General

J.B.M. Hertzog) had left the NP to form the party in 1969, because they were dissatisfied with Vorster's policies. With the rise of the Conservatives, the HNP, which found its support base in poorer sections of the Afrikaner community, had been pushed to the margins.

But there were also pressures from more progressive elements in the NP for meaningful reform and negotiation with the black majority. An opportunity came in 1989 when P.W. Botha suffered a stroke and was ousted as leader of the party and as state president. He was succeeded by F.W. de Klerk.

In his speech at the opening of Parliament on 2 February 1990, De Klerk announced the unbanning of the ANC and other political parties and said that the time to negotiate had arrived. Nine days later Nelson Mandela was released from Victor Verster Prison.

By now the concept of total onslaught had fallen into disfavour, and its proponents – the politicians and particularly the hard men and soldiers who had protected volk and fatherland from the communist threat – were swept aside by De Klerk. Discarded as surplus stock, they were filled with resentment, and their alienation was even more keenly felt when De Klerk unbanned and began negotiations with their old enemy, the ANC.

The former head of Military Intelligence, General Tienie Groenewald, was one of those men who had staffed the senior echelons of the SADF and who had been trusted by Botha and others before him to stop the communists from conquering South Africa through their surrogate ANC.

Groenewald grew up in an era when being an Afrikaans-speaker was dangerous in some parts of South Africa. As an Afrikaner at an English-speaking school in Ixopo, Natal, he quickly realised that hostilities between Boer and Brit had not ceased at the end of the Anglo-Boer War. 'I was chosen as the Afrikaner to be bullied at school,' he says. 'I still carry some of the scars of those fights. I always say I was beaten into being an Afrikaner. The fights did not stay on the playground. They were carried into the classrooms. One time I had to interrupt our history teacher, Miss Ormond, because I differed with her about her interpretation of the Anglo-Boer War.'

Groenewald was a gatherer of information, a handler of spies and a keeper of secrets for most of his professional career. For many years he managed people who had betrayed their organisations and/or countries, usually for money. His network of human assets fed Military Intelligence information that could be used for South Africa's benefit.

As part of his total-onslaught strategy, Botha appointed Groenewald head of the Tak Nasionale Vertolking (National Interpretation Branch), a shadowy organisation that worked with the secretariat of the SSC, and that met at precisely ten o'clock every morning to compare intelligence notes on the situation in South Africa. Two senior members from each intelligence-gathering organisation were required to be present at these meetings and a daily situational report was prepared for dissemination. Groenewald briefed the SSC every fortnight. The Branch also prepared an annual report.

'Let me emphasise that the Branch was a security and not a political organisation,' explains Groenewald. 'We had nothing to do with legal political organisations. We were monitoring banned organisations such as the ANC, Umkhonto we Sizwe and the Pan Africanist Congress, all of them organisations that posed a threat to South Africa. Naturally we looked intently at people such as Archbishop Desmond Tutu and Dr Allan Boesak. We also worked on men like Nelson Mandela, Thabo Mbeki and Jacob Zuma.'

In order to operate more effectively, Groenewald and Military Intelligence also recruited people inside the ANC. 'You'll fall on your back if you hear who worked for us,' he says. 'Those are names that I will never disclose. You can't betray a person who has risked everything to spy for you. We infiltrated the ANC quite successfully.'

Considered an authority on the level of insurrection against the state, Groenewald was in demand. He was called on to educate selected individuals, such as directors-general, about the extent of the threats. 'I knew just about every cabinet minister. I was incredibly surprised when F.W. de Klerk was elected as new leader of the National Party, because he'd never shown that he had any leadership qualities,' he says, unable to suppress a dismissive laugh.

As a member of Botha's trusted inner circle during the era of total onslaught, Groenewald attended the president's team-building sessions, where he was asked to give briefings. Over time he was afforded glimpses into cabinet's thinking, and was astonished by what he witnessed.

'One of the most shocking discoveries for me was that cabinet had realised apartheid was over but they were not taking any positive steps to look at an alternative policy,' he says.

Even in P.W. Botha's time? 'Yes,' answers Groenewald. 'I asked to be relieved as Branch manager in 1984 because I'd begun to experience the SSC trusted me a lot and was asking me more and more, "What must we do?" There is an important principle in the intelligence community that the man who delivers information should not be involved in the decision-making. He can come to you after you've made your decision and inform you what the enemy may or may not do, but he should not stand there and prescribe what must be done.'

When it comes to the security of their nations, spy chiefs will go beyond politics to cultivate relationships that may lead to tip-offs about possible threats. Nothing beats personal contact: meeting your counterpart, looking him or her in the eye and talking. Once a year,

Andries Viljoen, armed and ready to battle the Germans in South-West Africa

Andries Viljoen's wife, Geesie Maria Viljoen, later in life

Newborn twin boys Abraham and Constand Viljoen on leaving the hospital with their mother

The Viljoen brothers wait to be taken for a ride in their pram …

… and 'prepare' for careers in public speaking, using chairs as props

The Viljoen clan: Andries and Geesie with their three children, Sannetta, Abraham and Constand

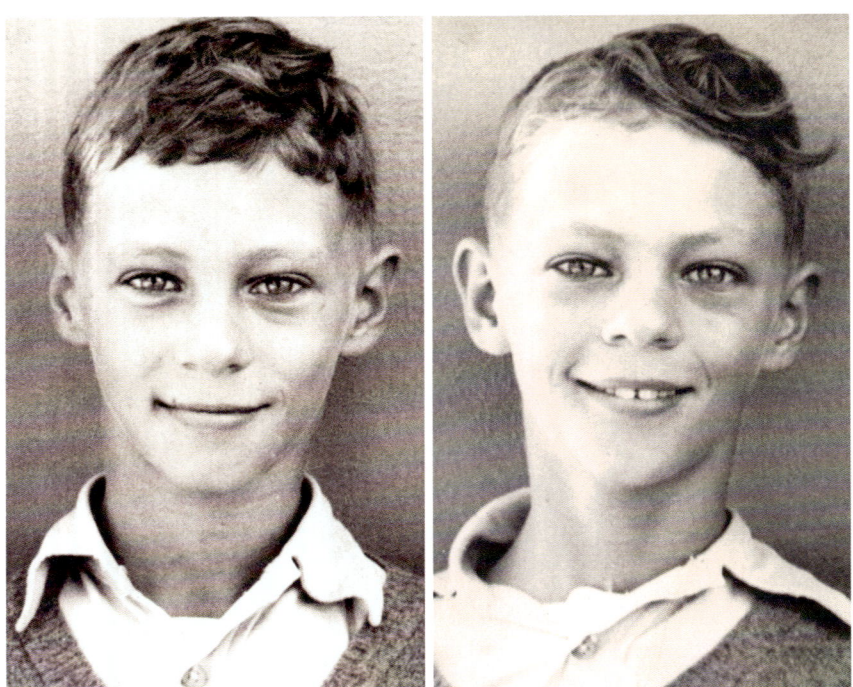

Constand (left) and Abraham (right) as schoolboys

Head boy Abraham (second from left in the middle row) and his brother Constand (second from right in the middle row) with the Standerton High School *leerlingraad* (student council) in their matric year

Constand, wearing his army uniform under his graduation gown, and Abraham on graduation day at Pretoria University

Abraham interviews his mentor, Ben Viljoen, in 1986

General Constand Viljoen carried on the family's military tradition

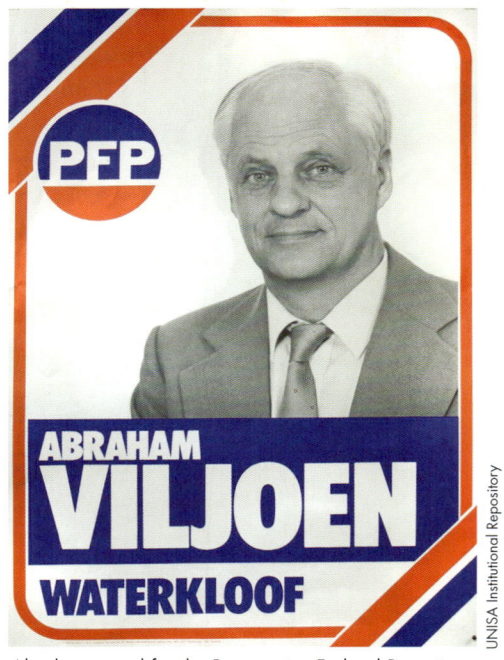
Abraham stood for the Progressive Federal Party in Waterkloof in 1987

The South African delegation in Burkina Faso, a few days after the Dakar talks, July 1987: (left to right) Revel Fox, Trudie de Ridder, Abraham Viljoen, Mike Savage, Jacques Kriel, Heribert Adams and Lourens du Plessis; (left to right, seated) Peter Gastrow, Errol Moorcroft, Ilse Naude and Andre du Pisani

Constand addresses an AVF rally in 1993

Constand steers the Freedom Front into the country's first democratic election, April 1994

Seated in front from left: Marietjie Viljoen, Ristie Viljoen and Sannetta Viljoen. Behind them are Abraham (left) and Constand

Constand with Nelson Mandela in 1997

Groenewald would attend a meeting of Western spy agencies, including the US Central Intelligence Agency and counterparts from West Germany and Switzerland. 'Through the military of each country we had a channel to most foreign ministers and prime ministers,' he says, but Military Intelligence kept a firm grip on its secrets and spies. 'We were never compromised. I can't say the same of the [former] Department of Foreign Affairs.'

By 1989 Groenewald was at the top of his game. For one who had given his professional life over to fighting communism, watching the Soviet Union crumble must have been immensely satisfying. In November, the Berlin Wall, the great barrier that had divided communist East Germany and capitalist West Germany since August 1953, fell, destroyed by a people thirsting for freedom. The event was the harbinger of a changing world: communism, white South Africa's worst enemy, was a spent force, a failed political system to be feared no longer.

From the Soviet Union, an asset who had been paid bags of money to spy on the Central Committee of the Communist Party of the Soviet Union in the heyday of Soviet Russia reported to Groenewald that the ANC had been urged to negotiate with the National Party government. 'The ANC heard it had "to take what it could get",' says Groenewald. 'I saw that we were in a position of power.' But then an acrimonious internal revolt in the National Party toppled the hard-as-granite Botha, opening the way for De Klerk to replace him as party leader and president of South Africa.

The change of guard at Tuynhuys, the office of the Presidency in Cape Town, heralded a change for Groenewald, too. 'In 1990 I asked for early retirement,' he says. 'F.W. de Klerk was president. I was shocked at the situation: the National Party still didn't have a solution. They were also so full of hubris that they thought they could roll over the ANC in negotiations. They were also under the influence of the US.'

Groenewald was angry that the government was being seduced by the ANC's call to level the playing field so that constitutional negotiations could take place between equals. Known for his candour, he did not hold back at a meeting with De Klerk. 'I couldn't believe that one would be so stupid as to negotiate himself out of power and put oneself at the mercy of the enemy,' he recalls. 'That's why I told De Klerk, "Your other name is Piet Retief." Piet Retief was right to negotiate with the Zulu king, Dingaan, in 1838. But it was ill-advised to leave his weapons outside Dingaan's kraal and sit with him as if he was a fellow Christian. This led to Retief's death and one of the biggest bloodbaths in the history of South Africa, the Battle of Blood River. I told him: "Mr President, you have neutralised your defence force. You've reached an agreement with Mandela. You've placed yourself in his hands and it will lead to the biggest bloodbath that South Africa's ever experienced."'

When De Klerk subsequently ordered him out of his office, Groenewald said: 'That will be a pleasure. You are my commander-in-chief. I can't remain loyal to you while you're wiping out South Africa.'

Responding to these allegations via email, De Klerk says he recalls that General Groenewald was one of the officers who regularly briefed the SSC on the security situation. Although he could not recall the specific information that Groenewald was referring to, he admits that the changing situation in the Soviet Union, the ANC's biggest sponsor and supporter, did have an influence on South Africa.

Lifting the prohibition on the ANC was an unexpected move calculated to exact the best deal from a weakened enemy, which, for the first time in decades, could no longer turn to Moscow for support and now found itself in uncharted waters. 'But I do remember intelligence to the effect that the Soviets had informed the ANC that they would no longer be able to support the organisation,' says De Klerk. 'Of course we realised that this would substantially weaken the ANC – also at the negotiating table. I certainly did not ignore the implications of this situation, which was a major factor in my decision to take the steps that I took on 2 February 1990.'

Regarding the incident in his office, De Klerk says he has no recollection of it: 'People in subordinate positions generally exaggerate the role that they play in the unfolding of history. If General Groenewald had made such comments, there is a strong possibility that I would have asked him to leave my office. However, whatever discussion may or may not have occurred, it apparently made a greater impression on General Groenewald than it did on me.'

By his own admission, neither De Klerk nor his decision to legalise the ANC and other banned organisations was popular with the military. It is true the military chiefs advocated that politicians would eventually have to thrash out a new constitution, but they were angry with De Klerk for acting unilaterally and without a mandate. In fact, willing as it was to be a part of the force resisting the total onslaught, and flushed with its military prowess, the SADF had taken a sober and honest look at the condition of the country and had begun to believe that the only solution to South Africa's conundrum was a political and not a military one.

General Constand Viljoen had begun to develop this view himself after studying the liberation wars that had been fought in Vietnam and Rhodesia.

'Do you know what I did when I was at the Army College?' he asks. 'We had some Rhodesian officers and I asked them to prepare a paper on the liberation war in their country: what they had done wrong, what had gone wrong and why they lost the war. I sent that report to the minister of defence. I had hoped that they would learn the lessons of time and diminishing options.' His recommendations were never followed up.

Constand reckons that if South Africa had acted in the 1960s and formed a federation, the country would have begun to solve its problems. He also believes a different country would have emerged if those who negotiated the Union of South Africa in 1910 had not done so as if the black majority could be ignored forever. By settling between themselves, Afrikaans- and English-speaking whites only postponed the negotiations that had to be held with black South Africans.

Be that as it may, the defence force provided regular assessments to the government, even dating back to the Border War, but its advice was usually spurned.

'A study of insurgency wars brought us to the conclusion that you don't win these wars through military power: you win them by arriving at a political solution,' Constand says. 'I recall that as head of the defence force I briefed cabinet. I was frank and told them, "The army can continue this war [in South West Africa] for a long time. We don't have a problem if you continue to give us the money to make war, but you must know that we need a political solution."' He also warned them that every year they failed to find a political solution, their options narrowed.

In his book *Days of the Generals*, author Hilton Hamann refers to this briefing. It took place in the operational area in South West Africa on 4 June 1981, nine years before De Klerk announced in Parliament that he was unbanning the ANC. In his presentation, Constand recalled two previous briefings, given to cabinet in 1977 and 1978, where the 'emphasis fell upon the need for a total national strategy to be developed in order to successfully combat the total onslaught'.[3]

Time had been lost, the general told them, because briefings had not been given in 1979 and 1980. And it was not only time that had suffered; they were running out of options. The advantages that flowed from making changes and then dictating the pace of reform and negotiations were being lost. Two and a half years had passed since their last meeting, and in that time the situation in South Africa had weakened considerably, argued General Viljoen, so much so that the Republic of South Africa, in his opinion, stood at a crossroads when it came to national security and survival.[4]

He then delivered his punchline: 'That brings me to the essence of the problem staring us in the face, namely the serious danger of ever-decreasing strategic options that go hand-in-hand with the passage of time in a multicultural population with a white minority where constitutional, social and economic problems are not solved in time – perhaps because of the inherent restrictions presented by the peacetime democratic process.'[5]

Like his friend and fellow anti-communist Groenewald, Constand monitored the constitutional negotiations that De Klerk had ushered in and was troubled by what he saw.

'Mr de Klerk and I had held several discussions about his strategy,' says Constand. 'We argued about the wisdom of a unitary state – in other words, majority government. I believed that we should have a transitional period of about twenty years. Mr de Klerk told me: "The ANC will not be able to govern. If they take over they'll come crawling on their knees to me and ask the National Party to take over the country again." I laughed and told him, "You don't know what you're talking about. I've studied every insurgent war that took place over the past forty years. What you're saying has never happened. It will not happen in South Africa."'

When asked about this particular conversation, De Klerk replies via email: 'Once again, I certainly don't recall having said any such thing to General Viljoen. He is either misquoting me or misremembering whatever communication I might have had with him. One would have to be extremely naive to think that after having fought so long for power, the ANC would simply hand it back to a leader from the National Party!'

Alleged arguments aside, like other discordant voices of former total-onslaught warriors, Constand was disturbed by De Klerk's refusal to use the defence force to bolster his position. Losing confidence in his leadership, Constand and others began to believe the president no longer spoke for all Afrikaners.

Afrikaner leaders in the agricultural sector, too, were apprehensive about the direction in which De Klerk was going, and believed his negotiations with the ANC should be blocked.[6] In 1990 they formed Boere Krisis Aksie (Boer Crisis Action), to give farmers a voice and to function as their armed wing.

The following year was an exceptionally bad one for farmers. Besides buckling under one of the worst droughts in living memory, they believed the government was coming off second best in negotiations with the ANC. A meeting between De Klerk and the Transvaal Agricultural Union in Cape Town in January 1991 ended acrimoniously. De Klerk had become aware of a plan by farmers to move in on Pretoria in a massive show of strength. As temperatures soared, the president accused the union's president, Dries Bruwer, of politicising the agricultural sector. Bruwer responded by saying, 'I want to tell you that the farmers will have their procession and you won't stop them. You are the cause of it because you don't talk to them.'[7]

De Klerk presumably made the accusation because Bruwer, the president of the union, was also a Conservative Party MP. But at least one member of Bruwer's delegation rebutted this allegation, doggedly saying that farmers in the Transvaal, and not the CP, had elected Bruwer as their president.

With the rift between De Klerk and the agricultural sector ever widening, Boere Krisis Aksie went ahead with its planned march on Pretoria on Tuesday 29 January 1991. Farmers began arriving the night before, by tractor, quad bike, bakkie and car, bringing the centre of the capital to a standstill. It was a show of force that registered not only with De Klerk and the ANC, but also with Constand and Abraham Viljoen, Groenewald and others.

In February 1992, the NP was defeated by the CP in a Potchefstroom by-election, and the CP used the result to argue that De Klerk was no longer speaking on behalf of the majority of whites. Undeterred, De Klerk announced that a national referendum for the white electorate would be held to test both his and the government's support. Although he had committed his National Party to reform, the president wanted an endorsement from the white electorate. He did not go for an election, because this mechanism would have brought up all kinds of other issues; he wanted a focused referendum.[8]

'I was determined to focus attention on one matter and one matter alone: the necessity for constitutional reform based on the National Party's commitment to a united South Africa; the abolition of racial discrimination; universal franchise; and a constitution which would extend fair democratic protection for minorities,' wrote De Klerk in 1998.[9]

The proposed referendum caused chaos in the Conservative Party: the younger MPs were against taking part because they thought De Klerk was disingenuous. They would have preferred an election in which, as the largest opposition, they could have fared well. Instead, they now faced a conundrum: no matter what they did, De Klerk was going to get his 'yes' for change. It was the beginning of the end for the Conservative Party.

'You can't vote against change,' explains Corné Mulder. 'We wanted to know what his change would look like. Our argument was not to take part in the referendum. The party caucus resolved not to partake in the referendum. But that night the minority went to work. The next day they called the caucus together. They wanted us to vote in the referendum, which they were confident De Klerk would lose and then have no option but to resign. They thought the Conservative Party would then become the next government. We opposed them. We voted on the issue and were tied. Dr Treurnicht cast his vote in favour of taking part. He held a press conference and enunciated all the reasons for staying out of the referendum, but then he announced our participation. That was the end of the Conservative Party.'

On 17 March 1992 white South Africans were asked if they supported the government's reform process, which would culminate in a power-sharing arrangement between different race groups. All those who decided to participate had to answer with a simple 'yes' or 'no'.

De Klerk, backed by the mainstream media, state-controlled radio and television, won the referendum with 68.73 per cent of the vote. As the negotiation process accelerated, the CP began to slip into oblivion. Eventually the telephones at the party's offices stopped ringing.

Part of the Conservative Party's planning for the future after the March 1992 referendum involved forming three groups: one to take part in negotiations; a second to get ready for elections if unavoidable; and a third to prepare for military action in case insurrection became necessary.

Some of the CP's members felt that their party was dithering about participating in the multiparty talks, and a few of its MPs broke away to form Afrikaner Volksunie (Afrikaner People's Union) in August 1992. The Afrikaner Volksunie wanted to rejoin the talks and seek a self-governing territory for Afrikaners. Among its founders were advocates Rosier de Ville, Chris de Jager, Moolman Mentz and Andries Beyers.

Meanwhile, in an effort to adapt to the new politics, the CP reached across ethnic lines to black homeland leaders on the right of the ANC to form the Concerned South Africans Group (COSAG) in October 1992. An alliance that promoted the idea of a federation based on ethnic lines, COSAG members included leaders such as Chief Mangosuthu Buthelezi, founder of the Inkatha Freedom Party (IFP) and prime minister of the KwaZulu bantustan; Lucas Mangope, president of Bophuthatswana; and Oupa Gqozo, military ruler of Ciskei.

'We realised that the ANC had formed its own coalition that included the Congress of Traditional Leaders of South Africa, homeland leaders and trade unions,' says Corné Mulder of the CP's overtures to the bantustans. 'The National Party also had its own coalition partners. We had to organise ourselves as well and try to save what we could.'

Further to the right, the HNP began to stir. Now brushed aside by the electorate and nearing obscurity, Jaap Marais issued a New Year's message on 1 January 1993, pleading with white (Afrikaner) parties to form a united front that would force De Klerk to call a general election.

Andries Breytenbach, current leader of the HNP and son of former Transvaal state archivist Dr J.H. Breytenbach, says that Marais 'never was in favour of violence. He believed we could win an election and was calling for a constitutional way to get change.'

But the HNP had nothing to offer. It had angered the CP by contesting a by-election in Pietersburg, thereby splitting the vote and opening the door to the NP.

'Some of us in the Conservative Party did not want to work with the HNP under any circumstances,' says Corné Mulder. 'The HNP was so discredited that we did not want to be associated with such a radical fringe group.'

While the CP and the HNP squabbled inside Parliament, outside Eugène Terre'Blanche's right-wing paramilitary Afrikaner Weerstandsbeweging (AWB, Afrikaner Resistance Movement) was a growing threat. In an attempt to build his own profile as a leader of right-wing Afrikaners and the leader of the white militia, Terre'Blanche was breathing fire and disrupting meetings. A brutal oaf, a bully and a modern-day Nazi, his violent and racist politics appealed to some Afrikaners harking back to the days of Verwoerd. He was king of the noise-makers and a menace.

Fired with racial hatred and white superiority, AWB members wore khaki uniforms and proudly displayed their emblem, one that recalled another era: three black sevens forming a triangle on a red background. Its resemblance to the Nazi swastika was not unintentional. Their charismatic, portly leader Terre'Blanche tapped into Afrikaner fears and fuelled them. He went around reassuring his audiences that it was not the end, that they were indeed racially superior. With his blue eyes blazing, he proclaimed: 'We will govern ourselves with our own superior white genes' and 'We will level the gravel with Nelson Mandela!'[10]

AWB units such as the black-clad Ystergarde (Iron Guard) and the Wenkommando emphasised the paramilitary nature of the organisation and were intended to simultaneously strike fear into the hearts of black people and convey to Afrikaners that they had a resistance movement fighting their corner. The AWB would stop the black communists from taking over their God-given fatherland.

There had been and were other right-wing militias, including the

Wit Kommando, which claimed responsibility for arson and bombings; the Order Boerevolk; the Order van die Dood, which planned to murder members of De Klerk's cabinet; the White Liberation Army; the World Apartheid Movement; and the neo-Nazi Blanke Bevrydingsbeweging, which was banned in 1988 after Barend Strydom shot and killed eight black people in Pretoria.[11] There was also the Afrikaner Vryheidstigting, founded by Verwoerd's son-in-law Carel Boshoff in 1988; and the Boere Weerstandsbeweging, started in 1986 to prepare Afrikaners for their third freedom war.[12]

De Klerk became even more unpopular in right-wing and military circles when he fired twenty-three senior army officers in December 1992 for allegedly instigating violence against the ANC. Among them was Major General Chris Thirion. Maintaining his innocence, Thirion sued De Klerk over his dismissal: 'I made it clear to his advocates I wasn't suing for money. I just wanted my name cleared.'[13]

When De Klerk's lawyers said the president was willing to make a statement, Thirion turned down the offer. 'I said: That's not what I want and I don't want an excuse from him. What I want is for him to say that he acted on unconfirmed information, that I asked him to be court-martialled and that was not done and he never gave me an answer. I also wanted him to state that there were investigations by the Attorney-General's office, the police and the Defence Force and that it was reported back to him that there were no grounds for action against me. That was it.'[14]

Thirion is a man who commands respect and guards his integrity, as De Klerk was to discover when he finally gave the general what he wanted. Taking on a sitting president shows the calibre of the man.

Constand was deeply shocked by De Klerk's purge, and he resigned from the Broederbond on principle when it failed to support the twenty-three men. 'I said that the government had made a big mistake. I urged the organisation to intervene. I resigned when it failed to do so. I said: "I don't want to be associated with the Broederbond any more."'

By the end of 1992, the world of informal right-wing politics was confused and disorganised, and looking for someone to take charge. Someone who was respected, authoritative and knew how to fight. Someone like General Constand Viljoen.

As more took up the chorus accusing De Klerk of being a sell-out, the former head of the SADF farming in Ohrigstad became a sought-after figurehead for those groupings contesting the president's legitimacy as an Afrikaner leader.

Given the rearranging that was occurring in Afrikaner politics, and the expressed need for a leader who had proved himself in battle, General Constand Viljoen's membership would have been a huge boost to any party. And so the wooing began. Betel was soon receiving all kinds of visitors, most of whom were not there to view the game. They were there to talk about the political situation and how their view of the future was being undermined.

Chris de Jager and Moolman Mentz from the Afrikaner Volksunie were among the first to come knocking. De Jager had known Constand and Abraham Viljoen for more than half a century. Born in Morgenzon, near Standerton, he, like the brothers, was indelibly tied to the Anglo-Boer War. His fourteen-year-old father had ridden alongside his own father (De Jager's grandfather) on the side of the Boer forces, and General Coen Brits was married to his father's sister, Aletta, a friendly and hospitable woman whom the Viljoen twins were fond of visiting as children.

With this connection, it was inevitable that De Jager, now deputy leader of the Afrikaner Volksunie, would be sent to call on Constand – only to find the general unwilling to enter the world of party politics.

'When we broke away from the Conservative Party,' recalls De Jager, 'Moolman Mentz and I went to Ohrigstad. Actually we didn't meet on his farm. We met in his butchery in Ohrigstad. We convinced General Viljoen to at least meet us on Rosier's farm, Kromdraai. There we talked to him. We asked him to be leader of the Afrikaner Volksunie. He said no. He stood outside politics and wanted to remain there. But he did say he was prepared to be an advisor.'

The Afrikaner Volksunie's meeting with the general and his subsequent role as their advisor did not remain a secret for long.

'When the Conservative Party heard about this they were worried because General Viljoen's presence would get us a lot of votes. The Conservative Party sent Transvaal Agricultural Union president Dries Bruwer and Herman Vercueil [also from the union] to see General Viljoen.'

I wonder if the Volksunie felt Constand had dropped them by entertaining the Conservative Party delegation. 'No,' De Jager reassures me. 'He was still sympathetic towards us. But he was adamant that he didn't want to enter politics. But he did end up there.'

At the end of the day, Constand advised both the Volksunie and the CP. 'He was slowly being drawn into politics,' says De Jager. 'I don't think he'd ever planned on a career in politics. I don't think he was happy in politics. He was an accidental politician.'

The hook that ultimately pulled the general into politics was his concern for the future of his people. Far removed from politics and living the life of a farmer on Betel, Constand had watched as, in his opinion, the NP capitulated to the ANC. When Bruwer and Vercueil came calling, they impressed on him that organised agriculture had lost confidence in De Klerk.

It was during this period that Corné Mulder met Constand.

'What's important was that we advocated that we were in a period similar to the Anglo-Boer War and during that war the generals got together and gave leadership,' recalls Mulder. 'Now it was a time for the generals to take the initiative and lead again.' This was exactly the right bait to ensure General Viljoen would join them: like the Boer War generals, he, too, wanted to save his people.

The ANC was also showing in negotiations that it only respected raw power.

'We saw that you can put the best plans on the table, be as friendly as you want, but it would bring you nowhere,' says Mulder. 'The ANC always talked about "balance of power". If you didn't have a military arm, you were powerless.'

Constand could provide the requisite military nous, and in Boere Krisis Aksie they had men spoiling for a fight.

'People were panicking when they saw that De Klerk was going to give over South Africa to the ANC,' Mulder continues. 'The stark reality was that the ANC would take over. General Viljoen is a brave man. He was a general who was in the front lines with his troops. He was a godsend, if I may put it like that, because our other example of Afrikaner "military" leadership was Eugène Terre'Blanche and his Mickey Mouse troops. Every Tom, Dick and Harry was a general in his forces. When General Viljoen became involved, he started a new phase and he was the man for that phase. He was a man of his people. For him everything was about his people. Absolutely.'

Although they were preparing for war, Mulder says it was to be their last option. Did they want a civil war? 'Absolutely not,' he answers, but they were sending a signal to the ANC that they should be taken more seriously, as they now had the capacity to shoot.

But it was a shooting that pushed South Africa to the edge of the precipice and shifted the balance of power in ways that no one could have predicted.

8

The general answers the call

O N EASTER SATURDAY, 10 April 1993, the hand of white right-wing terrorism reached into the East Rand suburb of Boksburg. Chris Hani, the general secretary of the South African Communist Party and arguably the most popular and revered black leader in South Africa after Mandela, pulled up at his Dawn Park home after driving to a café to get a newspaper and got out of his car. Parked across the street, with a view of his driveway, was a red Ford Laser. A man armed with a nine-millimetre Z88 army-issue pistol leant out of the window and fired two shots into the struggle hero. Hani staggered against his garage door and fell to the ground. The shooter got out of his vehicle, walked across the street and fired two more rounds into Hani's body. He then got back into his car and drove away.[1]

It would have been the perfect assassination and the perfect getaway had it not been for Hani's Afrikaans neighbour, Retha Harmse, who had returned from her shopping trip upon realising that she had left her purse at home.

She did not witness the shooting, but she heard the shots and saw the Laser drive off. She noted the registration number, PBX231T, committed it to memory and ran into her house, shouting to her husband as she did so. She then called the police flying squad.

About a quarter of an hour later, police pulled over the Laser. The driver was a thirty-eight-year-old Polish immigrant, Janusz Waluś, who had associations with the far right. The murder weapon was inside the vehicle. Following an interrogation, Clive Derby-Lewis, a leading member of the Conservative Party, and his wife Gaye were also arrested.

Fear took hold of South Africa that day, as civil war, the desired outcome of the assassination, now seemed a real possibility. An intervention was urgently needed to maintain balance, but it could not come from De Klerk. That night, Nelson Mandela and not the president spoke to the nation in a televised address. In a brave show and for the sake of peace, Mandela hid his true feelings, his pain, and remained calm as he talked about the man who had been like a son to him.[2]

The leader of the ANC knew that varying demands were being projected onto him. The black majority needed him to speak calmly and compassionately, and to keep them focused on the bigger goal: their freedom. The white minority needed assurance that vengeance was not in his heart. And the international community needed to see if he could bridge the divide separating liberation leaders from statesmen.

Mandela met all demands that night. He used the moment to grow from leader of the ANC to leader of South Africa. His message was clear: change was inevitable; all that was needed to cement it were elections; violence was what the killers wanted; but peace was his way. That night a new president was born.

Mandela reminded the nation that it was an immigrant who had murdered Chris Hani and that it was an Afrikaner woman who had given police the information that led to his arrest.

'This is a watershed moment for all of us,' he told South Africans. 'Our decisions and actions will determine whether we use our pain, our grief, and our outrage to move forward to what is the only lasting solution for our country, an elected government of the people ... I appeal, with all the authority at my command, to all our people to remain calm and honour the memory of Chris Hani by remaining a disciplined force for peace.'[3]

Mandela's words were not lost on the right wing, which, rather than being a monolithic organisation, was composed of several puzzle pieces tenuously held in place by fear, anger and hatred of blacks and communism.

For General Tienie Groenewald, Hani's assassination was a turning point. 'I realised that some bad things were going to happen,' he says.

Groenewald met with men who had a similar foreboding. Among them was his brother, Jan, who, with Eugène Terre'Blanche, had founded the AWB. Jan and others like Chris de Jager and Dr Wally Grant, former head of the Uranium Enrichment Corporation, had quit the organisation when they realised Terre'Blanche 'considered himself to be a god'. Together they had launched a new movement, calling it the Boere Vryheidsbeweging (Boer Freedom Movement), a name that reflected their fear of losing their political freedom and hegemony, and evoked images of Afrikaner freedom fighters in a war for liberation.

'People who formed the soul of the Boer community were in this movement,' says Groenewald. 'They were men like Wally Grant, my brother Jan, Adriaan Pont [former professor of church history at the University of Pretoria] and Professor Willie Lubbe [of the Afrikaans Protestant Church]. They were giants among Afrikaners. What's important is that they were Afrikaners who had no personal political ambitions. I wrote an assessment of the situation as I saw it. My brother urged me to present it to the movement.'

Present it he did. His assessment, compiled from information on communism, the ANC and revolutions gathered over many years of digging, impressed the group, which resolved to form a committee under the leadership of Dr Grant that would seek to unite Afrikaners, as well as convince them to accept self-determination. Other professionals were called in to form a committee of eleven, which later increased to twenty-three. Groenewald himself was among them.

In a departure from the usual Afrikaner approach of laying claim to the whole country, the committee put together a model for self-determination that it planned to sell to the volk. Shortly after Hani's assassination, they were ready. The Boere Vryheidsbeweging called a meeting, inviting all Afrikaner organisations. The NP and the AWB refused to attend, and Jaap Marais of the HNP accused the committee of stealing his party's ideas.

Groenewald had been busy drumming up support for the new movement. After several consultations with Treurnicht, he had given the Conservative Party leader a document in which he recommended that the party change its policies and embrace the concept of an Afrikaner volkstaat if it wanted to remain significant. He brutally predicted that the CP would disintegrate and disappear if it stayed out.

'Dr Treurnicht told me he was for self-determination, but his problem was that he was being opposed by some Young Turks in his own party,' recalls Groenewald. 'He asked me to come and help the Conservative Party. The party said I should join as an ordinary member and work my way up to the top. I said I wasn't prepared to do that.'

While he was not overly impressed by the CP or sure about its future, Groenewald admired the brilliance of certain men who had split from it, such as Bruwer, De Jager, Mentz, De Ville and the leader of the Free State Agricultural Union, Pieter Gouws. 'These were the people who said, "We have to do something about Afrikaner unity now."'

And so, in mid-April, a group of Afrikaner organisations got together in Silverton, Pretoria, for talks at the Boere Vryheidsbeweging's request. Despite his best efforts, events in South Africa were conspiring to elevate an unwilling Constand Viljoen onto a political platform beyond the role of advisor.

There were rumours that, shortly before his death on 22 April 1993, Treurnicht had asked Constand to lead the Afrikaner people. 'No, it's not true,' Constand says. 'I knew Treurnicht and had a lot of respect for him, but he never asked me to be leader of the Afrikaners.' But many Afrikaners did want him to lead them.

At a rally in Potchefstroom on 7 May, 15 000 farmers in brown uniforms sang songs and raised their voices as one, loudly demanding that General Viljoen come on stage and lead them. The atmosphere seethed with the anger and defiance of the white right, their feelings of betrayal only adding to the mounting insurrection. It was an emotional and dangerous situation, one that AWB leader Eugène Terre'Blanche was all too ready to capitalise on. The heavyweight orator could turn an Afrikaner audience inside out with his sense of the dramatic, his poetry and his hate-filled rhetoric that recalled the glorious past and vowed never to surrender.

He also knew how to flatter, seduce and deceive. Taking to the podium, he said he would be 'proud' to serve as a 'corporal' under a Boer hero of General Viljoen's stature. He was in top flight and knew that few would resist his spell.

Unsurprisingly, Constand was moved. He got up and spoke with fire, saying he was ready to lead the Afrikaner people against the 'unholy alliance' between Nelson Mandela and President de Klerk.

'The Afrikaner people must prepare to defend themselves,' he said. 'Every Afrikaner must be ready. Every farm, every school is a target. If they attack our churches, nowhere is safe. If we are stripped of our defensive capacity we will be destroyed. A bloody confrontation which will require sacrifices is inevitable, but we will gladly sacrifice because our cause is just.'[4]

His militant words resonated with the crowd, who responded: 'You lead, we will follow!' The militias present, which included the AWB-Wenkommando and the Boere Weerstandsbeweging, pledged their allegiance to the new leader of the Boer resistance, anticipating a war for Boer freedom that would stop the black advance towards democracy and keep political power in Afrikaner hands.

On that day, the Afrikaner Volksfront (AVF) was officially formed as an umbrella body uniting a number of right-wing Afrikaner organisations. Dries Bruwer recommended that a committee or directorate of generals be elected to plan the AVF's strategy. To this end, five generals were selected: Constand Viljoen, Tienie Groenewald, Dries Bischoff (former chief of operations of the army), Kobus Visser (former head of the police's criminal investigation department) and Lothar Neethling (former deputy commissioner of police and founder of the South African Police's forensic unit, which allegedly supplied assassination-squad members with toxins to use against freedom fighters).

Referring to the Boer War, Bruwer reportedly proclaimed at the rally: 'The time of the generals has arrived again.'[5]

The AVF welded together at least forty Afrikaner organisations with a common cause: the future of the volk. It also brought together men who had spearheaded the battle against communism in South Africa's neighbouring states for a last stand against an enemy now present within. In their view, the enemy was no longer at the door: he was inside the house, sitting at the president's table.

When Bruwer and Vercueil had visited Constand in Ohrigstad to impress upon him the crisis facing organised agriculture, they had asked him to get involved because he had the insight, experience and gumption to lead. He told them he was willing, provided they met one condition.

Constand recalls: 'They said, "You know war, we don't. Won't you please come in with us?" I said, "Yes, but I want a panel to help me."'

The directorate of generals was that panel.

'We made a thorough study of the situation. We saw that the negotiations had gone too far and could not be stopped. Our best option was to demand self-determination. Unfortunately the word "volkstaat" got to be used and was being commonly used. This was an error,' Constand admits.

Groenewald suggested that the directorate develop a three-tier strategy. The first phase would be to mobilise Afrikaners and build alliances with organisations with similar ideas. This would lead to the second phase, negotiations with the government and the ANC. If these negotiations failed, the third phase – violent resistance – would kick in. Throughout it all, the first phase would not cease.

The generals went around South Africa to test how their recommendations resonated.

'We held hundreds of meetings throughout South Africa,' says Groenewald. 'The enthusiasm of Afrikaans- and English-speakers was shocking. I was fearful when I saw it. I addressed a meeting in Richards Bay and spoke in English. English-speaking South Africans have always known that their future is safe in the hands of Afrikaners. They can criticise as much as they want, but when it came to action, they were only too happy for Afrikaners to dirty their hands.'

Now effectively saddled with the command of the Afrikaner right-wing forces, General Viljoen began to plan. There was no shortage of men willing to fight, and he had a database containing the names of at least 50 000 well-armed, battle-hardened and experienced soldiers.

He also reckoned he could get permanent officers in the SADF to throw in their lot with him.

'I didn't go from unit to unit recruiting them, but most officers had a special bond with me,' Constand told journalist and author Max du Preez. 'I knew that I wouldn't get the support of all the SADF units, but I knew which ones I would get. I had enough weapons and small arms, but I also needed armoured cars and heavier weapons. I knew that I would have to rely on certain units of the SADF to supply that.'[6]

While Constand focused on strategy, others pitched him with outlandish plans to fight a resistance war that would strike directly at their enemies. Some of the recommendations evinced a total disregard and disrespect for black human life. One such involved taking out the entire top structure of the ANC in a single explosion; another suggested killing about 15 000 blacks living in a town in the Western Transvaal and dumping their bodies in a mass grave.

But the general would have none of it: he would resist, but not in the manner that some in the right wing were advocating.

'Because of my upbringing, and the influences that had formed me, I would never agree to schemes such as these ones proposed to me,' he says.

How would he have resisted? Would he have taken power in a coup and set himself up as a military dictator?

'It's nonsense that I would have abused my position as former head of the South African Defence Force to execute a coup,' he replies. 'But we would have disrupted the April 27 elections. We would have activated our people across the country. You know, not a lot of people are required to make this happen. The moment you start to cause tension, people will be too scared to go to the polls. I think that they were afraid that this would happen. I will never give all the details of my plans, because I'm a soldier and a soldier never discloses his whole strategy.'

The ANC did not need to see the general's plans. Their experiences in Angola and the front line states had given them a pretty clear idea of the kind of havoc that men who had served in the SADF could wreak.

As the head of the ANC, Nelson Mandela was fully aware of the danger. Shortly before the formation of the AVF, Richard Stengel, who was collaborating with Mandela on his autobiography *Long Walk to Freedom*, asked the freedom fighter if he perceived the right wing to be the greatest threat to the negotiations and the peace process in South Africa.

Mandela replied: 'You see, this is one thing that Mr De Klerk does not want to emphasize and I think he's acting wrongly. He is emphasizing the conflict between black political organizations, not the conflict between the National Party, his National Party, and the right wing.

'The right wing is the greatest threat to South Africa because during the 1987 election they polled 400 000 votes. The Afrikaner vote was split almost equally between De Klerk and the right wing. What saved De Klerk was the English vote which they gave to him and then during the referendum the English vote was 800 000 and that's a big, what-you-call, support.

'And apart from that the right wing is entrenched in the civil service, in the security services, the police and the army. And they have got highly trained people, both in the civil service and in the security forces. They have got support of a certain section of the business so *that* is the real threat to South Africa – not the Bantustans, not Buthelezi, not Mangope. If De Klerk said to Buthelezi, or to Mangope or to Gqozo, "from now on I'm withdrawing, I'm withdrawing my financial support to you, you have to pay your own bills", they'll collapse. That will be the end of their political career. They are there simply because they are supported by De Klerk. Treurnicht, the right, the Conservative Party – they are there on their own not because you see they are supported by the [De Klerk] government. They have their own support base.'[7]

Mandela told Stengel that he was aware the right wing wanted a peaceful resolution on condition they were given self-determination in an area where they could govern themselves. He was willing to talk, had even made overtures to the right wing, but there had been no response. Yet he remained hopeful.

While De Klerk did not share Mandela's fears about the right wing, he knew the ANC took the right-wing threat seriously. He believed they had identified General Viljoen as one of the key figures in the ranks of the far-right Afrikaners. As he was a political babe, they hoped to play on his naivety.

'The ANC,' wrote De Klerk, 'was more concerned about the threat from the Afrikaner right than they were about the IFP. They felt that the IFP could, if necessary, be crushed, but they were worried about the military threat posed by right-wing Afrikaners. They feared the right wing's influence in the SADF and the police and its supposed ability to call up hundreds of thousands of trained commandos ... Nelson Mandela accordingly went out of his way to court General Viljoen.'[8]

In Ventersdorp, headquarters of the AWB, General Constand Viljoen's emergence as the Afrikaners' chosen saviour was not met with hallelujahs. Terre'Blanche, for all his posturing, was smarting. His inflated ego could not accept that Viljoen was the man the volk now trusted to save them from a communist takeover. Unlike him, Viljoen was a battle-hardened soldier surrounded by real generals. Terre'Blanche's generals were all men he had appointed, boorish paper tigers who loved to talk and boast about war as they downed their brandy and Coke. Jealousy was making Terre'Blanche and his straw generals dangerous; they believed they had something to prove.

The AWB had condemned the formation of the Afrikaner Volksfront. Suspicious of the united right-wing movement, they belligerently demanded to know who had instructed General Groenewald to start it. They found it strange, they said ominously, that the launch of the new organisation had not been discussed with their leader or their general staff.[9]

And yet, the AWB knew on which side its bread was buttered. In an effort to keep doors open, it stressed its willingness to talk to other right-wing organisations about unity and joint strategies, but it still had its eyes fixed on a revolution. The AWB believed it would lead this revolution, in which millions of blacks would be defeated. It was a dream world of threats, hunting rifles, ammunition stolen from the defence force and Dutch courage.[10]

On 25 June 1993, about 3 000 AWB militia stormed the World Trade Centre in Kempton Park, where the multiparty constitutional talks were taking place. Like the commander of an invading army, Terre'Blanche smashed through the glass doors of the building in a Viper armoured vehicle, opening the way for the rest of his heavily armed forces to stream inside.[11]

The invasion exposed the right wing's terrorism, brutality and racism. Once inside the building, AWB members shouted racial abuse, urinated and sang the South African anthem 'Die Stem', underscoring just how serious they were about keeping South Africa in white hands.[12]

9

Secret negotiations get under way

A BRAHAM VILJOEN KNEW how volatile the right wing was. He was afraid – for his country, his people, his brother, his family and himself. His instincts warned him that the volk was preparing for a war of attrition: he could smell it in the air, hanging over South Africa, waiting for the spark that would ignite right-wing Afrikaners against blacks. He had to act. He knew he had to get Constand, as the powerful military leader of the right wing, to do an about-turn and consider a more peaceful alternative.

The consequences of a modern civil war between black and white would have been far more dire than those of the Anglo-Boer War. Abraham had grown up in the aftermath of that war and had witnessed how it had divided his people. He had learnt how devastatingly cruel war could be and he did not wish it on any South African: he wanted peace, and he was willing to do almost anything for it.

He was convinced Constand held the key to preventing bloodshed. Blessed with an extraordinary reservoir of integrity, selflessness and love for country, Abraham longed to speak to his brother about a new South Africa, not that created by the National Party, but a new land where black and white would live together. If he could win Constand over, a peaceful transition from apartheid to democracy would be possible. If not, war was inevitable.

But there was a gulf between them, one that went beyond time and space. Created by their political differences, it would require nothing less than bridging the divide between racial differences.

Across from Abraham was the white right, marginalised by its choice not to be part of the constitutional discussions and threatening to wreck any chance for democracy. From the mouths of those standing in the colours of the right wing came the lies that they and their forebears had been fed. They were the descendants of heroic settlers, pioneers called to Africa to develop and civilise. Blacks were inferior, in extreme cases even baboons, mere children who would be lost without the white man, who was superior and civilised. It was a mass deceit that had infected generations of Afrikaners and driven them into laagers built on an implicit, almost childlike, trust in authority.

Now, in 1993, the National Party, which, together with the Dutch Reformed Church and the Broederbond, had peddled these lies for so long, was negotiating with the blacks. It was an about-turn that caused an identity crisis in the volk. For right-wingers to accept to share the country with blacks and to give them the franchise would be to admit that they, and their parents and grandparents, had been lied to, that they were not superior after all. It would be like surrendering to the barbarians.

Lost and afraid of the future, they were too angry to cut themselves loose from the lies. For many it was easier to hold on to the deceit – the fuel of their existence – than to change.

Abraham knew the power of hate: he had lived with it and seen its cumulative, corrosive effects. Desperate for peace, he began an intervention in the affairs of South Africa that would take him all the way to Nelson Mandela, where his search for peace would resonate with the former political prisoner's own wish for a peaceful transfer of power.

Because of Abraham's intervention, the ANC and Constand's directorate of generals would begin secret talks, parallel to the official negotiations. In a sense theirs were the real negotiations, because the outcome was less certain than it was with the official talks.

Abraham began by going to see Allister Sparks, the journalist and former editor of the liberal English *Rand Daily Mail*, whom he had first met in the middle of 1993. Abraham apprehensively told Sparks that the right wing was urging his brother to head an operation that would torpedo the constitutional negotiations and to fight for the establishment of a separate volkstaat for Afrikaners.[1]

This conversation was followed by a secret meeting at Sparks's home between ANC secretary general Cyril Ramaphosa and Z.B. du Toit, editor of the Conservative Party's newspaper. Ramaphosa and Du Toit agreed to try to persuade their respective party leaders to meet.

Restless, nervous and afraid of war, Abraham became more alarmed when he did not see any results. He resolved to approach the Dutch Reformed Church. But first he needed the help and support of a friend and fellow dissident, Professor Jaap Durand.

Like Abraham, Durand had been brutally bruised and scarred as a result of his opposition to apartheid. In August 1960 he had completed his PhD at the Vrije Universiteit Amsterdam, submitting a forthright and radical thesis that said a church divided on racial grounds did not pass the test of Christianity. He concluded that the churches making up the Dutch Reformed family of churches in South Africa (including those for blacks, coloureds and Indians) had to unite to form one church. He was the first theologian in the Dutch Reformed Church to voice this opinion. His belief that all people were equal was against the very foundations of apartheid, and, being voiced in the wake of Sharpeville, earned him the interest of the security police.

Of further concern to the government was the newly ordained Dutch Reformed Church minister's burgeoning friendship with dissident cleric Beyers Naudé. But Durand would cross the point of no return without the traitor's assistance. In 1982, he helped draft the Belhar Confession, a Christian statement of beliefs advocating that unity (non-segregation between Christians of different races) is both a gift and an obligation of the church.

The Dutch Reformed Church punished Durand for his involvement with the Belhar Confession by resolving to remove his status as an ordained minister. He wrote a letter to the elders, informing them that the church had no authority over him. When he became vice-rector at the University of the Western Cape (UWC) in 1980, Durand and the Dutch Reformed Mission Church (the coloured Dutch Reformed congregation) agreed that he would retain his status as an ordained minister despite his not being a member of UWC's theology faculty. His part of the agreement was to teach one class per week and to continue promoting PhD students. He received no reply from the church elders.[2]

Abraham and Durand first met in the late 1960s. In 1987 they were both part of the group that flew to Dakar for talks with the banned ANC. Decades later, in mid-1993, they were both present at another important meeting, this time at Jan Smuts International Airport, named after that Boer general who, with Louis Botha, was among the men who had laid the foundation stones of the Union of South Africa and who had enjoyed the political loyalty of the Viljoen twins' parents.

'Braam asked a few friends to urgently meet him,' says Durand. 'I can't remember who were all present. But I do remember that we were all Afrikaners.'

Abraham quickly elaborated on his reasons for calling them together.

'A shocked silence greeted Braam's first words,' recalls Durand.

'Without wasting any time, he told us we were standing on the verge of a bloodbath because the white right wing was exerting pressure on his brother, Constand, to go into armed revolt against the government. These groups were saying that the government was selling out the white man and thus the Afrikaner. They believed that nothing less than an armed insurrection would persuade the government to stop with its treason against Afrikaners.'

It would be dangerous to underestimate the powerful influence of these groups, Abraham warned them. Neither should their tactics be ignored, one of which was to keep him from his brother. In this they were succeeding, Durand recalled.

But what do we do, the others asked. How do we stop a war?

'Braam was convinced that the Dutch Reformed Church was the only institution that could convince Constand not to walk the road of violent resistance,' says Durand.

Constand was a member of the moderature of the Dutch Reformed Church's General Synod. Abraham believed his brother would listen if high-ranking representatives of the moderature spoke to him.

'He was hoping that they would counsel him not to carry out a coup,' explains Durand. 'He also felt that his brother could be won over if the ANC could be converted to believe it would be in their own interest, as well as that of South Africa, to allow that the possibility of a volkstaat for the Afrikaner be left open. The wind would be taken out of the sails of the right-wing pressure groups if this message was given to General Viljoen.'

Those at the hastily arranged meeting agreed with Abraham that the only counter-strategy was to get talks going between the ANC and Constand. But how were they to put his suggestion into action? Apart from him and Durand, the two mavericks of the group, none had access to the senior ranks of the ANC.

Durand says, 'It was easy to resolve that Braam Viljoen and Jaap Durand should run with the ball and see where they end [up].'

The two decided that one of their first steps would be to contact members of the General Synod moderature and impress upon them the need to exercise their influence over Constand.

'The other task,' Durand tells me, 'was to contact the ANC and make it clear to them that in their negotiations they would have to make concessions and accommodate the aspirations of right-wing Afrikaners; otherwise the country would fall into chaos.'

If the ANC agreed, then a way would have to be found to relay this information to the relevant Afrikaner ideologues, who could then influence Constand.

Because both men had in the past come under the scrutiny of the security police, they were well aware of the need for discretion. There was a high probability that ears other than theirs were listening in on their telephone conversations. They also knew that the ANC would have to be their first port of call. If the liberation movement was unwilling to accommodate the right wing, they may as well scrap the whole mission.

Back on the UWC campus, doubts began to creep into Durand's mind. Where would he even begin seeking out the ANC? Would they listen to him? And, if they did, would they grasp the gravity of the situation? He realised he had to find a trustworthy person to open the door to the ANC. Someone who would listen to him and take him seriously enough to put him in contact with the right people.

'This was something that I had learnt early on when I became part of the university's administration,' says Durand. 'One has to take care to enter at the right level in any form of negotiations. If one aims too high, they'll ignore one. And if one goes in too low, one may end up waiting with nothing happening.'

After deep reflection, he decided to approach Kader Asmal, a professor of human rights law at UWC. The previous year, Asmal (who was destined to become minister of water affairs and forestry in Mandela's first cabinet in 1994) had returned to South Africa from exile in Ireland, where he had been working as a law lecturer at Dublin's Trinity College.

Remembering that the security police had planted a bug in his own office a few years before, Durand walked to Asmal's office, thinking it would be a more secure place. 'Later I stupidly realised his office could have been bugged as well,' he remarks.

Asmal, who was known as a talker who loved the sound of his own rich, educated and eloquent voice, surprised the vice-rector by quietly listening to him. He did not once interrupt to ask a question or comment. He just listened. When Durand was finished, Asmal said he would arrange for him to meet ANC intelligence head Joe Nhlanhla. Then things took off.

Two days later, Asmal and Durand were on an aeroplane bound for Johannesburg, headed to a meeting at Shell House, then headquarters of the ANC.

A friendly Nhlanhla was waiting for them in his office. As they broke the ice with small talk, Durand learnt that Nhlanhla had been a cattle herder in his early youth on a farm in Frankfort in the Free State. Durand had also spent part of his childhood in the Free State, where his father had been a teacher. The two men hit it off. At times, Nhlanhla expressed himself in Zulu while the UWC vice-rector spoke Xhosa.

When they eventually got down to business, Durand switched to English, as his command of Xhosa was not adequate to explain fully what had brought him all the way from Cape Town. When he noticed that Nhlanhla was not taking any notes but listening to him intently, Durand assumed that the conversation was being recorded.

Nhlanhla surprised Durand at the end. He said the vice-rector could assure those around Constand Viljoen that the ANC would be sympathetic towards any suggestion that room be left in the new constitution for further discussions around an Afrikaner volkstaat. He further assured Durand that the ANC was not insensitive towards the Afrikaners and was very aware of their struggle against British colonialism.

'Kader didn't say a word,' recalls Durand. 'It's difficult to assess if he agreed or not. But it didn't matter to me, because I heard what I wanted to hear.'

At that stage it did not concern him whether or not Nhlanhla had the seniority required within the ANC to provide such an undertaking: 'All I wanted to do was to phone Braam Viljoen to plan our next move.'

Once back in Cape Town, Durand called Abraham from the UWC campus and they agreed to meet at Jan Smuts once again. There he got an inkling of just how difficult life could be as the identical twin brother of someone with Constand Viljoen's standing.

'Identical twins are rare,' Durand remarks. 'Few of General Viljoen's fans knew that he had an identical twin in Abraham. There was only one Constand Viljoen. Eyes followed us wherever we went at the airport. People watched us as we were having lunch. Then they would start whispering about Constand Viljoen being present.'

Irritated, the pair eventually gave up on the airport and moved to the Holiday Inn. Even there, 'Constand' was recognised. As they sat talking in a quiet corner, some young men walked past. They stopped and stared before one of them walked up to their table and, looking Abraham in the eyes, said, 'General, good day, General. It's a privilege to meet you. We are behind you, General.'

'I'm the wrong general,' Abraham replied.

The young man walked away laughing in disbelief.

While Durand had rather enjoyed the scene, he recalls, 'Braam didn't. His fears that things could go wrong bordered on being paranoid.'

Durand had concerns of his own: 'I'm ashamed to admit today I was afraid someone might recognise me and see that I was big mates with the general who was the hero of the Afrikaner right wing!'

Apprised of the ANC's position, Abraham agreed to fly to Cape Town to meet with the Western Cape leadership of the Dutch Reformed Church. He also hoped he could meet Chris Jooste, who, because of his association with the Broederbond-led South African Bureau for Racial Affairs (SABRA), was likely to have the ear of Verwoerd's son-in-law, Carel Boshoff.

Boshoff lived in Orania, an area in the Northern Cape where Afrikaners were implementing their idea of a volkstaat. Abraham was convinced that both Boshoff and Jooste could influence Constand. If they were told that the ANC was not unsympathetic to the idea of Afrikaner self-determination, it was certain that the message would reach the general.

In preparation for Abraham's visit, Durand began the process of re-entering the Dutch Reformed Church laager to raise the topic of the right wing's plans. Despite his acrimonious history with the main body of the church, his stepson was a minister. Durand had married a widow named Sonja Hanekom, whose son, Braam Hanekom, was a young minister who would later become moderator of the Western Cape Dutch Reformed Church. This gave Durand an advantage.

Hanekom loved the man who had married his mother and, as a minister, he understood the pain that the church's sanctions must have caused him.

'He was my stepfather,' says Hanekom today. 'He was declared persona non grata by the church. He also lost his status as a minister.

This was very painful for him. 'The godly irony is that today the same Jaap Durand whom the Dutch Reformed Church had kicked out and rejected is my mentor,' he adds with a smile. 'We talk to one another every day. When we talk it's with tenderness and intimacy. There is so much love between us.'

Hanekom's biological father, Christof, was a professor of ethnology and anthropology at the University of Stellenbosch and a member of SABRA.

Founded in September 1948, SABRA was a Broederbond initiative heavily subsidised by the secret organisation's executive committee. Its mission was to come up with an ideological underpinning for apartheid, to formulate policy and to address practical aspects, such as the creation of bantustans and the threat of communism and its effect on commerce.[3]

Christof Hanekom's close friend Solomon Johannes 'Sampie' Terreblanche, author, economist and professor emeritus of economics at Stellenbosch University, was one of those rare Afrikaner academics who had seen the light. He resigned from SABRA in 1972, taking Christof with him, and in 1987 parted ways with the NP to become a fierce critic of its policies.

'My father started to realise that things weren't right,' says Braam Hanekom. 'I came out of the anaesthesia that apartheid had caused. White children weren't always aware of what was going on in our country. Then I became a young minister in Stellenbosch and I was drawn into a new world. I developed a new sense of awareness.'

Durand was part of this new world. He called his stepson one evening, upset about the political situation in South Africa and perturbed about a right-wing strategy to persuade General Constand Viljoen to fight.

'I think that at that stage he and Braam Viljoen were looking to use any platform that could be used to send a moderate message to the right-wing Afrikaner groups that were supporting and influencing Constand Viljoen,' says Hanekom. 'They were looking for an entry point.'

While he appreciated his stepfather's faith in him and his abilities, the young minister realised that he was not senior enough in the church hierarchy to arrange a leadership meeting. He called then moderator of the Western Cape Dutch Reformed Church and scribe of the General Synod, Frits Gaum.

It was decided that a meeting would be held at Hanekom's parsonage in Stellenberg, Durbanville. About twenty people were invited. Both Abraham and Durand were present.

'It was a sombre evening,' recalls Hanekom. 'Tension was in the air. Those present felt that we had reached a breaking point in our country. We agreed we didn't want violence and conflict in South Africa.'

The two emissaries left with the clear message that, as it had not been a synod meeting, they did not have a mandate from the synod. However, they did have the support of those present.

Looking back at the attitudes present in the Dutch Reformed Church in 1993, Hanekom says there were three identifiable groups. The majority, in line with the two-thirds who voted 'yes' in De Klerk's referendum in 1992, were in favour of change and ready and willing to give themselves over to a new South Africa. A second group was afraid, nervously watching as the situation unfolded. They felt they did not have a choice, that they just had to go along with it.

The third group was the most dangerous. They represented the last frantic kicks of a people desperate to hold on to the past. Ideologically opposed to any change, 'if they had the chance to resist militarily, and this is important, they would have done so,' says Hanekom. 'That's why Constand Viljoen played such a pivotal role.'

After the meeting in Stellenberg, Abraham and Durand turned their attention to Chris Jooste, who lived in the West Coast town of Vredendal.

At first they weren't assured that Jooste would even agree to see them. Abraham's unpopularity within the Afrikaner establishment was no secret and Durand had had his own run-in with SABRA in 1970, when the organisation condemned his book *Swartman, stad en toekoms* and sent Jooste to impart its feelings. 'Afterwards both of us knew that a beautiful friendship wasn't waiting somewhere in the future,' says Durand wryly.

Again, as with Asmal, they just needed someone to open the door. They first turned to Jooste's daughter Christine and her husband, Carl Antonissen, who lived in the Boland.

'I asked them, "How about it? Won't you try to persuade your father to meet with Braam and me?"' recalls Durand. 'A promise was made that they'd do their best.'

The next day, they heard that Jooste would see them. 'I must say that I wasn't wildly enthusiastic,' says Durand. 'I didn't expect too much. I told Sonja about my misgivings as she was preparing sandwiches for the road.'

Abraham and Durand listened to music in the car as they drove to Jooste's house in Vredendal. One of the songs was about the Boipatong massacre. Situated south of Johannesburg, Boipatong was the scene of a horrific slaughter on the night of 17 June 1992. Under the cover of darkness, a group of Zulu migrant workers had crept out of their hostel and hacked and shot to death thirty-eight people in one of South Africa's most violent nights in the decade before democracy. Among the dead were a nine-month-old baby, a four-year-old child and twenty-four women, one of whom was pregnant. The ghosts of Boipatong were present in Abraham and Durand's car.

'It made a big impression on Braam Viljoen,' remembers Durand. 'It was almost as if the lyrics underscored the seriousness of our journey to Vredendal.'

On arriving in the town, the men asked two coloured people for directions to Jooste's house. 'Baas Jooste?' they responded in Afrikaans. 'Up the street, turn left. It's the second house.'

A friendly woman answered the door and led them to the stoep, where Jooste was waiting. Wasting no time, Abraham asked him what the attitude of the right wing would be if the new constitution contained a clause that said they could negotiate for self-determination. He was not prepared for Jooste's response.

'I still remember Chris Jooste's reaction quite clearly,' Durand recalls. 'He hesitated for a moment, as if he hadn't heard properly, then he raised a clenched fist and said, "If you can accomplish this …"'

Overwhelmed by the man's enthusiasm, Abraham and Durand did not tell him they were merely the messengers and not the deal-makers.

'Although Braam was silent about our status or lack thereof, I still believe today that in the mind of Chris Jooste we were more than messengers,' chuckles Durand. 'It wasn't in the interest of our goal to emphasise that we were nothing more than figures on the edge of the whole situation.'

The visit to Jooste brought to an end Durand's role as Abraham's fellow seeker of peace. Now it was up to Braam to continue. He alone carried the burden of persuading his twin brother to consider talking to the ANC.

Unbeknown to him, that which he feared was being discussed in the ANC. Nelson Mandela, Thabo Mbeki and Jacob Zuma, three men destined to lead democratic South Africa, were very wary of the right wing. While they had locked De Klerk and his National Party into constitutional negotiations, they knew that this was no guarantee of a peaceful settlement, election or transition. The right wing was accusing De Klerk of treason against Afrikaners, and belligerently threatening violence, armed resistance and even war. The ANC could not afford to dismiss these threats, especially in the wake of Chris Hani's murder and events at the Kempton Park World Trade Centre.

With Hani dead and Terre'Blanche's AWB running rampant, the ANC leaders were desperately casting around for someone to neutralise the right-wing threat. They recognised the need for a leader with stature, a respected military and/or religious man, in essence the antithesis of the verbose Terre'Blanche. History had shown that many Afrikaners had an almost inborn instinct to follow such men.

If he could be found, he could become their partner in peace, another negotiator, separate from the official deal-makers and perhaps even more important, because he would tame the right-wing beast.

It was Abraham Viljoen who would give them that man.

10

Bridging the divides

IN JULY 1993, the CP and the IFP charged out of the multiparty constitutional talks, essentially clearing the decks for the AVF and its directorate of generals. The Conservative Party's withdrawal from the negotiations was unexpected.

'We were surprised,' recalls Constand Viljoen. 'They didn't warn us that they were leaving negotiations. The five generals got together and pondered, how does one negotiate if you've left the negotiating chambers? They had abdicated.'

By now Abraham was working for IDASA on the Conservative Dialogue Project, which was promoting talks between several interest groups in the Afrikaner community. The project created a safe place where Afrikaners could openly articulate their fears, hopes and concerns.

After the AVF leadership was bestowed on Constand in Potchefstroom, the head of the IDASA office in Pretoria, Ivor Jenkins, was beset by the thought that time was running out.

'Constand's rise in Potchefstroom sounded like a curse to me,' says Jenkins, an ordained Baptist minister. 'At that time Constand wasn't talking to Abraham. I don't think that they had had any contact with one another. There was a total break between them. The family was split as well. I said to Abraham, "If you don't use this gap, it will be wasted forever."'

Knowing the volk as he did, Abraham did not need a reminder of how precarious the situation was, and in July 1993 he acted. Knowing the risk and the possibility of rejection, he arrived at the Volksfront's offices in Hatfield and asked to see his brother.

Although already aware that the right wing was prepared for war, Abraham nonetheless asked Constand, 'What are your options?' His brother told him straight up: 'As things stand now, we have only one option, and that is to fight.' Furthermore, he said, he could muster a force of 50 000 if he were to choose resistance.

Abraham, leaning heavily on Joe Nhlanhla's assurances, suggested to his brother that there was another way, albeit one that would require a measure of risk.

'The day when I went to see him,' says Abraham, 'I said, "There's an option. If you are willing I can arrange a meeting with the ANC. You can meet in camera. The press and the general public won't know about it."

'Constand said nine others had brought similar propositions to him. The Dutch Reformed Church leader, Johan Heyns, was one. He had turned down each one of them. But he was willing to listen to my proposal. Constand could not give me an answer, as he still had to discuss my proposal with his colleagues.'

Abraham left his brother's office unsure of what to expect, but he did not have to wait long. A short while later, Constand informed him that it had been decided he could follow up on Braam's proposal and arrange a meeting with the ANC.

Never in his wildest dreams had Abraham thought he would be involved at this level, or that leaders of the right wing would trust him with such a secret mission.

'They knew me,' he explains. 'They trusted me, not because I had been on a hit list, but because I made no secret of my feelings about South Africa's future. I was fortunate to have good relationships with many so-called right-wingers.'

'Many tried to do this,' Constand later told Max du Preez. 'Johan Heyns also came to me. But I didn't want to get involved with others. I thought Abraham was reasonably objective. It was important that the negotiations with the ANC should be kept secret. It was important to them and to us. People were queuing up to introduce me to Mandela, but I chose Abraham to do that. We are politically far apart, but he is an honest man and I trusted him.'[1]

Armed with his brother's blessing, Abraham contacted Carl Niehaus, one of his former theology students. Niehaus had been incarcerated for his ANC activities, but was now a party spokesman with access to Mandela. At Ivor Jenkins's house in Garsfontein, Pretoria, Niehaus was asked to arrange a meeting between Abraham and Mandela.

With that, Abraham was squeezed into the struggle icon's hectic schedule, and they met at Jan Smuts International Airport. During those few precious minutes, Abraham talked and Nelson Mandela listened. Then the ANC president said the words: 'Go ahead. It's on.'

Subsequent to his meetings with Mbeki and Zuma, Mandela himself had been using back channels like the Dutch Reformed Church to approach disaffected Afrikaners. He had first developed a bond with the Afrikaner church when he was incarcerated on Robben Island. After his release, he had shared his fears about the right wing's plans with Dutch Reformed Church leaders, who then held a meeting with Constand Viljoen in Pretoria in 1993. The former moderator of the church, Professor Pieter Potgieter, approached the general in that meeting.

'We knew what the AWB was threatening to do,' says Potgieter. 'The big fear was what General Viljoen would do. I told him I'd heard that people were considering going to the extremes of a civil war. I related to him how our people in Zimbabwe had warned us that such an option should be the very last one because people suffered in times of war. His reaction was that he didn't want to be ruled by a communist government. I think his opposition to change was not about race: it came from a deep ideological feeling against communism.'

That meeting was just one of Mandela's numerous bids to negotiate a peaceful transition with the right wing. Some months later he asked the church delegation to meet with another far-right leader.

'At Mandela's request we went to Ventersdorp in 1994, just before the election,' continues Potgieter. 'We talked to Eugène Terre'Blanche. He listened to us. His reaction was the same as that of General Viljoen: communism was unacceptable to him.'

Asking intermediaries to approach the neo-Nazi Terre'Blanche showed Mandela's seriousness about wanting peace. And his involvement of the Dutch Reformed Church underscored his willingness to inform and include the spiritual leaders of Afrikanerdom, and by extension their flock. Mandela's trust in the church and his closeness with Potgieter especially is highlighted in two incidents on either side of the 1994 election. One day, sitting next to him at the church's main offices in Pretoria, the clergyman asked Mandela directly if he was a Christian.

Potgieter recalls: 'I said: "You often talk in public about God and His will. May I ask you if you're a Christian?" He said he had done some evangelisation as a student at Fort Hare University. He acknowledged that he was a Christian.'

On another occasion, after the election, Potgieter and his colleagues received a call from President Nelson Mandela's official aircraft, asking them to meet the head of state, who was on his way home from abroad, at Libertas, his official residence in Pretoria.

'We were the president's first appointment on that day,' says Potgieter. 'Then he told us he wanted to introduce us to his new wife. It was a huge honour for us. The president was informing us that he was going to get married.'

As Abraham gleefully reported the result of his meeting with Mandela to his brother, he was oblivious to all these other overtures and to the fact that he alone had succeeded.

On the night of 12 August 1993, a gracious and hospitable Mandela welcomed the Viljoen brothers and their party into his home. He asked Constand to sit next to him, a symbolic acknowledgement of the general's leadership role, as well as a way of honouring him that did not go unnoticed. Mandela called their gathering a meeting of the generals, since the Viljoens were accompanied by a number of other generals.

The most famous political prisoner in the world offered his guests tea, which he then proceeded to pour. Addressing Constand, he asked: 'Do you take milk, General? Would you like some sugar?' 'Yes, please, Mr Mandela.'[2]

'Meeting Nelson Mandela,' Constand tells me, 'was part of the strategy of the directorate of generals to talk directly to the enemy. This strategy opened when the Conservative Party rejected negotiations.'

'It was important that the talks remain a secret,' says Groenewald. 'And they did. Very few people knew that we were in talks with the ANC. Constand's brother Abraham was involved. We met under the utmost secrecy. We knew that we were being watched twenty-four hours a day by others [state spies], but we had our own intelligence network and kept our secrets. The army taught us how to protect our secrets. Our first meeting wasn't a long one. Mandela basically asked us what we wanted. General Viljoen said we had only one goal:

self-determination. Mandela said, "Listen, the way that we're going on now we could end up being like Ireland or the Middle East and be caught up in a civil war." He said he knew that the ANC and the Afrikaners couldn't neutralise one another. He asked us if we were prepared to negotiate with the ANC. We said yes.'

They only reached this point after some honest discussion. At one stage Mandela said, 'Look, General, I know that the military forces you can muster are powerful and well armed and well trained, and that they are far more powerful than mine. Militarily we cannot fight you; we cannot win. If, however, you do go to war, you assuredly will not win either, not in the long run. Because, one, we are too many, and you cannot kill us all. So then, what kind of life will there be for your people in this country? My people will go to the bush, the international pressure on you will be enormous and this country will become a living hell for all of us. Is that what you want? No, General, there can be no winners if we go to war.'[3]

Constand, who had witnessed the havoc, destruction and pain of war, agreed. 'There can be no winners,' he said.[4]

Mandela and Constand agreed to negotiate, but the ANC president's heavy workload would prevent him from taking a direct role, and so he proposed ANC deputy president Thabo Mbeki and deputy secretary general Jacob Zuma as his proxies.

If the negotiations were to succeed, they had to be conducted in a spirit of mutual trust, respect and willingness. Moreover, the facilitator would have to be someone of impeccable character, with a reputation beyond reproach. Jürgen Kögl was identified as the right man for the job.

Kögl, a Namibian-German businessman, had been involved in the resistance to South Africa's occupation of South West Africa and had lived through that country's transition.

In April 1989, Martti Ahtisaari, who would go on to become president of Finland and win a Nobel Peace Prize, arrived in Windhoek as the United Nations (UN) special representative heading the UN Transition Assistance Group. Ahtisaari was responsible for the implementation of UN Security Council Resolution 435 in the territory that was to become Namibia.

'Ahtisaari asked me to support him, to assist him in understanding the South African military regime,' says Kögl. 'I ended up advising him and being a back channel to that which is part of the South African nuts and bolts: the soldiers. When Resolution 435 was implemented, it gave the UN credibility. The Berlin Wall came down during that time. Martti Ahtisaari could prove, because he didn't have to look at a bipolar world any more, that the UN could be a significant partner in these matters.'

Kögl was trusted by both sides in the conflict, and would pass on in person messages considered too sensitive to be shared on the telephone. Even SWAPO president Sam Nujoma recognised his qualities and the trust he enjoyed.

Kögl tells me, 'The night before the elections [Nujoma] called me up and ordered: "Jürgen, get all the generals to come." We met in the boardroom of the family business. There were Sam Nujoma, Hage Geingob [future prime minister of an independent Namibia] and Aaron Mushimba [Nujoma's brother-in-law] on the SWAPO side. On the other side were Hans Dreyer and Lloyd Gouws, whom I will call the Constand Viljoens of Namibia. We sat down. Mr Nujoma said, "Gentlemen, I give you my word that no PLAN [People's Liberation Army of Namibia, the military wing of SWAPO] fighter will rise against the ballot box tomorrow. I want the same from you." These guys gasped. They agreed. They said yes.'

The elections took place from 7 November 1989, and SWAPO

obtained the majority. In the weeks that followed, the elected parties introduced a blueprint for a constitution, and a date was set for official independence on 21 March 1990. President F.W. de Klerk would be the last South African head of state to see the South African flag lowered in Windhoek. It was the end of an era, a change that did not carry the approval of all South Africans, and, unbeknown to all including his wife Marike, it was the beginning of a huge transformation. On 2 February 1990, De Klerk announced the unbanning of the ANC and other proscribed organisations.

'No matter what people may say,' says Kögl, 'he did it on his own. De Klerk is right when he says so. He really did it on his own. Nobody knew what he was going to do. That's why I still think he deserves the Nobel Peace Prize.'

Kögl had followed the announcement, but, about to become a father for the second time, he had in mind to resume his life as a stockbroker based in Johannesburg now that Namibia was about to become independent.

Nujoma, now president elect, had also been following events in South Africa. Remembering the lessons SWAPO had learnt in its own constitutional negotiations and the role that Kögl had played, Nujoma contacted his old ally and said: 'You must help.' He did not, however, say how.

Kögl and Frederik van Zyl Slabbert, who had returned to South Africa from the UK, where he had been a visiting lecturer at Oxford University, then started a black investment trust called Khula Consultancy, advising blue-chip companies on how to adapt to the new South Africa, as well as how to treat southern Africa, which was taking on a new identity.[5]

Because of his involvement in bringing about the implementation of Resolution 435, Kögl was spending time with Mbeki and Zuma, gaining their confidence and helping them find suitable accommodation.

'Because of SWAPO's credentials and through Jacob Zuma, I was brought in,' says Kögl. 'I bought a flat for JZ [Zuma] in the Esplanade. I also owned a penthouse in Hillbrow in a block of flats that used to be a safe house for the ANC. I said to Thabo Mbeki, "Where are you staying?" Because he was at the Carlton Court I said, "You can move in. I'm moving out and you can stay there until further notice." Then, in the first week of September 1990, a microbus from the Carlton Court dropped Zanele and Thabo Mbeki in front of Park Mansions. They stayed at my largesse until he became deputy president. They tried to pay. I said no.'

Zuma and Mbeki shared their concerns with Kögl about the rise of the right wing. 'Everybody knew that they were formidable,' says Kögl. 'De Klerk had lost the support of most Afrikaners. He had won the referendum. But he was not seen as a leader any more.'

The AWB's actions at the World Trade Centre had further underscored that someone other than De Klerk was beginning to speak for conservative Afrikaners. The seemingly cosy relationship between Constand Viljoen and the AWB was causing serious jitters among the ANC leadership.

'There are two things one needs to say that's really the context,' Kögl continues. 'Nelson Mandela was really cautious, if not afraid. Firstly, it was an understated and very obvious design from Mandela to become the very first black president. Former ANC president Oliver Tambo was really quite sick already. The second thing is that certain members of the party and the United Democratic Front had common cause with Mandela in putting into the post [1991] conference leadership folks who were much more loyal to a Mandela process.'

In August 1993, Mbeki and Zuma began urging Kögl to become involved with the secret negotiations between the ANC and the right wing. They needed a facilitator and someone who was prepared to raise certain issues in the discussions. Their main concerns were the farmers' hold on agricultural production and the exact size of the right-wing armed forces.

'First of all there was food security,' explains Kögl. 'One hundred per cent of staple foods in this country were produced by white farmers. The second thing was that they never knew how many in the right wing were armed. The leadership around General Viljoen said 8 200 people were under guns. They were all ex-military people. Mandela understood this. Mbeki understood it. Zuma understood it very much so.'

Once Kögl agreed to facilitate, the negotiations commenced.

Eight secret meetings were held, each taking place at a carefully selected venue, including a private residence and the racing-pigeon club in Atterbury Road, Pretoria. Success was contingent on everyone agreeing to maintain secrecy. To avoid drawing unnecessary attention, the meetings conveniently coincided with ANC national executive committee meetings so that Kögl could pick up Mbeki and Zuma in his white Fiat Uno without arousing any suspicions.

Mbeki led the ANC team and Constand led the group of generals. Regular briefings kept Mandela in the loop. Officially, the South African government was completely unaware of these secret parallel negotiations.

'Mandela was always there,' recalls Kögl. 'Whenever we had documents to sign, Mandela would sign them. We phoned up the house: even if he was sleeping, he would get up and receive us.'

The negotiations were a lifeline for Mbeki, who had fallen victim to serious jockeying among the exiles for influential positions in and control of the ANC. Senior SACP leaders like Joe Slovo had not forgiven him for leaving their fold in 1990, and had vented their displeasure by supporting Hani for deputy president at the movement's July 1991 national conference in Durban. The ANC resolved the crisis by persuading Walter Sisulu to contest the position, which they knew he would win. But notice had been publicly served: Mbeki was not a darling of the left and would do well to tread carefully.

Earlier in 1993, the SACP had thwarted Mbeki from leading the ANC at the formal constitutional talks by backing Cyril Ramaphosa, the 'inzile' whom it had helped elect ANC secretary general in July 1991. Mbeki's detractors thought he had been successfully muscled out, but they had underestimated him and the fight was far from over.[6]

'As the negotiations unfolded Mbeki focused his attention and energy on wooing the reluctant political groups to the table,' wrote William Gumede in *Thabo Mbeki and the Battle for the Soul of the ANC*. 'The spectre of a right-wing coup or violent insurrection loomed large, and he worked tirelessly to bring the noisy white and black-right groups to the negotiating table.'[7]

Far from being the man on the outside looking in, Mbeki was in fact driving the real negotiations for Mandela.

'That's Mandela,' says Kögl. 'When it came to backing up this channel for negotiations and backing [Mbeki] against Cyril, it was also Mandela. Nobody went against him. You know, Mandela was decisive.'

One of Ramaphosa's miscalculations was that he dismissed the secret negotiations, privately referring to the talks with the Volksfront generals as a sideshow.[8] He underestimated General Viljoen's stature, and failed to grasp Mbeki's prickly character. Mbeki believed Constand had enough of a following in the SADF to command a secessionist force that would split the army.[9] Ramaphosa's words would have undoubtedly reached his ears and wounded his pride. And they would not be forgotten.

Beneath the veneer of the diplomatic, eloquent and avuncular pipe-smoking poetry lover, Mbeki was a survivalist politician who had lived the ANC way and witnessed several internecine battles while in exile. He understood that power could be conceded and gained through conspiracy. It was not for nothing that he had developed a reputation in exile for being enigmatic, manipulative and devious. Joe Slovo had once referred to him as Zhukov, after General Georgy Zhukov, the most successful Russian general in the Second World War and a cold-blooded schemer.[10]

For now, Mbeki had to help get the country to the polls. Everything hinged on the secret negotiations that Kögl was facilitating.

Among the Namibian's recollections of those meetings is an observation about General Viljoen. 'Look, first of all this is a country of big men, going back to Shaka, Paul Kruger, Jannie Smuts, and he's one of them. He was a formidable infantry general and was suspicious of politicians. He heard that Jacob Zuma, as head of ANC intelligence, was so well informed that half an hour before the Matola raid by the SADF against the ANC in Maputo [on 30 January 1981], he knew it was coming and was out. It was fascinating to see the interaction between these actors.'

IDASA's Ivor Jenkins was also present at the secret meetings. The son of an English-speaking railway worker, Jenkins says one of his most memorable moments in the negotiations involved Zuma and the general. It took place in an Anglican church in Lynnwood Road, Menlo Park.

'They were standing around,' recalls Jenkins. 'Jacob Zuma said to General Viljoen, "General, why are we busy with all this nonsense? Why don't we just go back to our farms and boer with our oxen?" They laughed and hugged before walking up the stairs to the meeting. It was such a beautiful moment.'

The Anglicans of Menlo Park would have no idea what a significant encounter had just occurred on their church premises.

Jenkins recalls carefully and meticulously assessing the venue for the second meeting: the home of Dawid and Annatjie Theron in Wapadrand, Pretoria.

'I told Oom Dawie that this was an important meeting,' he says. 'It was in the interest of the future of the country. You can never talk about it. I think that that meeting changed their lives.'

Today the Therons' house is in a gated part of the busy suburb. To get there, one has to stop at an access boom, produce identification and sign in. It is a way of keeping tabs on non-residents. In 1993, however, Wapadrand was a quiet area, with far fewer residents than it has today and no boom. It was a neighbourhood made for clandestine meetings.

Dawid Theron owned one of Pretoria's most successful and popular butcheries in 1993. On returning home from hunting trips, cabinet ministers such as Pik Botha and F.W. de Klerk would bring their kill to Lynnpark Butchery in Lynnwood Road to be turned into biltong and steaks by the respected and skilled butcher. The Therons describe themselves as ordinary people. They believed the propaganda about the evils of communism and diligently voted NP election after election. Their eyes were finally opened after visiting Europe in 1981 and Japan in 1984, where they realised that they had been lied to.

In late 1993, Jenkins was invited to a braai at the Theron home by their son-in-law. When he saw the place, he knew it would be ideal. 'The long table on the porch is perfect,' he said aloud. Wondering what on earth he was talking about, the Therons pressed him. 'Uncle Dawie,' said Jenkins, 'we want to hold a bosberaad here.'[11] Nobody must know about it. You won't even get an advance warning that we'll come in a few days' time. You'll only get a telephone call a day before the meeting. I will only say we are there tomorrow. I will tell you when we will arrive.'

'He didn't tell us what this bosberaad was all about,' says Annatjie Theron. 'No names were given.'

When the call came, Jenkins told Dawid, 'We'll be there tomorrow. We're coming to talk at your house ... Don't tell anyone about it.'

'Mbeki was here first,' Annatjie remembers. 'All of them arrived at about the same time. I will never forget his eyes. That smile ... They were all so calm and peaceful. I can't recall who provided the food. But I know they prayed. One of them, it might have been Abraham Viljoen, said they should pray for the hostess.'

Also present were MK head Joe Modise, Joe Nhlanhla and Constand Viljoen. Fourteen chairs were put out around the Therons' table and each was occupied. Mbeki was the only one to be accompanied by a bodyguard.

'I had to work,' recalls Dawid. 'But I did pop in to see if they were really here. Today we're sorry we never thought of asking each one of them to sign a visitors' book ... We only have the memories that live in our heads.'

No photographs were taken; there is no official record of the meeting. Annatjie says this with a touch of regret, before adding philosophically, 'Actually it was none of our business.'

The Therons kept their secret for more than twenty years. When Mbeki was sworn in as one of Mandela's two deputy presidents in 1994, they realised that the talks held at their home were part of the history of the formation of the new South Africa, but their lips remained sealed. It was only after Jenkins told me the story and I said I'd like to interview the Therons that he called them to release them from their promise not to talk about that meeting in 1993.

At some point the National Intelligence Service got wise to the negotiations. According to Jenkins, agency head Niel Barnard insisted that the government had an interest in the talks. Despite this, Jenkins firmly believes that De Klerk was not aware of what was going on: 'He did not know, certainly not about the first three meetings. It's phenomenal that we kept the negotiations under wraps for so long.'

Kögl is proud that the sanctity of the parallel negotiations was maintained: 'Not even President de Klerk was aware that the ANC was talking to the right wing. They were not aware of the talks. The money to help us with that [the negotiations] did not come from the church; it was from the German government. I still have the contract: it's still with me.'

In an email reply to the question of whether or not he knew about the bilateral negotiations between the ANC and Constand Viljoen, De Klerk says he recalls reports that the general had played such a role and that 'if he did, I would have welcomed it. At that stage it was very important to try to persuade the right wing to participate in the elections – and we realised that the ANC could play a key role in this regard ... One must remember that during the negotiations all the participating parties frequently met with one another behind the scenes to try to cut deals.'

11

The Freedom Front is born

THE ANC AND the generals both ruthlessly exercised the lessons they had learnt about negotiation when they sat down to talk. They bluffed, cajoled and feinted. They talked peace, but kept war at the back of their minds. The right wing kept preparing for armed conflict and the now legal ANC exerted pressure with vocal mass action.

A military strategist and student of insurrection, Constand was not averse to borrowing ideas and tactics from the hated communists. The need for utmost secrecy was one such. His supporters could not know what he was up to. The talks had to remain a secret for as long as possible. The ANC was in agreement.

In order to achieve this, Constand maintained a belligerent façade. He had to appear unwavering and ready for war so that his supporters retained their confidence and trust in him. With his bellicose language and dire threats, not one of them would have suspected him of talking to the enemy. He also had to be hard-hitting in his public messages to the ANC: even though he was now prepared to negotiate with them, he was still holding his gun.

Both sides knew theirs was a dangerous dance in the dark.

As the ANC's lead negotiator in the parallel talks, Thabo Mbeki did not deviate from his usual style of negotiation. He kept the talks going and, as was his wont, raised questions, all the while slowly and imperceptibly winning everyone to his point of view, fitting in compromises along the way, creating the impression that everyone wins.[1]

As the negotiations continued, the AVF came to realise and regret that it did not have easy access to the airwaves to keep in touch with its support base. Although the ANC did not own a radio station, among the rewards for being Africa's oldest liberation movement and having Nelson Mandela as its leader was unfettered media access. Whether via radio, television or print, the organisation had a healthy ability to communicate with its supporters. The NP was not doing too badly either, given its control of state media.

Because of its reputation and the actions of certain people identified with its cause, the right wing did not always get positive media coverage. And because it did not have a licence to launch a radio station, the AVF was unable to give its news and views in its own words and uncensored to its supporters. In September 1993, it defiantly took the law into its own hands and launched Radio Pretoria, illegally, without a licence.

They chose the name of South Africa's capital to remind Afrikaners, especially those on the right, of another era, when Pretoria was the capital of the Transvaal Republic. At the launch of the station, Constand drew a clear line between Radio Pretoria and others professing to represent Afrikaners, saying the volk required a credible voice to speak to it.[2]

In October, the general addressed a crowd in Church Square, a location in central Pretoria dominated by imposing statues of Paul Kruger and other Boer fighters. As a place that evoked patriotism and recalled a time of Afrikaner independence, it was the perfect venue for speaking to the volk. The Volksfront was spiritually strong, he said, and prepared for the struggle awaiting them. They were looking for a political answer that would satisfy everyone, but if Afrikaners were not given a chance to negotiate for their rights, they would be driven to war. It was no empty threat. Under Constand's direction, the AVF was thought to be responsible for more than twenty explosions targeting railway lines, electricity pylons, a childcare centre and ANC offices. No casualties were reported, but fear was rampant.

'The purpose of these operations was to apply pressure on the De Klerk–ANC government in order to get them to make concessions regarding Afrikaner self-determination,' said Constand some time later, 'and I think some good came of it, because eventually in the negotiations for the new constitution in 1996 we succeeded in getting some concessions from the ANC, and I'm sure the whole negotiation process would not have been as well carried out in 1993/1994 had it not been for the military potential that we had.'[3]

In October 1993, the AVF joined COSAG, the alliance formed a year earlier between the CP and the leaders of KwaZulu, Ciskei and Bophuthatswana. With the inclusion of the AVF, COSAG was renamed the Freedom Alliance. This alliance continued to oppose the negotiations between the NP and the ANC and promised to boycott the upcoming elections.

In their quest for an Afrikaner volkstaat, many right-wingers were more extreme than Constand, and the general found himself on the receiving end of their rage.

On the last Saturday of January 1994, thousands of rebellious right-wingers streamed into Pretoria for a big meeting, many loudly demanding immediate violence to secure a white homeland. It was no place for moderates. More restrained leaders who suggested they participate in the election if only to show their strength and support were shouted down. When Constand took to the stage, offering a voice of reason and suggesting violence as a last resort only, outraged right-wingers turned on him and pushed him away from the microphone, shouting 'Now! Now!' as they demanded war.

The mood was dark, dreadful and racist. Uniformed AWB members removed an African American reporter from the *Philadelphia Inquirer*. A Boer republic was declared and Conservative Party leader Dr Ferdi Hartzenberg was appointed president of the AVF. This was not completely unexpected, as the CP formed the biggest part of the Volksfront. A chastened Constand, who was given the security portfolio, told reporters: 'When I warn people, they just say you're crying wolf. Here today you have seen the anger of the Afrikaner people.'[4]

By now the ANC was not the only organisation keeping an eye on the AVF. As the general engaged in unashamed brinkmanship and tried to juggle his preparations for war with the secret negotiations, he received a blunt warning from an unexpected source.

General Georg Meiring, chief of the SADF and one of Constand's former fellow officers, was determined to be loyal to the Constitution of the Republic of South Africa. And as long as he was head of the defence force, it, too, would be loyal to the government and would not be swayed by chatter of rebellion.

In February 1994, Meiring, who has the distinction of being the last chief of the SADF and the first of the new South African National Defence Force, called a meeting with the AVF leadership. Among those present were Constand Viljoen, Joseph Chiole, Willie Snyman, Dries Bruwer, Colonel Piet Uys and General Tienie Groenewald. Rumours of a right-wing coup and of mammoth support for the right within the defence force were rife. Though he had served under some of the generals present at this meeting, he was now the man in charge and it was his show. Meiring laid down the law: the election would take place as scheduled. He did not tell them that he was planning to send a trusted envoy to Europe in April to assure the heads of ten national defence forces that the SADF was not planning a coup. But he was confident and not shy to say he could count on the loyalty of his defence force.

It was a defining moment, one that showed the right wing the futility of insurrection and also drove fear into the hearts of some of the men Meiring had called together. Here was an officer who, unlike the politicians, would not be intimidated by threats of war, but who would stand up to them if needs be. The message was clear: they would be killed or imprisoned if they went ahead.

A South African Air Force intelligence colonel, Callie Stein, also briefed the group. He candidly told the AVF that the defence force was fully aware of their plans. He then outlined some scenarios, using a map to make his point, and shocked those present by reviewing the Volksfront's strategies and actions. There was no denying it: the SADF was up to date with their plans for rebellion. Stein, an experienced intelligence operator, made General Viljoen think very hard.

Chiole could not believe what he was hearing. 'General Meiring, will you use Afrikaners against fellow Afrikaners?' he asked. Meiring replied: 'You know our soldiers are in place already. You may win small, insignificant towns. But we will act against the Afrikaner leaders. You'll either be shot dead or end up in jail.'

There it was, then: the most senior officer in the SADF had thrown down the gauntlet; his troops were ready for war and would crush any and all armed resistance.

According to Uys, who served as Constand's personal assistant, Snyman, the Conservative Party MP for Pietersburg and a staunch anti-communist, tried to play on the fear of communism that had been an essential part of the Afrikaner diet. 'General Meiring,' he asked, 'are you prepared to be the head of a defence force under a man [Mandela] who is a communist?' He had not reckoned on Meiring's professionalism. 'Dr Snyman, how dare you ask me such a question,' he replied.

Another AVF member piped up: 'General, what are you going to do when the right wing revolts?' 'We will shoot them' was the direct, unambiguous and cold reply.

In his biography of Cyril Ramaphosa, Anthony Butler related a similar conversation between Meiring and Viljoen in the lead-up to the 1994 election. When Viljoen asked what would happen if soldiers mutinied, Meiring said that they would be shot and that such an order had already been given.[5]

I asked F.W. de Klerk in an email if he had been aware of this order, if he had issued it and, if so, how he had communicated it to General Meiring. 'I certainly never gave such an order,' he wrote back, 'and was not even aware that such an order had been given.'

Nonetheless, and harsh as Meiring's warning was, a few days later Volksfront president Ferdi Hartzenberg announced that the AVF would boycott the coming April election. General Viljoen and Eugène Terre'Blanche, the acceptable and ugly sides of the right wing respectively, stood on either side of him as he roared: 'I must tell you I'm not prepared to say that retaliation won't take place because there is violence, there is a revolution, and there will come a time when people will say things have gone far enough and they won't tolerate it anymore. In fact we must use a bit of violence to protect ourselves.'[6]

Hartzenberg's rhetoric and Terre'Blanche's presence were portents of right-wing aggression. Hartzenberg himself was feeling the heady after-effects of Constand's fall from grace in January.

But even though he was negotiating with the ANC privately and suggesting temperance publicly, Constand never stopped preparing for war. He reached out to an old ally in Angola, Jonas Savimbi, the leader of the rebel movement UNITA, a once favoured recipient of South African aid and arms. Constand sent Groenewald to meet Savimbi in Huambo in February 1994.

'My request to Savimbi, as Viljoen had instructed me,' said Groenewald afterwards, 'was to ask him if he would be willing to give us a base and weapons if we were to start a guerrilla war.'[7] Savimbi was willing to help. He told Groenewald: 'Everything I have is at Constand's disposal.'[8]

While Hartzenberg blustered about boycotts and General Viljoen sought help from Angola, there were some in the right wing who were readying themselves for the election. The CP's election committee was tasked with making recommendations on whether or not to contest the election. Chiole, a member of the Conservative Party caucus and secretary of the AVF, was its chairman. The committee recommended that the party begin immediately to position itself to take part; if it did not, it would risk entering the election underprepared.

The truth was, Chiole was rattled by what General Meiring had told them. The chief of the SADF had been clear: he would use the army against the right wing. For Chiole it evoked images of the 1914 Rebellion, when Afrikaners loyal to the government had shot at Afrikaner rebels. He imagined the might of the defence force bearing down on them, ground attacks by tanks and air assaults by fighter jets. Theirs was a lost cause if the military was not in their corner. It was in their interests, he felt, to choose the ballot over the bullet.

Chiole went to see Constand at his Hatfield office in Pretoria. Knowing that the general was not interested in looking at long memoranda, he had specially prepared a short version. The last section recommended that the CP take part in the election scheduled for 27 April. It was a fundamental departure from the official stance, but it was a proposal made after deep appraisal.

'General, I'm a Conservative Party MP,' Chiole said. 'I'm here to tell you that I shall be seeing Dr Ferdi Hartzenberg to recommend to him that the party participates in the 1994 elections.'

Constand agreed with Chiole's assessment and volunteered to accompany the young man in a show of support to the party's offices two blocks away in Schoeman Street. The meeting with Hartzenberg would be difficult. The party leader had already menacingly hinted that Afrikaners would protect themselves at all cost, and it was widely known that he opposed having the CP on the first ever non-racial ballot. However, Chiole feared a shoot-out between Afrikaners more than his leader's annoyance.

Bravely laying his memorandum on the table, he told Hartzenberg: 'We've all listened to General Meiring. This is the situation and this is my analysis. General Meiring made it absolutely clear that the defence force is in on our plans. They are aware of our strategies, everything. We have to change gears and take part in the elections.'

Chiole thought Hartzenberg would accept his recommendations, because, as he had said in his memorandum, it would be fatal for the CP not to. Furthermore, three months earlier he and Hartzenberg had attended a meeting in Lichtenburg where some hot-headed farmers were unwavering in their opposition to taking part in the ballot. The farmers were asked how the non-participation of a handful of whites compared to the participation of more than twenty million blacks. A boycott would only lower the percentage of the number of voters who went to the ballot box, the leader had explained.

But three months is a long time in politics. Now Hartzenberg was unyielding, his attitude hardened: the Conservative Party would not be on the ballot.

When they were alone again, Chiole turned to Constand. They had to get ready for a possible involvement in the election, he said, and look at forming a new party.

'Josef, do it,' the general said. Although Chiole's first name is Joseph, Afrikaners seldom use the anglicised version, preferring to call him by its Afrikaans pronunciation, Josef.

Chiole did exactly that. He acquired the necessary documentation for registering a party, read up on the requirements and wrote the as-yet-unnamed party's founding principles, which were largely based on those of the Conservative Party.

The first hurdle was that the deadline for registration of a political party was Friday 4 March 1994. Also, to register, the party would have to put down an amount of R70 000 in the form of a bank-guaranteed cheque with the Independent Electoral Commission (IEC). Time was running out.

Then there were the hardliners in the CP who tried to keep those getting ready for the election inside the party. As a compromise, and in the interest of unity, it was resolved at a meeting in Pretoria that the CP would participate. A group, including Chiole, left happy in the belief that they had an agreement to enter the election.

United in purpose, they retired to Chiole's home. Professor Carel Boshoff said a prayer. 'It's wonderful that we were able to find one another and that the party had not fractured. Now we can be part of the elections,' said the theologian from Orania.

But unbeknown to them, the boycott faction approached Hartzenberg that same evening and persuaded him to reverse the decision. He did, and Chiole and three other MPs were expelled from the Conservative Party. The hardliners had won, but the victory would break up the party.

The group of MPs heard the news of their expulsion over the radio. Far from being dejected, they viewed being kicked out as an opportunity to take off the old outdated coat of apartheid South Africa and put on a new one that represented the future. Relieved and optimistic, they went to see General Viljoen, the man who was to lead them.

Convincing Constand to lead a new party was one thing, inducting him into the political way was another entirely. He was like a child learning to walk, taking his first tentative steps towards becoming a political leader. He now had to talk and act like a politician, a role vastly different to that of a soldier. He had to learn to juggle many balls simultaneously, and always appear at ease and in control of the act.

Corné Mulder was one of those showing him how to bob and weave in the political arena. On occasion their classroom was the roof of the Volksfront offices in Hatfield, where they would talk. Or rather, Mulder talked and Constand listened, as the younger man explained the Electoral Act line by line, article by article.

The new party's name, Vryheidsfront (Freedom Front, or FF), was carefully chosen to comfort, inspire and signal to Afrikaners that they had a solid body taking their predicament onto the political battlefield. It also reminded Afrikaners what the new struggle was all about: freedom. Their freedom was linked to this party.

The name Freedom Front was also an olive branch to their COSAG/Freedom Alliance friends, a sign that the struggle continued.

Moulded in the military and schooled to operate on a strict need-to-know basis when it came to subordinates, the general did not always share the outcomes of his meetings with the rest of his party's leadership. Being kept out of the loop was frustrating for Chiole, but there was not much he could do about it. It was just the general's way. However, the military way was not the political way and it could potentially trip them up. For now, though, Chiole had to put up with the unorthodox style of management and start raising the R70 000 needed to register the party.

The cut-off date was fast approaching and Chiole was getting worried that they would miss the deadline and suffer the embarrassment of being absent from the ballot paper, despite all the trouble they had gone to. They would be the butt of jokes for years to come.

Chiole emptied his personal bank account of the R70 000 he had received as a pension payout from Parliament, phoned his bank and had a bank-guaranteed cheque prepared. Little did he know that Constand had already managed to raise the registration money. Chiole only discovered this on the eve of 4 March when he was advised that a bank-guaranteed cheque was ready and waiting to be collected from the home of Johan and Karin Leibbrandt in Kempton Park.

Tall, sincere and kind, Johan Leibbrandt was a former army officer who had gone into municipal management. One Friday, at a lunchtime information briefing given by the NP's chief constitutional negotiator, Roelf Meyer, Leibbrandt heard something that grabbed his attention. Meyer was concerned that the CP had once again terminated their participation in the multiparty negotiations and that they had indicated they would not contest the election. Their departure robbed a group of people who were not National Party or Democratic Party (DP) supporters of a political home.

Leibbrandt immediately recognised that if Constand Viljoen launched a political party, it would at least provide these aggrieved CP members and others like them with the option to participate in the first democratic election. He believed it would be disastrous for the country if these voters were denied the opportunity to take part. It could lead to civil war, something he desperately wanted to prevent. So he decided to get involved.

The next day, he got hold of the AVF's office number. He called and was put through to General Viljoen.

Leibbrandt related what Meyer had said and explained that he was convinced there would be enough support at the polls for the general to succeed should he decide to register a political party. Leibbrandt promised he would assist in raising the registration money.

Constand could not give him an answer immediately, because he had a specific mandate from the farmers and would have to go back and consult with them. His secretary would be in touch.

Not long thereafter, Leibbrandt received a call from Constand's office. Would he keep his word about the deposit required to register a party? He would.

Leibbrandt immediately contacted a wealthy business associate. He explained and emphasised that Contand's participation in the election would contribute to a peaceful transition. He reiterated that if the right wing was excluded, the risk of destabilisation was high. So, too, was the possibility of casualties on all sides.

Leibbrandt had found a kindred spirit. The businessman gave one condition: the money would not have to be returned if General Viljoen failed at the polls, but if he got enough votes to go to Parliament, it would have to be repaid. He handed over the R70 000 to Leibbrandt, who arranged a bank-guaranteed cheque as prescribed by the IEC.

In the days approaching the 4 March cut-off date for registration, Constand came under pressure from various quarters. The section of the right wing that could not see past the barrel of a gun vied with Volksfront members who wanted to be part of the election. On top of that, the general had his own fears about the damage that asymmetric warfare could inflict on his people and the rest of South Africa, and then there was the question of Afrikaner-on-Afrikaner violence. He was a conflicted man, wavering between boycotting the election and taking part. As the deadline neared, his emotions pulled and pushed him in different directions at greater frequency. Unscrupulous opponents within the right wing were also threatening his personal safety, and death threats were not uncommon.

Friday 4 March began with the *Pretoria News* informing its readers that Hartzenberg had made his stand in Roodepoort the previous evening and defiantly declared that the AVF would not take part in the election on 27 April. The general's dilemma was clear: should he listen to his chairman's public declaration or should he rebel and face the consequences? He had been told that if he missed the election boat, he would become as politically irrelevant as the Conservative Party because the ballot would go ahead no matter what. Those who boycotted would be left behind and violence would be their only recourse if they wanted to be heard.

Not even the general knew what he would do that Friday. As evening approached, the South African Broadcasting Corporation (SABC) reported that he would not be registering a party. It appeared that he had capitulated to Hartzenberg. Aghast at the news, Pieter Mulder called Constand to warn him he would be finished as a leader if he failed to meet the deadline. Many friendships would be lost and bridges burnt.

While the general wrestled with his decision, Karin Leibbrandt was waiting in Kempton Park. Pregnant with her first child and just a few weeks shy of her due date, she was alone at home. Her husband was in Stellenbosch, where he was studying towards his MBA. Before he left, he had shown her a brown envelope locked in their safe. It contained the bank-guaranteed cheque needed by General Viljoen to register a political party. Karin knew that an emissary would collect the cheque at some stage, but by early evening on Friday 4 March no one had contacted her. She waited by her telephone, wondering what was going on.

Hours later she got the call from Chiole: he was on his way to collect the cheque. General Constand Viljoen had decided to register the Freedom Front.

Some time went by and Karin began to worry that Chiole had got lost. But eventually, about an hour before midnight, he arrived at her front door. He took the envelope, got back in his car and raced off to the IEC offices, which were approximately fifteen minutes from the Leibbrandt residence.

The new party was registered with mere moments to spare. The Freedom Front would officially appear on the ballot papers in each of South Africa's nine provinces.[9]

'I don't think that General Viljoen ever got the full recognition due to him for his role in the peaceful transition of South Africa,' says Johan Leibbrandt. 'I know that there are those on the far right who were spoiling for a war and were disappointed when he launched a political party. He defused the talk of war. As a country we owe him recognition. He was never a politician; he was a military man.'

Justice Johann Kriegler, head of the IEC at the time, recalls that the IEC offices were in that 'godforsaken place' called the World Trade Centre. That weekend the IEC was moving to new premises. When the sun went down the majority of officials called it a day, but Kriegler, his wife and colleague Betty Weltz and two officials from the Department of Home Affairs waited behind for parties that still wanted to register. Kriegler had felt it would be wrong to let two juniors work late while all their colleagues had gone, so he and Weltz had remained at their stations.

Contrary to urban legend, the Freedom Front was not the only party to register late and Kriegler had not been waiting specifically for General Viljoen. It was the judge's understanding that a number of parties still had to register. He did not know how many would come, but he would be ready nonetheless. He went down to the reception area a few times that night to check what was going on and to indicate to the two remaining officials that they were not the only ones still working. At 9.05 p.m. the IFP's Frank Mdlalose arrived to register his party, which had also been threatening to cause mayhem.

'Someone said the Afrikaner Volksfront was coming to register,' says Kriegler. 'I can't remember who it was. We anticipated that he [General Viljoen] would come. I expected him to register a political party. Expected, but did not know.'

Kriegler was in his office when Constand turned up.

Despite the SABC's report, the media were keeping a watchful eye on the IEC offices. Few pictures would be as newsworthy as those of General Viljoen arriving to register. The later he arrived, the more dramatic the story.

As expected, it was the big news of the night, overshadowing that of the IFP. Representatives from the print and electronic media recorded the moment for posterity and the following day it was a major news item all over South Africa.

It was a watershed moment. Registering the FF increased the inclusivity of the whole election; but it was also part of a bluff that would keep Constand in the game. He was still not ready to rule out war. Furthermore, it showed that a significant crack had appeared in the granite monolith of the Afrikaner right-wing movement.

'There was no way in which his decision would win over hotheads such as Eugène Terre'Blanche,' says Kriegler. 'By registering, General Viljoen had completed half of the process. He still had to submit his list of candidates to the IEC.'

Afrikaners in the AVF who were vehemently against the election did not take kindly to the news. Outraged that their general had betrayed them, they sharpened their knives in anticipation of the People's Representative Council to be held that Saturday, 5 March, where

Constand would be called to account. The council was a parliament of sorts, made up of Afrikaner leaders.

On this day, all niceties were absent as the broedertwis over the FF's registration dominated the meeting. Those who less than a year before had begged the general to lead them were now determined to crush him. His explanation that he had registered the party to keep the door open was dismissed out of hand by emotional men. They wanted blood, preferably his.

Even though the IFP, a Freedom Alliance partner, had also registered, the meeting was livid and unforgiving: General Viljoen had violated an earlier decision which held that the Freedom Alliance, a grouping of the right wing and black homelands, would boycott the elections. They had made a pledge to their partners and they would keep it. Hartzenberg sided with the angry mob, which applauded him when he defiantly announced the boycott would not be lifted. Constand was rejected, pushed out into the cold.

Some of the younger AVF members, however, made a stand, saying they would follow through on the registration and would be among the starting line-up in South Africa's first democratic election. It caused a crisis in right-wing circles.

Two days later, on Monday 7 March, Groenewald told the South African Press Association that AVF members who supported the registration were hopeful they would win over the boycotters. Once again it was right-winger against right-winger, Afrikaner against Afrikaner, Boer against Boer. The broedertwis that had bedevilled the Botha/Smuts/Hertzog era was back in full swing.

By midweek, Constand was attempting to placate the dissenters. He still had to give the IEC his candidates list, which meant the door to backing out of the elections was still open. He started giving the impression that he would not follow through on the registration by failing to submit the list. According to the *Pretoria News*, without a list the FF's registration would be invalid, the registration fee would be returned to them and the warmongers would have won.

As the general and his lieutenants agonised over what to do, the AWB made the decision for them. At an AVF public meeting in February, Constand had argued for a final mandate to continue with the struggle for an Afrikaner volkstaat. He had also audaciously declared, 'There is only one man who will decide if we will go over to violence and that is me', before saying he could not be kicked out because he was the military leader of the AVF.

His boldness had fuelled the anger and resentment of the AWB, who had been pushed to the sidelines and were feeling marginalised. They tried to shout him down, screaming 'AWB! AWB! AWB! Terre'Blanche! Terre'Blanche! Terre'Blanche!' It was a loud and clear warning that they were displeased with Viljoen's leadership.[10]

Now the AWB was ready for a showdown, an opportunity to show the general who was really in charge. He and the world would learn the hard way just how dangerous Terre'Blanche and his delusions of grandeur really were.

12

The game changer: the Bophuthatswana coup

IN THE FAIRY TALES about the good intentions of apartheid spun by an adroit propaganda machine and sold to the world, the independent homeland of Bophuthatswana was held up as a success story of a black-governed country within South Africa, different from and more successful than other independent African countries.

In distributing their lies about the so-called independent homelands, it did not matter to the propaganda-makers that the United Nations recognised the African countries they were deriding as independent in the real sense of the word. They simply had to prove to the world that their homelands were more successful and viable than many black-governed African countries.

Bophuthatswana was one such homeland, made up of disconnected pieces of land. Kept financially alive by South Africa, it was neither a country, nor was it independent. President Lucas Mangope could not be considered the head of a free country. He was a kept president, beholden to his paymasters in Pretoria. But he had no desire to participate in the election for a democratic South Africa.

Courtesy of the AWB, Mangope was to find out in 1994 just how expendable he was, and how little Pretoria really cared. And also thanks to the AWB, Constand Viljoen was finally to be jolted from playing both sides into taking decisive action.

The homelands created by the apartheid machine deliberately encouraged the growth of tribal identities. Carefully screened and selected strongmen were put in charge to bolster and entrench apartheid policies and create a favourable climate for new alliances. But the political changes blowing through South Africa in the early nineties were rocking old alliances.

The National Party was accused of deserting its old allies and ditching them for constitutional negotiations with the ANC. The white right, recognising the possibilities for new alliances, had stepped into the gap and formed COSAG (later the Freedom Alliance) with the leaders of territories such as Bophuthatswana, Ciskei and KwaZulu as part of a strategy to stop democracy.

The Freedom Alliance partners believed that by boycotting the 27 April election they could place its legitimacy under a cloud. Cognisant of the ANC's method of using mass action to destabilise, they pledged to come to a fellow member's assistance if its sovereignty was ever threatened. The Ciskei was the first to be tested, and the homeland could not withstand ANC mass action. But the real target was Bophuthatswana, the jewel in the crown of quasi-independent states created by the South African nationalist government.

In early March 1994, while Constand was resolutely withholding his list of candidates from the IEC, Mangope started to send out distress signals. His decision to not participate in the election had sparked a civil service strike.[1] He begged his right-wing allies for help against the ANC-fanned mass action, but with a firm request that the AWB not be sent into the homeland, because he feared their brutal racism would antagonise his people.

The AWB were notorious as the most visible and belligerent expression of the right wing. These pseudo-Nazis had been committing sadistic and cruel deeds within South Africa since the organisation's formation. They were often divided into small groups and given orders to kill people, thereby creating chaos. In one incident, on 12 December 1993, AWB members were stopping cars with black occupants at a roadblock between Krugersdorp and Randfontein. Non-ANC members were allowed to proceed. At one point, two vehicles were pulled over and their ten occupants were ordered out to be questioned. One of the AWB men, Deon Martin, fired the first shot that set off the others. Altogether, nine AWB members executed four black people and injured six others. Martin's 'commanding officer', Phil Kloppers, told him to remove an ear from one of the bodies because 'General' Japie Oelofse wanted it. 'I cut off the ear and put it in a plastic bag,' he said later.[2] Such was the brutality of the organisation.

If more moderate right-wingers could help Mangope survive, his homeland could stay out of a democratic South Africa and remain 'independent'. The ANC knew it, President Mangope knew it, the South African government knew it, and the right wing knew it. The shape of South Africa would be decided in Bophuthatswana.

'If we could help President Mangope to stay in power, we could thwart the whole concept of a united South Africa,' says Ferdi Hartzenberg. 'It was a difficult operation. We lost, but it was not General Viljoen's fault.'

The AVF's military wing, Boere Krisis Aksie, assembled a 3 000-strong force ready to drive into Bophuthatswana in disciplined formation, to be armed by Mangope's army, and with orders and Mangope's clearance to defeat any and all ANC supporters out to remove him and his government. They were primed to go in at short notice. This was to be an operation in which Constand's men would show South Africa what they were capable of. This was to be their big moment: history was reaching out to embrace them, or so they thought, and they were not going to miss it. They would defeat the ANC and its surrogates.

Then, on Friday 11 March, Terre'Blanche and his armed AWB militia rumbled uninvited into Bophuthatswana, against Mangope's wishes and Constand's orders, and thoroughly messed up the day. They opened fire indiscriminately on the black population, wounding, terrorising, killing and sowing fear.

Fired up on brandy, their coarse language, superior attitude and boorish behaviour rekindled bitter memories of apartheid oppression, opening a toxic mix of anti-Afrikaner sentiment that turned Mangope's people, who believed he had invited the racists in, against him.

Back in Pretoria, Colonel Piet Uys knew that Constand and his men from Boere Krisis Aksie were preparing to assist Mangope if summoned. On Thursday 10 March, filled with foreboding about Bophuthatswana, he had decided to sleep in his Volksfront office in case a call came through. The shrill ringing of the telephone woke him at about three that Friday morning.

'Oom, die AWB is hier. Julle moet hulle uitkry,' said a frantic voice in Afrikaans. (Uncle, the AWB is here. You must get them out.)

Uys immediately phoned Constand, who decided that Colonel Jan Breytenbach was one of the few men who could be trusted to go to Bophuthatswana. The tough veteran was called to the general's office in Pretoria for a military-type briefing: the army was revolting against President Mangope because of the AWB. There was an aeroplane ready. Breytenbach was to make his way to the airport without delay.

'Your job is to sort out the AWB,' Constand ordered.

'General, I told you not to trust Terre'Blanche,' Breytenbach replied.

With that, Breytenbach, Uys and Herman Vercueil hastened to Mafikeng on a chartered plane.

In the meantime, in Bophuthatswana, three wounded AWB members – Jacobus Stephanus Uys, Alwyn Wolfaardt and Nicolaas Fourie – were executed in the capital Mmabatho by a black Bophuthatswana policeman, Constable Ontlametse Bernstein Menyatsoe. The shooting was captured by nearby journalists and broadcast worldwide.

In 1997 Menyatsoe gave a vivid and graphic first-hand account of the shooting to the Tebbutt Commission of Inquiry. It was the first time the shooter was publicly identified and his account told. In Menyatsoe's judgement, Bophuthatswana was in a state of war: defenceless members of the public were being shot at indiscriminately. Attempts on his life had also angered him.

'My actions on March 11, 1994, should not just be seen through the lens of the camera that focused on that dramatic moment showing a black policeman firing at three khaki-clad, swastika-bearing white men,' Menyatsoe said. 'We should bear in mind that during that period more than 40 people had died and many were injured. I see myself as an ordinary policeman who obliged when duty called to defend human lives and dignity and to prevent anarchy.'[3]

Armed with an R4 rifle and with instructions to guard Mmabatho police headquarters against a possible right-wing assault, Menyatsoe had heard gunshots in the street outside. He and his colleagues saw a group of khaki-clad white men in a bakkie. A shot was fired at him from the vehicle, striking next to his boot. He dived for cover. Civilians were panicking. Furious, some even broke down the gates of the police headquarters. They were dubious of the police's ability to protect them and demanded that he hand over his rifle so that they could defend themselves.

'I refused to hand over the rifle as it is against the rules of the police force,' Menyatsoe told the commission. 'I chose to protect them from this attack myself in order to prevent further disorder and chaos. I considered giving arms to members of the public irresponsible.'[4]

He had moved to the other side of the road when he heard shots coming from a blue Mercedes-Benz.

'When the Mercedes-Benz drove past where I was lying, the people in the Mercedes started firing shots at me. I heard a man screaming that he had been shot. He was bleeding from the knee. I took aim at the Mercedes-Benz and fired several shots. The Mercedes-Benz stopped a distance away. As I was moving towards the Mercedes-Benz, I saw a woman lying on the ground, bleeding from the stomach. I approached the occupants of the Mercedes-Benz and fired shots at them.'[5]

Wolfaardt had stumbled out of the car and pleaded for his life and the lives of his injured colleagues. In response, the policeman shot the three wounded men dead at point-blank range.

By the time Constand arrived on a different flight, Breytenbach had ordered the AWB to withdraw to South Africa. For their own safety it was agreed that they would leave at nightfall. They did so violently, throwing smoke grenades and shooting at residences. As he was getting ready to fly back to Pretoria, Constand ordered those who were driving home not to stop, but to return fire if they were shot at.

Meanwhile, the SADF was on the Bophuthatswana border busy with exercises, not, as many have speculated, to invade the homeland – the military exercises had been planned months before. Mangope asked South Africa for assistance, thinking the NP government still championed homeland leaders. The Presidency wanted General Meiring to enter Bophuthatswana to help restore order, but he refused to dispatch South African troops until he received official confirmation. When the official request came by fax, the SADF moved in. It was the end of Bophuthatswana's short history as an independent state.

Officially, ninety-two people died violently in the coup. And the right wing lost in a big way. The bloody killings of the three AWB militiamen, broadcast across the world, signalled the end of right-wing resistance, the myth of Afrikaner superiority and black inferiority, black fear, Bophuthatswana's independence and Eugène Terre'Blanche, and the beginning of the final stretch of the long walk to democracy.

The coup had not been the date with history that Constand had thought it would be. 'The AWB completely buggered up the whole thing,' he told Padraig O'Malley in 2001.[6]

'The AWB turned President Mangope's army against him,' says Hartzenberg. 'It was chaos. They [the AWB] were drinking. They looted shops. President Mangope's people turned against him because of the AWB. It was absolutely tragic.'

The execution of the three AWB men was a humiliation and an event that convinced Constand that the time for brinkmanship was over. He had not read Terre'Blanche's character properly. When Constand had become military leader of the AVF, Terre'Blanche had been cut adrift. On his own and no longer constrained by the semblance of discipline that Constand had brought to the right wing, the AWB leader had become increasingly volatile and dangerous, something that seemingly bypassed the general. Driven by ego and behaving like the braggart he was, Terre'Blanche had decided to prove his credentials by sending his ill-disciplined AWB militia into Bophuthatswana against Mangope's express wishes.

By the time the South African troops entered, Mangope had lost the loyalty of his civil service, defence force and police, and had fled to his home in Motswedi. On Saturday 12 March a delegation from the Transitional Executive Council went to see him there. The council represented the first grip on state power for the extra-parliamentary liberation movements of South Africa. Its basic purpose was to 'promote the preparation for and transition to a democratic order in South Africa'. In other words, to 'level the political playing fields and create a climate for free political activity in the run-up to the elections in April 1994'.[7]

South African foreign minister Pik Botha, like a judge summing up before pronouncing on the guilt of an accused, reminded Mangope that he was on record saying he would not allow free and fair elections to take place in Bophuthatswana. As Mangope was no longer in control of Bophuthatswana, it was time to restore order. It was his painful duty, said Botha, to inform President Mangope that the South African presidency and country had no other option but to remove him as head of state. South Africa's ambassador, Tjaart van der Walt, would take over administration of the homeland.

Mangope argued that he had followed the constitution and had not acted unlawfully. He asked to be allowed to inform Parliament in an address the following Tuesday, as well as for an opportunity to address his nation. Botha acknowledged that Mangope had not acted unlawfully or unconstitutionally, but said he was merely the messenger.

More discussions followed, but the writing was on the wall. Although Mangope did not see it, his son Eddie did. He spoke to his father in Tswana. After that conversation, Mangope accepted his fate, and the same party that had boasted about their progress in another era dissolved his presidency and country.[8]

The AVF had failed to save Mangope's presidency and the AWB had done irreparable damage to the right wing. 'My assistance to Bophuthatswana was firstly because of our joint membership of COSAG,' says Constand. 'We had a joint political goal – a very acceptable one considering the 1994 election.' COSAG wanted to 'form a multiracial political alliance to oppose the single black ANC party in the elections to come'. Terre'Blanche had destroyed this goal.

Flying back to Air Force Base Waterkloof on Friday night, 11 March, an ashen-faced Constand was seething. Shocked, shaken and humiliated, his military training had not prepared him for what he had witnessed earlier that day.

Breytenbach and Uys saw that their general was weighing some heavy matters and staring into the abyss. 'Do you know what they'll do if we don't participate?' he asked his colonels, referring to the AWB. 'They'll burn town after town just as they did in Mafikeng. We will have to take part because we'll ignite something that we won't be able to stop.'

'Never again,' said Breytenbach as they winged their way to Pretoria. 'I'm sorry; I don't want to have anything to do with the AWB. You must get away from those farmer types.'

'What must I do now?' Constand asked. Should he register his candidates?

'Yes,' Breytenbach replied.

Spoken straight and businesslike, it was this conversation that steered Constand towards a decision he had procrastinated over since registering the Freedom Front a mere week before.

Upon landing, he and Uys went directly to the AVF offices in Hatfield. Chiole and his wife were still working, even though it was already about 9.30 p.m.

Constand, still as white as a sheet, in severe distress and undecided, asked: 'Piet, what must we do?'

'General, don't ask me. I can't make out head or tail.'

'I can't do this to the Afrikaner people,' said the general. 'I can't allow what I've seen in Bophuthatswana today to happen in Belfast, Machadodorp, Ohrigstad, Brits and places like that.'

With these words, he crossed the line between indecision and resolve; between being a Machiavelli who pushed his people into war and a hero who saved them from one; between infamy and respect. The time for playing games was over. In an instant, it was as if he had been transported to the battlefield, where the commanding officer does not ask subordinates what course of action to take. He became the general, the decision-maker thousands of South African soldiers were proud of. He was self-assured and in charge, the chief who had led the SADF with distinction. He was once again General Constand Viljoen, leading from the front.

'Get Herman Vercueil on the line.' Then: 'Herman, you got me into this thing. I will take part in the elections.'

The next call was to Dries Bruwer: 'Dries, I'm telling you now that we will take part.'

The decision alone did not guarantee participation. The final, irrevocable commitment would be to hand in a list of candidates at the IEC that very night. Once that was done, there would be no turning back.

'Take the candidates list to the IEC,' said Constand.

The final list was entrusted to Pieter Groenewald, who drove off to seal the Freedom Front's fate. The divorce with Hartzenberg was final.

It had been a week since Constand had registered the FF as a political party. As former Labour Party leader and British prime minister Harold Wilson once famously said, a week is a long time in politics. The general had just discovered how right he was.

As with the registration, the Freedom Front's candidates submission dominated the news the following day. 'Poll: Viljoen says yes', read the headline in the *Pretoria News*. 'General Constand Viljoen has restored hope to a threatened election process by shattering the last remnants of the Freedom Alliance and confirming his registration of the Vryheidsfront,' wrote reporters Dale Lautenbach and Robert Brand.[9]

THE GAME CHANGER: THE BOPHUTHATSWANA COUP

Not only was it good news to a country nervous about the possibility of civil war, but it was also music to Nelson Mandela's ears. Buoyed and grateful to Constand for turning his back on violence, Mandela said any subsequent disturbances caused by the right wing would now simply be a matter for the police.[10]

General Meiring was also hugely relieved by the news. Unlike the rest of the country, he did not have to wait for his morning newspaper to read all about it. Constand rang him in the middle of the night to share his decision. Meiring then phoned the defence force chaplain general. 'Dominee,' he said, 'this is a time for prayer. Please pray. General Viljoen will participate in the elections.'

While it was happy news for some, it predictably inflamed those in opposition. The denunciations from Constand's former right-wing allies came in thick and fast, and were filled with venom, insults and disgust. AWB spokesman Fred Rundle was quoted in the *Pretoria News* saying, 'We don't trust him. He has no credibility left with our people.'[11] His remarks were carried next to a photograph of the three AWB members executed in Bophuthatswana the day before.

Terre'Blanche was less polite than Rundle. He condemned the general as a 'political Judas goat', a 'Brutus' and a 'government agent sent to split and lead the Afrikaners to slaughter'.[12]

Andries Breytenbach, then leader of the far-right HNP and a former soldier, had been under the impression when Constand led the AVF that he would give military resistance. It was actually the HNP that had first become aware of the general's secret negotiations with the ANC. Former party leader Jaap Marais had read a report about it in the *Christian Science Monitor*. 'Viljoen is busy negotiating with the ANC,' he had charged at the time. Although the HNP was not a member of the AVF, party members were present at the meeting where Constand had sought to justify his reasons for registering in the election. His defiant stance at the volatile meeting was fresh in Breytenbach's mind and he, too, condemned the general's actions.

Breytenbach still maintains it was correct not to contest the elections. 'We did not want to negotiate and give our country away,' he tells me. 'If I get my way, then F.W. de Klerk, Roelof [Pik] Botha and Roelf Meyer must be taken somewhere, lined up and shot. They were traitors who caused more damage to our people than anyone else.'

Amid the congratulations and condemnations on 12 March, Constand announced his resignation from the Volksfront, citing the AWB's behaviour in Bophuthatswana. He doubted he could ever work with the organisation again. Two days later, he broke ranks with the Freedom Alliance.

General Viljoen was now quite alone.

President Mandela established the Tebbutt Commission of Inquiry in 1996 to investigate the Bophuthatswana invasion. The commission ruled that the AWB had to carry the majority of the blame for the deaths in the homeland, but the AVF was also criticised for encouraging President Mangope to walk his own road. The commission also laid blame with the Transitional Executive Committee, Mangope and his government, General Constand Viljoen, Dr Ferdi Hartzenberg, the SADF and the South African Police.

Mangope had made a major blunder by calling on General Viljoen and the AVF. In saying it was naive of the general to believe that the AWB would not come with the AVF, the commission questioned his political wisdom. The AVF was harangued for encouraging Mangope 'to go it alone, in the light of the reality of what was then happening in South Africa'. It 'was not only irresponsible, but provocative'.[13]

During the commission hearings, Eugène Terre'Blanche claimed that Mangope had invited him and the AWB into Bophuthatswana.

Mangope denied this. The commission was scathing about the intentions of the AWB and its reasons for the attack: there was overwhelming evidence that AWB members had gone into Bophuthatswana with the deliberate intent of killing black people. 'The chilling and horrendous prayer of the AWB dominee that "it will be expected of us today to shoot dead kaffirs" is testimony to this,' the commission concluded.[14]

The far right is still furious about the events in Bophuthatswana. Louis van der Schyff has been in the right-wing corner for decades, and experience has taught the HNP veteran to be sanguine about politics. 'You win some battles but we couldn't win the war,' he says. 'Some battles also damage your cause. Bophuthatswana was a very bad case.'

13

The ultimatum

ALTHOUGH IT IS commonly held that time heals all wounds, certain words and accusations can cut so deep as to leave scars that not even the passing of years can heal.

Being rejected and branded a traitor by fellow Afrikaners still burns Constand Viljoen. Few outside his inner circle suspected the strain he was under while with the AVF. When he got involved in 1993 it was because he had been asked to give strategic guidance to the volk; it was a task into which he threw his heart and soul.

'For nine months we worked flat out on this [political, economic and propaganda strategy], also preparing the military strategy itself,' Constand said later. 'I always said: "I may be preparing for a military option but I will decide whether and if it is the time to launch an offensive." I always said I was prepared to wage a war and was prepared to sacrifice lives if I regarded that as the only and last possibility.'[1]

He held onto the option of war, hoping to use it to extract more concessions from the ANC. But when he made his momentous decision to put his party's name on South Africa's first democratic ballot paper, men such as Hartzenberg gave him the cold shoulder.

'Some of them called me a traitor because they somehow thought I was in a position to keep the old South Africa standing,' he said.[2]

While his character was being ripped apart and his reputation sullied by his erstwhile comrades, Viljoen felt increasing pressure from the ANC.

Princeton Lyman was the US ambassador to South Africa from 1992 to 1995. He witnessed first hand how the official and secret negotiations were progressing. In several meetings with him, Mandela alluded to his concerns about the right wing, but remained optimistic that he would handle the threat, and his confidence only grew in the second half of 1993.

In Lyman's mind, General Viljoen was the key to defusing the right's threat of civil war. So the US began a dialogue with Constand in October 1993. As the secret negotiations between the ANC and the AVF intensified, so did the discourse between the ambassador and the general. At their first meeting, Constand told Lyman that the situation was on a knife-edge and urged the US to support a delay in the installation of the Transitional Executive Council, but not the election. Ambassador Lyman explained that this was not possible because the council was an ANC precondition for lifting economic sanctions. The US, therefore, could not support a delay, but the two agreed to stay in touch.

'Increasingly over the next few months, Viljoen called or visited me to express either his hopes or frustrations over his negotiations with the government and the ANC and to ask for our intervention,' wrote Lyman in *Partner to History: The U.S. Role in South Africa's Transition to Democracy*. 'For our part, we appealed to Viljoen's patriotism, his love of country, and his sense of honour to encourage him to eschew thoughts of violent resistance, and to find his way into the election process.'[3]

At the time, Constand still had his dream of a volkstaat, a place where Afrikaners could live according to their own culture and be independent. It was a view that did not fit in with the ANC's determination to end race-based structures in South Africa. Because of his conversations with Mandela and others, Lyman knew that the ANC were resolute about some things, so he tried to change Constand's mind.

'We urged, as did the ANC, that Viljoen search for other ways than a Volkstaat to achieve the preservation of his people's heritage and culture,' he wrote.[4]

Lyman was familiar with the ANC's arguments against a volkstaat. Firstly, because of the way in which groups had migrated in South Africa, there was no part of the country in which Afrikaners were in the majority and therefore a volkstaat was inherently impractical. Secondly, even if a volkstaat could be created it would not be economically sustainable, unless it was given some of South Africa's economic assets, something that the black majority would never agree to. Thirdly, if Afrikaners were to stay in power in a volkstaat, some form of race-based franchise would have to be introduced, another non-negotiable for the ANC. Then there was the question of what to do with Afrikaners who refused to move to the volkstaat and their status inside South Africa proper.

'But General Viljoen and his supporters had to reach these conclusions themselves,' explained Lyman. 'Thus in our conversations my staff and I would raise these practical questions, press Viljoen and his staff for answers, and suggest the problems that resulted. One of Viljoen's greatest difficulties was that he could never get his people to agree to produce a map of the proposed Volkstaat. When he did, and it included the capital, Pretoria, the impracticality of it all was evident.'[5]

ANC negotiators Mbeki and Zuma saw things in very much the same light as the Americans: 'Their purpose, like ours, was not to ask Viljoen to abandon his fundamental objective, that is to protect the lives, the culture and identity of the Afrikaners; for Viljoen to do so would mean the loss of his constituency. The objective was to see if it was possible to define the future in different ways.'[6]

Lyman saw how Mbeki and Zuma, whom he called the consummate negotiators, engaged Constand in almost endless discussions and proposals: 'They toyed with the concept of self-determination, how to accept it in principle without creating a new apartheid. By late December [1993] they had negotiated with Viljoen's Afrikanervryheidsfront an "interim strategic agreement" which would have pledged both parties on the one hand to a "non-racial democracy" and on the other to seeking ways to address expeditiously the commitment of many Afrikaners to "the ideal of self-determination in a Volkstaat".'[7]

However, the ANC pushed the envelope even further: 'The ANC wanted evidence that there really was sentiment for a Volkstaat. If the AVF would stand in the elections, its vote could be seen as a referendum on the idea.'[8]

With hindsight it is easy to see that the ANC never had any intention of granting Constand his volkstaat. Their goal from the beginning had been to trap the general into taking part in the election. How else could he show how much support he had except through the ballot? The negotiators had smiled affably and praised him, but ultimately sought to outmanoeuvre him.

But Constand would not have been the leader he was if he had not had a sharpened intuition when it came to traps. On 7 December 1993 he met with Lyman to complain. In turn, Lyman phoned Mbeki to get a sense of the ANC's position before calling the general back 'to explain that the ANC would accept a commitment from the AVF to participate "if agreements were reached between them"'.[9]

Mandela was increasingly pulling Lyman into the secret negotiations. He also wanted Ferdi Hartzenberg in on election day, so he asked the ambassador to visit the CP leader.

Lyman did as he was asked and advanced a case for why the AVF should participate in the ballot. A sceptical Hartzenberg was not convinced. He thought there was a bigger advantage to be had by staying out. If the AVF took part, he argued, 'no one would listen to us or negotiate with us anymore'.[10] The old fear of communism was also still alive as he alleged that the elections would produce a communist state. Positions had hardened and the white right was intransigent. The meeting 'became circular' and Lyman left empty-handed.

Following the death of Andries Treurnicht in April 1993, Hartzenberg was one of the last spiritual fathers of the right-wing movement. His participation would have given the elections more credibility, but he would have none of it: he was not going to take his Conservative Party into a communist state. Besides sending Lyman, Mandela himself had at least thirteen discussions with Hartzenberg, but the AVF president remained unmoved.

One of these discussions took place in a private residence in Johannesburg, at a dinner hosted by Jürgen Kögl. Mandela was very gracious. He wanted to know from Hartzenberg if he would participate in the election.

Kögl remembers: 'Halfway into the dinner Dr Hartzenberg says, "Mr Mandela, I'm a man of God. I'm not a man of communism." That's his way of saying I'm not a man of black people, because communism was equated with black people. And he stood up and walked out of my dinner. He didn't even say goodbye.'

Now retired from politics, Hartzenberg farms in Lichtenburg, in the North West. The area is a haven for mielie farmers, but the neglect is evident: there are potholes in the main road and the lake in front of Hartzenberg's house that once teemed with birds and fish is now dry.

The former CP leader politely declines to dwell on the past, criticise anyone or say anything that could turn anyone's world upside down. He recalls the example of General Koos de la Rey, who, when the South African Party was being formed, opined that it was time for bittereinders and joiners/collaborators to work together because the future of the Afrikaner was at stake. Because of their split, Hartzenberg did not witness all the tension and brinkmanship that characterised General Viljoen's final days before the election.

Constand's suspicions that he was being cheated at the negotiating table were exacerbated when various others told him that the ANC would con him. Uneasy, filled with a growing disquiet and doubtful of the liberation movement's real intentions, for his own protection and as a guarantee of the ANC's commitment, he called for a written agreement that would recognise the Afrikaners' wish for self-determination and sanction the establishment of a volkstaatraad (volkstaat council) to examine the possibility of establishing an Afrikaner enclave. To bind the ANC, he insisted the accord be signed before the election.

The agreement was ready by 12 April 1994, but the ANC kept postponing the signing ceremony, thereby adding to Constand's stress. Frantic and losing confidence in the liberation movement, he began to think they were playing him for a fool, pushing him closer to 27 April, when he would have no other alternative but to accept that the elections were happening and that he was not going to get anything from the ANC. His credibility and integrity were on the line.

He eventually snapped under the mounting pressure and reverted to threats. Angry, he went to the Union Buildings in Pretoria to deliver a message to Pik Botha: was the NP government aware of the heavy emotions running through Afrikaner veins? These emotions could lead to a bloodbath if Afrikaners stood their ground. Already some were preparing themselves for such an outcome by stockpiling canned food.

Botha countered that he could hardly believe Afrikaners would take up arms against a democratically elected government. Dissatisfied, Constand left, but not before warning the government to tread softly.[11]

On 16 April, eleven days before the election, the crisis had not yet been resolved. Constand was at his wits' end with the ANC's apparent inability to sign off on the accord. He was aggrieved that the ANC was taking him for a ride and told Mbeki, 'I can't trust you completely. Give me something in writing.' An accord was again drawn up but never signed. He decided to see Lyman again.

He confided in his wife before he sought out the ambassador. This time he had been pushed far enough and was ready to take up arms. 'I have to let the dogs loose, the ANC is difficult,' he told Ristie. Even as he spoke the words, he recalled his promise to Lyman that he would see him before he resorted to any military action.[12]

Constand phoned Lyman, recalling their conversation of December 1993: 'You remember, between you and me, we had a gentleman's agreement. We met quite often and you said, "Before you do anything, promise me you will first come to me." And I said "Yes I will do so" and you remember we used that eventually ... I came to you and said "I'm going to let the dogs loose," and you said "Give me half an hour."'[13]

Lyman had been around long enough to know that the elections would be sabotaged. He took action immediately, calling Mbeki's office and explaining that Constand believed he had been betrayed. All their hard work at the negotiating table was in jeopardy.

The gravity of the situation sank in. Finally.

Yusuf Saloojee, the man who had taken Lyman's call, phoned back within minutes. The accord would make provision for a volkstaatraad, which would be appointed after the election to investigate the feasibility of an Afrikaner volkstaat (see Appendix). It would be signed at the Union Buildings on Saturday 23 April, three days before the election.

Constand asked Lyman if he would sign the agreement as a guarantor, but the ambassador could not for various reasons. He would, however, be present as a witness if the other parties consented.

'On Saturday, in the cold, imposing Union Buildings, which houses the South African government, the signing ceremony took place. Although other ambassadors were invited, I was the only one to attend,' wrote Lyman.[14]

The general had been serious about going to war. 'As a matter of fact I had the war machine ready,' he said later. 'The final decision not to go to war was taken just after 23 April 1994.'[15]

During his application for amnesty on 16 May 1997, Constand told the Truth and Reconciliation Commission that during the elections phase in 1994 there were many who had plans to use violence. His followers, however, were in a commanding position as far as military capacity was concerned. They were ready to die for their cause. But he thought about the situation rationally. He was haunted by the devastating effects that the Anglo-Boer War had had on Afrikaners, and therefore decided against war, even though his decision disappointed many of his followers.[16]

A few years later, in an interview with Hilton Hamann, Constand said that a large portion of his forces disintegrated when he decided not to go to war. He had planned to use a so-called thick arrow – one big operation – followed by a thin arrow – the type of warfare waged by the Irish Republican Army in Northern Ireland. Both strategies collapsed when he chose the election over war.

'I don't regret the decision, but maybe I should say give me another five years then I'll tell you whether I regret it, because the situation in politics doesn't change that quickly and whether I made the right or wrong decision may only come out in another five or 10 years,' he told Hamann. 'Things in South Africa might turn like that in Zimbabwe: then I would certainly regret it.'[17]

In August 2013, thirteen years after Hamann's book was published, I ask the general again. Do you regret your decision?

'You know, I thought today that we made a mistake in 1910 when South Africa became a union,' he tells me. 'We did not take the realities of people's emotions into consideration. We made the same flop in 1994. I was involved in 1994. I think I should have fought harder. I often think we should have gone to war.'

It is increasingly apparent that we narrowly escaped a guerrilla war on par with Northern Ireland, Lebanon and Syria. It was a close call, but in April 1994 there was no time to reflect. The elections had arrived.

Under General Viljoen's leadership, the Freedom Front, then less than three months old, won 640 000 provincial and 424 555 national votes. The number of votes easily met the threshold, as set out in the accord between the ANC and the AVF, required to establish the volkstaatraad.

Voting in the election that would end white political domination was difficult for Constand. 'Of course it was not an easy day for us to vote,' he said in a recent television documentary. 'It could have been a bloodbath. There's no doubt about it.'[18]

To date, former UWC vice-chancellor Jakes Gerwel is the only black person to publicly declare that he voted for the Freedom Front on 27 April 1994.

Journalist Zubeida Jaffer recalls: 'He did this because he felt the

ANC did not need help, but the Afrikaners did ... he disclosed this fact to Madiba who was rather amused and completely at ease with the decision.'[19]

Gerwel, who had turned his UWC campus in Bellville into the intellectual home of the left, was appointed director-general of the Presidency when Mandela took office. His vote helped send General Constand Viljoen and eight others – Joseph Chiole, Corné and Pieter Mulder, Pieter Groenewald, Leon Louw, Willem Botha, Dr Willie Botha and Pieter Grobbelaar – to the National Assembly, and five FF members – Tienie Groenewald, Rosier de Ville, Dries Bruwer, Carl Werth and Piet Gouws – to the Senate in South Africa's first democratically elected Parliament.

14

Time to go

There comes a time in the life of every political party leader when he or she reaches that fork in the road and must decide whether to stay or go. Invariably the one who has led the way is no longer needed; they have served their purpose and must leave to make way for another. Many resist, choosing instead to fight their corner. A few recognise the inevitable and bow out gracefully. Whether they leave quietly or are pushed, leave they must.

Not many have the privilege of choosing their moment of departure. For some, the separation comes as a surprise, giving rise to feelings of betrayal. For others, it is foreshadowed by whispers that start off innocently enough but gradually become more personal and vicious. Party leaders require a single-minded focus, high levels of concentration and a thick skin, all qualities that may cause temporary blindness and deafness to the reality of succession.

By 1999 the signs were well and truly there for Constand Viljoen: whispers that he was a military man unsuited to the daily life of full-time politics, that it was time for new blood, time for change, time for a new leader. Politics being what it is, the manner of his exit was not gentle. And it has left a bitter aftertaste. He has not remained close to the party he helped create.

The unhappiness was not all directed at the general. Since Abraham's involvement in the secret talks, the twins had regained their connection. The bond between them was strong; they were a team, a unit once more. Abraham had gone with Constand to Parliament and their closeness made some uneasy. Those who were unhappy with Abraham's past thought he was exercising too strong an influence over his brother. Abraham was a left-wing intellectual whose views did not sit comfortably with the Afrikaner establishment, and now he was advising the leader of the Freedom Front.

Abraham, according to Jürgen Kögl, had bet everything on a political career when he lost in Waterkloof in 1987, but he came into his own during the negotiations.

'He was crucial in contextualising that which the ANC put on the table and relating it to the negotiations,' says Kögl. General Groenewald had military intelligence, but lacked the intellectual capacity and political finesse to match the ANC negotiators.

'Abraham was magnificent in contextualising, which was very helpful,' Kögl continues. 'On the other hand he was a man of the church in a different way than his brother. His brother was more observant. Abraham was more open. He had access to Beyers Naudé. He was a different kettle of fish. That's why he was able to contribute. He ended up advising his brother in Parliament. People in the Freedom Front were irked by this.'

Constand's reputation and integrity were savaged in 1997 when the far-right HNP published a book, *Die IDASA-komplot teen Afrikanernasionalisme* (*The IDASA Plot Against Afrikaner Nationalism*). In it, HNP leader Jaap Marais claimed that Abraham, who according to him was a well-known leftist, and IDASA had hatched a plot to seduce the right wing into constitutional negotiations. He accused Abraham and IDASA of plotting to have Constand appointed as military advisor to the Afrikaner Volksunie at a time when he was at a political dead end. From this position, the general could exert influence and launch the AVF, which was a deliberate step to unite the right before taking it into constitutional talks.

Marais accused the Viljoen brothers of using the Conservative Party and the Transvaal and Free State agricultural unions in a plot to hoodwink Afrikaners with talks of self-determination while they were being robbed of their fatherland and freedom.[1]

Today HNP official Louis van der Schyff is reluctant to use the word 'betrayal': 'I don't want to use that word because it's a strong one,' he says. 'But General Viljoen played a role that was not in the interest of the Afrikaner people. He was a brilliant soldier and loved by his troops. But he was not a politician.'

Some of the general's statements were also causing tension, but the tipping point was probably reached when one-time ally and former Broederbond chairman Carel Boshoff began to show concern about some of their leader's beliefs. Firstly, Constand wanted a volkstaat situated in the economic hub of the Transvaal, whereas Boshoff preferred the Northern Cape, where Afrikaners were already living in their own enclave, Orania. Secondly, they were at odds over the demand that Afrikaners be the only workers in the proposed volkstaat. Both issues were key to the success of the scheme. Gradually, and most damaging of all, Constand came to realise that a volkstaat would not be viable.

The whispers against the general grew louder and more vehement, vindictive and urgent.

'More party members began to talk about this,' recorded Boshoff in his autobiography *Dis nou ek*. 'In the judgement of some, General Viljoen's real talents lay in the military terrain and not in his political abilities.'[2]

The mounting dissatisfaction turned into open rebellion at a Freedom Front federal council meeting in Bloemfontein on 21 August

1999. Boshoff, who had positioned himself as a political adversary, now proposed a motion of no-confidence in the party leader and called for an immediate change in leadership. He also proposed that Pieter Mulder replace the general, a clear indication that the coup had been thoroughly planned.

It was all out in the open at last: some wanted Constand to go, and go now. The chairman, Abrie Oosthuizen, adjourned the meeting after recording the motion. It was a time-out measure, but the challenge had been delivered and a leadership tussle could not be avoided.

When the meeting resumed, Mulder was given the opportunity to make his case. He explained why a leadership change was necessary and why he should be named successor. Then it was Constand's turn. He told the delegates what he had achieved and outlined his vision for the future. A vote was taken. The general triumphed by three votes.

He had prevailed, but his challengers could smell victory and they were not going to give up. Constand's assurance that he would leave at a moment most beneficial to the party was not enough; change was in the air and his departure was no longer up to him.

The August showdown in Bloemfontein irreversibly damaged the FF. The relationship between Constand and Boshoff was hostile, and the incumbent felt unappreciated. But today the general is philosophical when he reflects on that meeting.

'Don't they say that all political careers end in tears?' he says. 'It is so that I did not have the political ambitions that others had. Yes, the tide began to turn against me because of the volkstaat issue. I so wanted a volkstaat, but it was beginning to become clear to me that there was no place where we could have a volkstaat in South Africa. I suggested that we should ask for cultural self-determination. If and when we reached a stage where we could get a volkstaat, then we should take it.'

Chiole vividly recalls the intrigue and shadowy machinations before the no-confidence vote. Approached to contest the chairmanship of the party, then held by Pieter Mulder, he had declined, but was resolute that he would change his mind if Mulder stood against Constand. When it happened and the general won, Chiole went up against Mulder for chairman, losing by one vote. Chiole believes he lost because two delegates voted contrary to their mandate.

Advocate Rosier de Ville, the FF's chief whip in the Senate, describes the leadership challenge in Bloemfontein as a close shave. He counted the votes and later pointed out that, although newspaper reports suggested Constand had won by one vote, he had actually come in by three. De Ville, like Chiole, supported the general.

Constand's diminishing support within the party was mirrored in the waning appetite for the Freedom Front's policies. In the June 1999 general election, only 127 000 voters (a mere 13 per cent of the Afrikaner franchise) cast their ballot for the FF. It signalled a huge drop in confidence, which plunged both the party and its leader into trouble. Their constituency had rejected them: many Afrikaner votes had gone to the Democratic Party, led by Tony Leon. It was surprising given that Leon was a Jew, a group that Afrikaners were not generally enthusiastic about.

It was thus a betrayal of the worst kind – to vote for a party representing a constituency and culture formally despised by Afrikaner leaders. But it was not only the Freedom Front that was rebuffed at the polls. The National Party managed to garner only 20 per cent of the Afrikaner franchise, while at least 54 per cent voted for the DP. The message was clear and unambiguous: Afrikaner voters had lost confidence in the parties they had previously supported and found a better political home in the DP.[3]

The Afrikaner voters' desertion shocked and distressed Constand,

and he commissioned a study by Professor Lawrence Schlemmer, a sociologist and former director of the Helen Suzman Foundation. The study cost more than R160 000 and concluded that Afrikaners were no longer interested in identity-based politics. After the election, the report was presented to the FF and roundly rejected. Raw emotion took over once again, as some critics said Schlemmer had written a report that supported the general's views.

The general could take a challenge to his leadership, but being accused of dishonesty and of manipulating Schlemmer's investigation was an assault on his integrity.

'We also began having problems in party structures,' Constand says, recalling that time. 'I considered the matter very carefully. I came to the conclusion that in the usable political years ahead of me, I would not be able to do anything about Afrikaner unity. I still had the ideal to be a farmer. I also wanted to finish the things that I'd started before I died. I decided to quit. That's why I left politics.'

On Thursday 14 June 2001, General Viljoen rose to speak in the National Assembly as Ristie sat watching from the public gallery. Ever dignified, she dried her tears as her husband announced he was stepping down from the leadership of the Freedom Front, as well as from Parliament.

'I am relinquishing set party structures and entering a wilderness where there is nothing,' he said. 'There's a new upsurge among the volk and other groups over their language. We have been disempowered politically. We have to find solidarity and strengthen our own social structures.'

When he sat down, he was given a standing ovation in the chamber where the representatives of South Africa's electorate were gathered. It was a fitting farewell and a public recognition of all he had done.

With his resignation as party leader and his departure from Parliament, Constand broke completely with the party he had led for seven years. He has not attended a single Freedom Front event since. There is a striking sadness about his departure. Like Generals Botha and Smuts, whose politics he detested, he has had to dance with the enemy for the sake of his people. And like Smuts he was shown the door by voters.

'We have had the same problems and divisions since the Anglo-Boer War,' he says. 'I experienced it in 1994. You reach a stage when you see people are stuck like a gramophone.'

One of his major regrets is that the volkstaatraad, which was the fruit of his negotiations with Mbeki, was beset by so many differing opinions that it was eventually rendered impotent.

'Remember Thabo Mbeki and I signed an accord,' Constand says. 'The volkstaatraad was so divided that it could not come to an agreement and make definite proposals to Parliament. I've told you about the divisions among Afrikaners that pushed me. It was the same with the volkstaat. The one group said we should have a volkstaat in this region, another group preferred a different area. It was an absolute waste of the state's money.'

Rosier de Ville still practises law in Standerton and is still involved in politics, but at local government level. These days he is also a member of the Democratic Alliance, the biggest opposition party in Parliament. Steeped in politics, he has watched more than a few Afrikaner leaders up close. For him Constand was not a political leader in the tradition of Treurnicht and Hartzenberg, both career politicians who thrived on debate and understood that all politicians want to be heard. Constand came from the military, where the commanding officer made the final decision because he was in charge. The general's background was bound to cause resentment in the game of politics.

'I respected him a lot,' says De Ville. 'I don't think that he had the wherewithal to act like a political leader in Parliament. There you have to execute politics if you want to make a success. I've served under a lot of political leaders. I was always in the opposition and never in the ruling party. Dr Treurnicht was honest and upright. He knew how to sidestep in Parliament. Dr Treurnicht was a cultural leader. General Viljoen was a different calibre of leader. General Viljoen also had to keep the Afrikaners united when he was in Parliament. He was respected in Parliament. The ANC tried to show their respect and appreciation in different ways.'

Constand is under no illusions about his lack of experience. He was an opposition novice in a democratically elected parliament. In one portfolio committee meeting he made a point and was told that the ANC had heard him, that they appreciated what he was trying to say, but that it was time for him to understand that the majority would have its way.

As the Freedom Front's chief whip in Parliament, Joseph Chiole was close to the centre of power. He knew that right-wingers who called Constand a traitor were making threats against his life, even after the 1994 election. Taking advantage of the unwritten rule that the chief whips of different parties may cross the floor before Parliament is in session to discuss delicate matters or raise concerns, one day he walked over to confide in ANC chief whip Jannie Momberg.

'Listen, Jannie, I have a situation,' said Chiole. 'I want to talk to Nelson Mandela for ten minutes. Alone.'

Discreet arrangements were made. Mandela had meetings scheduled for 1.30, 1.45 and 2 p.m. the following day, but he would squeeze Chiole in at 1.40 p.m. At the appointed time, Chiole walked over to Tuynhuys, taking assistant whip Deon Louw with him.

'What can I do for you?' the president asked in his friendly and open manner.

'Mr President, I believe that there are threats being made against my leader's life,' replied Chiole. 'He doesn't know that I'm here, but I want to ask you if you can't arrange for a bodyguard?'

'You know what, I should have thought about that myself,' said Mandela.

Less than an hour later, Constand had protection. His life was secure and he could sleep well at night.

Although his style as leader of a political party was not popular, General Viljoen was responsible for the significant inclusion of Article 235 in the Constitution of South Africa, says Advocate Chris de Jager. Article 235 recognises the right of self-determination by any community that shares a common cultural heritage.[4]

However, according to Andries Breytenbach and the HNP, this section is clumsily written and gives limited autonomy. 'We [Afrikaners] don't have the means or tools to get out of this mess,' he huffs. You can never please everyone.

'It's sad that General Viljoen could not play a bigger role,' De Jager says.

As far as twin brother Abraham is concerned, he often wonders why his friend David Webster was killed and not him. Through welled-up eyes he says he was lucky. But it is we who were lucky. Of Abraham, Jaap Durand says simply, 'I think that he saved South Africa from a bloodbath.'[5]

Abraham still farms outside Pretoria, nowadays with cattle, which he and his black partners have to protect against rustlers. He still carries an air of loneliness and isolation from having been shunned by his community. He does not have much money. Marietjie still works as a state doctor at age seventy-six. Abraham and his good friend Johan Wolfaardt still talk about changing the world. And he still plans for and dreams of a better country. He is a change-maker, after all.

Abraham and Constand Viljoen are reconciled. They still have their political differences, but they and their families know that blood is indeed thicker than water.

When it comes to the Dutch Reformed Church, Constand is still involved. He moves in clerical circles, where his brother would have been if he had chosen to be ordained. Abraham is still estranged from the church and the hurt is still there, but he has made peace with it. His decisions cost him dearly – intimacy with his loved ones and friends, family, opportunities, promotion, pension and medical aid among other things – but he acted according to his convictions.

In a memoir to his family, Durand recounts that a UN representative once told him that South Africans did not know how much they owed General Viljoen, because he could have turned South Africa into a bloodbath if he had wanted to. 'I said amen to that,' says Durand. 'But I still wonder if Abraham Viljoen's role in all of this will get the recognition it deserves.'

The ox that broke the yoke, the jukskeibreker, as Abraham refers to himself, had to run yoked together with the other ox, pulling as one, to prevent them veering off course. He succeeded and the brothers stayed together as they had all those years ago on the farm in Standerton when, armed with whistles, they searched for stray cattle in thick mist, or when they hitched the horse to the cart and set off for primary school. These tasks required teamwork and, as a team, they secretly negotiated to bring democracy to South Africa.

They could not have done it, though, without Nelson Rolihlahla Mandela. Mandela understood the Afrikaners' fear of losing their culture, religion and language. But he also knew black aspirations, which had been crushed for decades by Afrikaner rule. He realised he was walking on a razor's edge when he engaged the right wing in secret negotiations.[6] Touch the Afrikaner at his core and raise fears about those things he holds most dear and you risk unleashing uncontrollable anger. But Mandela also knew that South Africa was their home, a home that they had and would shed blood to hold onto. The British had learnt a bloody lesson. The ANC could walk that same road or it could build a new country through compromise and negotiation.

The secret negotiations boosted the mutual respect that Mandela and Constand had for each other. Both were principled leaders. The general's sincerity won over the freedom fighter and, according to many who knew them, Constand was the only opposition politician that Mandela trusted.

On the day when South Africa's newly elected Parliament met for the first time, Mandela entered the House of Assembly, the chamber built by former state president P.W. Botha, as part of a dignified procession. In an unscripted move, but one that illustrated his trademark penchant for breaking with convention, Mandela broke from the group and walked up to General Constand Viljoen. With all eyes in the House on him, he reached out for the general's hand and told him how happy he was that they had found each other. It was a profound moment, a public acknowledgement by President Nelson Mandela. Constand was close to embarrassment, because it is not his way to seek public tributes.

Constand regrets that the larger-than-life leader did not serve more than one term in office: if he had, Afrikaners might be better off today, he says.

In his life Mandela lived to bring about a democratic South Africa. In the Viljoen brothers he found two Afrikaners willing to put the country first, and not in the racist manner that the likes of General Hertzog had advocated.

Largely because of a set of twin farm boys, one on the left and the other on the right, a bloody civil war was averted and a new South Africa was born.

Epilogue

I F THERE'S ONE set of buildings that symbolises the heart of political power in South Africa, it is the Union Buildings, the architectural masterpiece designed by Sir Herbert Baker and deliberately built on Meintjieskop, the highest point in Pretoria, to give it a commanding presence over the city. Designed in 1908 and completed in 1913, three years after the formation of the Union of South Africa, the Union Buildings have been home to prime ministers and presidents of the Union and the Republic of South Africa.

On 10 May 1994, Nelson Mandela became the first black man to be sworn in as president of South Africa after his ANC won the election in a landslide victory.

Majestic as the Union Buildings are, up until 1994 they did not resonate with the majority of South Africans. To them they were a symbol of disenfranchisement and may as well have been located in a foreign land. But on 10 May, the majority accepted the Union Buildings as theirs. They were no longer those buildings on the hill; they were now the official office of a democratically elected president, a man who truly represented all South Africans. Apartheid was no more. Democracy had won.

During the swearing-in ceremony, aircraft flew over the Union Buildings, among them a group of helicopters flying the new South

African flag, and drew a huge roar of approval from a mainly black crowd, the likes of which had never been seen before on Meintjieskop. The celebration signified a new patriotism for a new country with its one rainbow nation.

Among those present at the changing of the guard on 10 May 1994 were F.W. de Klerk, the man who had started the whole process of political reform with his announcement in Parliament on 2 February 1990, and General Georg Meiring, the head of the defence force who had held together the military and whose leadership and professionalism as a soldier had hugely contributed to a peaceful transition.

A conversation took place between the two.

'We really needn't have given in so easily,' said De Klerk.

'But you never used your strong base to negotiate from,' replied Meiring, 'you never used the military as a base for strength, which you had available to you, you never wanted to use it.'[1]

When I ask General Meiring whether this conversation, which appeared in Hamann's *Days of the Generals*, actually took place, he is adamant that it did. De Klerk, however, gives me a different response.

'I certainly don't recall ever having said any such thing to General Meiring,' he writes in an email. 'He is either misquoting me or misremembering whatever conversation I might have had with him. At no point in the process did I believe that we had "given in".'

As for Meiring's allegation that he never used his base, De Klerk says, 'The SADF and the [South African Police] played an indispensable role in maintaining order – under very difficult circumstances – during the negotiations. However, there was never any prospect before or after 1990 of achieving a military solution to our problems.'

De Klerk acknowledges his policies were not met with unanimous approval by the upper echelons of the military. 'Some did, others didn't,' he says. 'The important thing is that they unreservedly accepted the principle that they were subordinate to the civilian government.'

The forefathers' arrogance in consigning black people to non-citizen status and failing to recognise that they would one day demand their rights as full citizens in the land of their birth meant that Afrikaners like Constand and Abraham Viljoen had to step up and rectify the mistakes of the past.

Unlike the generals and Union politicians of old, they had to face up to their enemy and negotiate a new country, one to be shared with the very people their forefathers had beaten down and stripped of citizenship. The wheel had finally turned full circle.

APPENDIX I

Letter from Nelson Mandela to Constand Viljoen

General Constand Viljoen,
Pretoria.

Dear General,

I was keen to meet you and your colleagues on Saturday 18 December 1993, and I regret it very much that this did not occur. I have now left on holiday until January 3 1994, and hope to see you on my return.

Meanwhile I wish to let you know that the attached memorandum of agreement between the African National Congress and the Afrikaner Volksfront was discussed and approved by the officials of the ANC and it enjoys my support.

Sincerely,

NRMandela

APPENDIX II

Accord on Afrikaner self-determination

BETWEEN THE FREEDOM FRONT, THE AFRICAN NATIONAL CONGRESS AND THE SOUTH AFRICAN GOVERNMENT/ NATIONAL PARTY taking note of the Constitution of the Republic of South Africa, Act 200 of 1993 as amended; and taking note of the unsigned Memorandum of Agreement between the African National Congress (ANC) and the Afrikaner Volksfront (AVF), dated December 21, 1993; and taking note of Constitutional Principle XXXIV, dealing with the issue of self-determination; and subsequent to the discussions between the delegations of the ANC, the AVF, the South African Government and eventually the Freedom Front (FF) -

The parties represented by these delegations record the following agreement:

1. The parties agree to address, through a process of negotiations, the idea of Afrikaner self-determination, including the concept of a Volkstaat.
2. The parties further agree that in the consideration of these matters, they shall not exclude the possibility of local and/or regional and other forms of expression of such self-determination.
3. They agree that their negotiations shall be guided by the need to be consistent with and shall be governed by the requirement to pay due consideration to Constitutional Principle XXXIV, other provisions of the Constitution of the Republic of South Africa, Act 200 of 1993 as amended, and that the parties take note of the Memorandum of

Agreement, as referred to above.

3.1 Such consideration shall therefore include matters such as:

3.1.1 substantial proven support for the idea of self-determination including the concept of a Volkstaat;

3.1.2 the principles of democracy, non-racialism and fundamental rights; and

3.1.3 the promotion of peace and national reconciliation.

4. The parties further agree that in pursuit of 3.1.1 above, the support for the idea of self-determination in a Volkstaat will be indicated by the electoral support which parties with a specific mandate to pursue the realisation of a Volkstaat, will gain in the forthcoming election.

4.1 The parties also agree that, to facilitate the consideration of the idea of a Volkstaat after the elections, such electoral support should be measured not only nationally, but also by counting the provincial votes at the level of:

4.1.1 the electoral district, and

4.1.2 wherever practical the polling stations as indicated by the parties to, and agreed to by, the Independent Electoral Commission.

5. The parties agree that the task of the Volkstaatraad shall be to investigate and report to the Constitutional Assembly and the Commission on the Provincial Government on measures which can give effect to the idea of Afrikaner self-determination, including the concept of the Volkstaat.

6. The parties further agree that the Volkstaatraad shall form such advisory bodies as it may determine.

7. In addition to the issue of self-determination, the parties also undertake to discuss among themselves and reach agreement on matters relating to matters affecting stability in the agricultural sector and the impact of the process of transition on this sector, and also matters of stability including the issue of indemnity inasmuch as the matter has not been resolved.

8. The parties further agree that they will address all matters of concern to them through negotiations and that this shall not exclude the possibility of international mediation to help resolve such matters as may be in dispute and/or difficult to conclude.

   8.1 The parties also agree that paragraph 8.0 shall not be read to mean that any of the deliberations of the Constitutional Assembly are subject to international mediation, unless the Constitutional Assembly duly amends the Constitution to enable this to happen.

   8.2 The parties also affirm that, where this Accord refers to the South African Government, it refers to the South African Government which will rule South Africa until the April 1994 elections.

Signed by:
Gen. Constand Viljoen, Leader: Freedom Front
Mr Thabo Mbeki, National Chairman: African National Congress
Mr Roelf Meyer, Minister of Constitutional Development and of Communication on behalf of the Government and the National Party

Witnessed by:
Prof. Abraham Viljoen & Mr Jurgen Kögl
April 23, 1994

(From 'The O'Malley Archives', as hosted by the Nelson Mandela Foundation, available at http://www.nelsonmandela.org/omalley/)

Notes

CHAPTER 1: AFRIKANER LEGACY OF THE ANGLO-BOER WAR
1. S. Dubow, *Scientific Racism in Modern South Africa*, Cambridge: Cambridge University Press, 2005, p. 225.
2. H. Giliomee, *Die Afrikaners*, Cape Town: Tafelberg, 2004, p. 206.
3. T. Pakenham, *The Boer War*, Johannesburg and Cape Town: Jonathan Ball, 1979, p. xv.
4. Ibid., p. 47.
5. Ibid., p. 20.
6. Ibid., p. 119.
7. Ibid., p. xvii.
8. Ibid., p. 64.
9. Ibid.
10. Ibid., p. 68.
11. Ibid.
12. Ibid., p. xvi.
13. S.B. Spies and G. Nattrass (eds), *Jan Smuts: Memoirs of the Boer War*, Johannesburg: Jonathan Ball, 1994, p. 16.
14. Pakenham, *The Boer War*, p. 506.
15. Ibid., p. 507.
16. Ibid.
17. Ibid.
18. A.J.J. du Preez, *Standerton 100*, Johannesburg: Caxton, 1978.
19. Pakenham, *The Boer War*, p. 568.
20. Ibid., p. 569.
21. Ibid.
22. Ibid., p. 567.

CHAPTER 2: STARTING ALL OVER AGAIN
1. H. Deegan, *The Politics of the New South Africa*, Essex: Pearson Education, 2001, p. 14.
2. C. van der Westhuizen, *White Power and the Rise and Fall of the National Party*, Cape Town: Zebra Press, 2007, p. 18.
3. W.A. de Klerk, *The Puritans in Africa*, Harmondsworth: Penguin, 1975, p. 93.
4. I. Wilkens and H. Strydom, *The Super Afrikaners*, Johannesburg and Cape Town: Jonathan Ball, 2012, p. 53.
5. Van der Westhuizen, *White Power and the Rise and Fall of the National Party*, p. 19.
6. Ibid.
7. De Klerk, *The Puritans in Africa*, p. 99.
8. Ibid.
9. Ibid., p. 100.
10. K. Ingham, *Jan Christian Smuts*, Johannesburg: Jonathan Ball, 1986, p. 87.
11. Ibid., p. 79.
12. Wilkens and Strydom, *The Super Afrikaners*.
13. De Klerk, *The Puritans in Africa*, p. 101.
14. Du Preez, *Standerton 100*.
15. De Klerk, *The Puritans in Africa*, p. 102.
16. Ibid., p. 103.
17. Ibid., p. 104.
18. Giliomee, *Die Afrikaners*, p. 284.
19. De Klerk, *The Puritans in Africa*, p. 106.
20. Van der Westhuizen, *White Power and the Rise and Fall of the National Party*.
21. De Klerk, *The Puritans in Africa*, p. 107.
22. Ibid., p. 110.
23. J.H.P. Serfontein, *Brotherhood of Power*, London: Rex Collings, 1979, p. 31.
24. Ibid., p. 29.
25. Ibid., p. 34.
26. H. Giliomee, *Die laaste Afrikanerleiers*, Cape Town: Tafelberg, 2012, p. 19.
27. Wilkens and Strydom, *The Super Afrikaners*, p. 53.
28. Serfontein, *Brotherhood of Power*, p. 42.
29. Ibid.
30. D. Reitz, *The Deneys Reitz Trilogy: Adrift on the Open Veld*, Cape Town: Stormberg Publishers, 1999, p. 518.

31 Ibid.
32 De Klerk, *The Puritans in Africa*, p. 122.

CHAPTER 3: EARLY POLITICS OF THE VILJOEN FAMILY
1 De Klerk, *The Puritans in Africa*, p. 199.
2 A.P. Treurnicht, *Credo van 'n Afrikaner*, Cape Town: Tafelberg, 1975, p. 78.
3 Giliomee, *Die laaste Afrikanerleiers*, p. 28.
4 Giliomee, *Die Afrikaners*, p. 303.
5 De Klerk, *The Puritans in Africa*, p. 220.
6 Giliomee, *Die Afrikaners*, p. 393.
7 Ibid.
8 Reitz, *The Deneys Reitz Trilogy*, p. 541.
9 Ibid.
10 Wilkens and Strydom, *The Super Afrikaners*, p. 82.
11 Ibid., p. 84.
12 Ibid., p. 91.
13 De Klerk, *The Puritans in Africa*, p. 196.
14 Ibid., p. 225.
15 Ibid., p. 206.
16 Ibid., p. 213.
17 Ibid., p. 224.
18 Wilkens and Strydom, *The Super Afrikaners*, p. 93.
19 Giliomee, *Die Afrikaners*, p. 306.
20 De Klerk, *The Puritans in Africa*, p. 224.

CHAPTER 4: THE DISSIDENT AFRIKANER
1 Giliomee, *Die Afrikaners*, p. 431.
2 Wilkens and Strydom, *The Super Afrikaners*, p. 300.
3 Ibid., pp. xviii–xix.
4 Serfontein, *Brotherhood of Power*, p. 20.
5 Beyers Naudé, letter published in the *Cape Times*, 20 November 1963.
6 Wilkens and Strydom, *The Super Afrikaners*.

CHAPTER 5: MILITARY IN THE BLOOD
1 H. Hamann, *Days of the Generals*, Cape Town: Zebra Press, 2001, pp. 23–24.
2 Ibid., p. 56.

3   J. Geldenhuys, *At the Front: A General's Account of South Africa's Border War*, Johannesburg: Jonathan Ball, 1994, p. 129.
4   L. Scholtz, *The SADF in the Border War 1966–1989*, Cape Town: Tafelberg, 2013, p. 41.
5   J. Sanders, *Apartheid's Friends*, London: John Murray, 2006, p. 326.
6   S. Ellis and T. Sechaba, *Comrades Against Apartheid*, London: James Currey; Bloomington, Indiana: Indiana University Press, 1992, p. 77.
7   M. Spaarwater, *A Spook's Progress*, Cape Town: Zebra Press, 2012, p. 65.
8   Ibid.

CHAPTER 6: IN ENEMY COLOURS
1   Giliomee, *Die laaste Afrikanerleiers*, p. 214.
2   F. van Zyl Slabbert, *Duskant die geskiedenis*, Cape Town: Tafelberg, 2006, p. 58.
3   Ibid.
4   F.W. de Klerk, *The Last Trek: A New Beginning*, New York: St. Martin's Press, 1998.

CHAPTER 7: RIVEN BY POLITICS
1   Giliomee, *Die Afrikaners*, p. 537.
2   Malan, *My Life with the SA Defence Force*, Pretoria: Pretoria Book House, 2006, p. 187.
3   Hamann, *Days of the Generals*, p. 54.
4   Ibid., p. 56.
5   Ibid.
6   D.W. Potgieter, *Kwart voor 'n bloedbad*, Pretoria: LAPA Uitgewers, 2012, p. 24.
7   Ibid., p. 31.
8   M. Schönteich and H. Boshoff, *Volk, Faith and Fatherland*, Pretoria: Institute for Security Studies, 2003, p. 22.
9   De Klerk, *The Last Trek: A New Beginning*, p. 232.
10 J. Carlin, *Invictus*, London: Atlantic Books, 2008, p. 127.
11 Schönteich and Boshoff, *Volk, Faith and Fatherland*.
12 Potgieter, *Kwart voor 'n bloedbad*.
13 Hamann, *Days of the Generals*, p. 204.
14 Ibid., p. 205.

NOTES

CHAPTER 8: THE GENERAL ANSWERS THE CALL
1. A. Sparks, *Tomorrow is Another Country*, Johannesburg and Cape Town: Jonathan Ball, 1995, p. 146.
2. Carlin, *Invictus*, p. 119.
3. Ibid., p. 120.
4. Carlin, *Invictus*, p. 123.
5. Potgieter, *Kwart voor 'n bloedbad*, p. 46.
6. M. du Preez, *Of Warriors, Lovers and Prophets*, Cape Town: Zebra Press, 2004, p. 225.
7. Unpublished comments made by Nelson Mandela to Richard Stengel during a series of interviews for *Long Walk to Freedom*, April/May 1993. Courtesy of the Nelson Mandela Foundation.
8. De Klerk, *The Last Trek: A New Beginning*, p. 310.
9. Potgieter, *Kwaart voor 'n bloedbad*, p. 49.
10. All the talk and bravado could not save Terre'Blanche when he had to face the South African legal system in 2001. He was imprisoned for the attempted murder of a security guard and for assaulting a petrol attendant. He was paroled in 2004. He suffered the ignominy of being murdered in his bed on his farm by black workers in 2010. He died with his boots off, not gloriously in battle, a victim of crime in the new South Africa, the country whose birth he and his neo-Nazis had tried to stop.
11. Potgieter, *Kwart voor 'n bloedbad*, p. 61.
12. Van der Westhuizen, *White Power and the Rise and Fall of the National Party*.

CHAPTER 9: SECRET NEGOTIATIONS GET UNDER WAY
1. A. Sparks, *Beyond the Miracle*, Johannesburg and Cape Town: Jonathan Ball, 2003, p. 127.
2. Jaap Durand, unpublished notes given to the author.
3. Wilkens and Strydom, *The Super Afrikaners*, p. 195.

CHAPTER 10: BRIDGING THE DIVIDES
1. Du Preez, *Of Warriors, Lovers and Prophets*, p. 226.
2. Carlin, *Invictus*, p. 138.
3. Ibid., p. 140.
4. Ibid.
5. Khula means 'growth' in Swahili.

6   W. Gumede, *Thabo Mbeki and the Battle for the Soul of the ANC*, Cape Town: Zebra Press, 2005, p. 42; and M. Gevisser, *Thabo Mbeki: The Dream Deferred*, Johannesburg: Jonathan Ball, 2007, p. 601.
7   Gumede, *Thabo Mbeki and the Battle for the Soul of the ANC*, p. 43.
8   P. Waldmeir, *Anatomy of a Miracle*, London: Penguin, 1997, p. 240.
9   Gevisser, *Thabo Mbeki: The Dream Deferred*, p. 617.
10 Ibid., pp. 415, 460 and 650. In 1994, Mbeki would show his mastery of the art of survival when Mandela named him one of his two deputy presidents, thus launching him on the trajectory to president of South Africa. 'Ramaphosa was devastated,' wrote Adrian Hadland and Jovial Rantao in *The Life and Times of Thabo Mbeki*. 'For some days after the election on 27 April 1994, as the results began to pour in to the offices of the Independent Electoral Commission in Johannesburg, people who knew Ramaphosa could see the tension he was having to endure. Then, suddenly, just before the new cabinet was announced in early May, Ramaphosa relaxed. He knew he had lost out. The decision, which had been Mandela's alone, had gone Thabo's way.' A. Hadland and J. Rantao, *The Life and Times of Thabo Mbeki*, Johannesburg: Zebra Press, 1999, p. 75.
11 A bosberaad, or 'council in the bush', is conventionally considered a strategy meeting in isolated, neutral territory, where complex political issues can be discussed.

CHAPTER 11: THE FREEDOM FRONT IS BORN
1   Gevisser, *Thabo Mbeki: The Dream Deferred*, p. 620.
2   Potgieter, *Kwart voor 'n bloedbad*, p. 53.
3   Hamann, *Days of the Generals*, p. 211.
4   Reported in the *Chicago Tribune*, 30 January 1994.
5   A. Butler, *Cyril Ramaphosa*, Johannesburg: Jacana, 2011.
6   Reported in the *Chicago Tribune*, 11 February 1994.
7   Potgieter, *Kwart voor 'n bloedbad*, p. 210.
8   *The Bloody Miracle*, Boondogle Films, produced for Sabido Productions, 2013.
9   The FF did well enough in the elections to have its registration fee returned. The cheque was duly handed back to the kind unnamed businessman who had provided it.
10 Potgieter, *Kwart voor 'n bloedbad*, p. 204.

CHAPTER 12: THE GAME CHANGER: THE BOPHUTHATSWANA COUP

1. M. Evans, *Broadcasting the End of Apartheid: Live Television and the Birth of the New South Africa*, London: I.B. Tauris, 2014, p. 160.
2. P. Meiring, *Kroniek van die Waarheidskommissie*, Vanderbijlpark: Carpe Diem Boeke, 1999, p. 347.
3. Reported in the *Mail & Guardian*, 6 May 1997.
4. Ibid.
5. Ibid.
6. J.D.F. Jones, *Storyteller: The Many Lives of Laurens van der Post*, London: John Murray, 2001, p. 425.
7. Padraig O'Malley, 'The O'Malley Archives', available at http://www.nelsonmandela.org/omalley/.
8. T. Papenfus, *Pik Botha en sy tyd*, Pretoria: Litera Publikasies, 2010, pp. 691, 692 and 693.
9. Reported in the *Pretoria News*, 12 March 1994.
10. A. Sampson, *Mandela: The Authorised Biography*, New York: Knopf, 1999, p. 475.
11. Reported in the *Pretoria News*, 12 March 1994.
12. Schönteich and Boshoff, *Volk, Faith and Fatherland*, p. 28.
13. Reported in the *Daily Dispatch*, 31 July 1998.
14. Ibid.

CHAPTER 13: THE ANC PUSHES

1. Hamann, *Days of the Generals*, p. 212.
2. Ibid.
3. P.N. Lyman, *Partner to History: The U.S. Role in South Africa's Transition to Democracy*, Washington, DC: United States Institute of Peace, 2001, p. 172.
4. Ibid.
5. Ibid.
6. Ibid.
7. Ibid., p. 173.
8. Ibid.
9. Ibid.
10. Ibid., p. 176.
11. Papenfus, *Pik Botha en sy tyd*, p. 695.

12 Jones, *Storyteller*, p. 425.
13 Lyman, *Partner to History*, p. 178.
14 Ibid.
15 Jones, *Storyteller*, p. 425.
16 Meiring, *Kroniek van die Waarheidskommissie*, p. 144.
17 Hamann, *Days of the Generals*.
18 *The Bloody Miracle*, Boondogle Films, produced for Sabido Productions, 2013.
19 Quoted on Zubeida Jaffer's website: www.zubeidajaffer.co.za/articles.

CHAPTER 14: TIME TO GO
1 J. Marais, *Die IDASA-komplot teen Afrikanernasionalisme*, Pretoria: Bienedell Uitgewers, 1997, p. 1.
2 C. Boshoff, *Dis nou ek*, Pretoria: LAPA Uitgewers, 2012, p. 441.
3 Giliomee, *Die Afrikaners*, p. 625.
4 Article 235 of the South African Constitution reads: 'The right of the South African people as a whole to self-determination, as manifested in this Constitution, does not preclude, within the framework of this right, recognition of the notion of self-determination of any community sharing a common cultural and language heritage, within a territorial entity in the Republic or in any other way, determined by national legislation.'
5 Jaap Durand, unpublished notes given to the author.
6 Sparks, *Beyond the Miracle*, p. 126; and Waldmeir, *Anatomy of a Miracle*, p. 238.

EPILOGUE
1 Hamann, *Days of the Generals*, p. 227.

Bibliography

BOOKS AND ARTICLES

Boshoff, C. *Dis nou ek*. Pretoria: LAPA Uitgewers, 2012
Breytenbach, J. *Eagle Strike*. Johannesburg: Manie Grove Publishing, 2008
Butler, A. *Cyril Ramaphosa*. Johannesburg: Jacana, 2011
Carlin, J. *Invictus*. London: Atlantic Books, 2008
Cassidy, M. *A Witness For Ever*. London: Hodder and Stoughton, 1995
Deegan, H. *The Politics of the New South Africa*. Essex: Pearson Education, 2001
De Klerk, F.W. *The Last Trek: A New Beginning*. New York: St. Martin's Press, 1998
De Klerk, W.A. *The Puritans in Africa*. Harmondsworth: Penguin, 1975
De Villiers, D., and J. de Villiers. *P.W.* Cape Town: Tafelberg, 1984
Dubow, S. *Scientific Racism in Modern South Africa*. Cambridge: Cambridge University Press, 2005
Du Preez, A.J.J. *Standerton 100*. Johannesburg: Caxton, 1978
Du Preez, M. *Of Warriors, Lovers and Prophets*. Cape Town: Zebra Press, 2004
Durand, J. 'Sommige dinge is die moeite werd om te onthou'. Private paper given to the author
Ellis, S., and T. Sechaba. *Comrades Against Apartheid*. London: James Currey; Bloomington, Indiana: Indiana University Press, 1992
Evans, M. *Broadcasting the End of Apartheid: Live Television and the Birth of the New South Africa*, London: I.B. Tauris, 2014
Evans, R.J. *The Third Reich in Power*. London: Penguin, 2005
Fisher, J. *That Miss Hobhouse*. London: Martin Secker & Warburg, 1971
Fourie, B. *Buitelandse woelinge om Suid-Afrika 1939–1985*. Private publication, 1991
Geldenhuys, J. *At the Front: A General's Account of South Africa's Border War*. Johannesburg: Jonathan Ball, 1994

Gevisser, M. *Thabo Mbeki: The Dream Deferred*. Johannesburg: Jonathan Ball, 2007

Giliomee, H. *Die Afrikaners*. Cape Town: Tafelberg, 2004

———. *Die laaste Afrikanerleiers*. Cape Town: Tafelberg, 2012

Gumede, W. *Thabo Mbeki and the Battle for the Soul of the ANC*. Cape Town: Zebra Press, 2005

Hadland, A., and J. Rantao. *The Life and Times of Thabo Mbeki*. Johannesburg: Zebra Press, 1999

Hamann, H. *Days of the Generals*. Cape Town: Zebra Press, 2001

Ingham, K. *Jan Christian Smuts*. Johannesburg: Jonathan Ball, 1986

Jones, J.D.F. *Storyteller: The Many Lives of Laurens van der Post*. London: John Murray, 2001

Kessler, S. *The Black Concentration Camps of the Anglo-Boer War 1899–1902*. Bloemfontein: War Museum of the Boer Republics, 2012

Lyman, P.N. *Partner to History: The U.S. Role in South Africa's Transition to Democracy*. Washington, DC: United States Institute of Peace, 2001

Malan, M. *My Life with the SA Defence Force*. Pretoria: Pretoria Book House, 2006

Marais, J. *Die IDASA-komplot teen Afrikanernasionalisme*. Pretoria: Bienedell Uitgewers, 1997

Meiring, P. *Kroniek van die Waarheidskommissie*. Vanderbijlpark: Carpe Diem Boeke, 1999

Nasson, B. *Abraham Esau's War*. Cape Town: David Philip, 1991

Odendaal, A. *The Founders: The Origins of the ANC and the Struggle for Democracy in South Africa*. Johannesburg: Jacana, 2012

Pakenham, T. *The Boer War*. Johannesburg and Cape Town: Jonathan Ball, 1979

Papenfus, T. *Pik Botha en sy tyd*. Pretoria: Litera Publikasies, 2010

Plaatje, S. *Native Life in South Africa*. Johannesburg: Picador Africa, 2007

Potgieter, D.W. *Kwart voor 'n bloedbad*. Pretoria: LAPA Uitgewers, 2012

Pottiez, J. 'Obituary: Sir Laurens van der Post'. London: *The Independent*, 1996

Rees, M., and C. Day. *Muldergate: The Story of the Info Scandal*. Johannesburg: Macmillan, 1980

Reitz, D. *The Deneys Reitz Trilogy: Adrift on the Open Veld*. Cape Town: Stormberg Publishers, 1999

Sampson, A. *Mandela: The Authorised Biography*. New York: Knopf, 1999

Sanders, J. *Apartheid's Friends*. London: John Murray, 2006

Scholtz, L. *The SADF in the Border War 1966–1989*. Cape Town: Tafelberg, 2013
Schönteich, M., and H. Boshoff. *Volk, Faith and Fatherland*. Pretoria: Institute for Security Studies, 2003
Serfontein, J.H.P. *Brotherhood of Power*. London: Rex Collings, 1979
Spaarwater, M. *A Spook's Progress*. Cape Town: Zebra Press, 2012
Sparks, A. *Beyond the Miracle*. Johannesburg and Cape Town: Jonathan Ball, 2003
———. *Tomorrow is Another Country*. Johannesburg and Cape Town: Jonathan Ball, 1995
Spies, S.B., and G. Nattrass (eds). *Jan Smuts: Memoirs of the Boer War*. Johannesburg: Jonathan Ball, 1994
Treurnicht, A.P. *Credo van 'n Afrikaner*. Cape Town: Tafelberg, 1975
Van der Westhuizen, C. *White Power and the Rise and Fall of the National Party*. Cape Town: Zebra Press, 2007
Van Zyl Slabbert, F. *Duskant die geskiedenis*. Cape Town: Tafelberg, 2006
———. *The Last White Parliament*. Johannesburg: Hans Strydom Publishers, 1985
Waldmeir, P. *Anatomy of a Miracle*. London: Penguin, 1997
Wilkens, I., and H. Strydom. *The Super Afrikaners*. Johannesburg and Cape Town: Jonathan Ball, 2012
Willan, B. (ed.). *Sol Plaatje: Selected Writings*. Johannesburg: Witwatersrand University Press, 1986

NEWSPAPERS
Beeld
Cape Times
Chicago Tribune
Daily Dispatch
Mail & Guardian
Pretoria News
Rapport
Sunday Times
The Star

WEBSITES
IOL: http://www.iol.co.za
News24: http://www.news24.com
South African History Online: http://www.sahistory.org.za

The O'Malley Archives: http://www.nelsonmandela.org/omalley/
Wikipedia: http://en.wikipedia.org/wiki/Main_Page
Zubeida Jaffer: http://www.zubeidajaffer.co.za/articles

INTERVIEWS
De Klerk, Frederik Willem
Durand, Jaap
Groenewald, General Tienie
Haasbroek, Marie
Hanekom, Braam
Kögl, Jürgen
Marais, Augusta
Meiring, General Georg
Mulder, Corné
Thirion, General Chris
Uys, Colonel Piet
Viljoen, Abraham
Viljoen, General Constand

Index

32 Battalion 81–82, 85–87, 89

AB *see* Afrikaner Broederbond
African National Congress *see* ANC
Afrikaanse Taal en Kultuurbond (Afrikaans Language and Cultural Board) 28
   Afrikaner Bond 18
Afrikaner Broederbond (Afrikaner Brotherhood)
   Abraham Viljoen and 63, 69
   apartheid and 41, 51
   Beyers Naudé and 63–66
   Constand Viljoen and 75–76, 127–128
   constitutional negotiations 144
   Cottesloe Declaration 57–58
   elections 40
   founding of 26–27
   Jan Smuts and 44–47, 49
   SABRA 152
   in schools 35
Afrikaner Party 42, 50
Afrikaner People's Union *see* Afrikaner Volksunie
Afrikaner Resistance Movement *see* AWB
Afrikaners
   Anglo-Boer War 5–16, 25, 31, 33, 74–75, 128, 130, 136, 143, 212
   English-speakers and 45, 74, 114–115
   nationalism 15, 24, 47
   poverty and 6, 25, 33–34, 41
   Rebellion of 1914 20–23, 96, 179
   Second World War and 46
   urbanisation 25, 46
Afrikaner Volksfront *see* AVF
Afrikaner Volksunie (Afrikaner People's Union) 124–125, 128–129
Afrikaner Vryheidstigting 127
Afrikaner Weerstandsbeweging *see* AWB
agricultural sector 5–6, 122–123, 129, 166
Ahtisaari, Martti 163
ANC
   AVF and 138–140
   Bophuthatswana and 192–194
   Constand Viljoen and 222
   constitutional negotiations 117–119, 121, 130
   Dakar meeting 104
   Military Intelligence and 115–116
   secret talks 147–150, 155–156, 173–174, 206–211
   total-onslaught concept 112–113
   unbanning of 114
Anglo-Boer War 5–16, 25, 31, 33, 74–75, 128, 130, 136, 143, 212
Angola 76–78, 80–81, 91, 139, 178–179
Antonissen, Carl 154
Antonissen, Christine 154
apartheid 36, 40–42, 50–51, 54–55, 57, 191
Asmal, Kader 149–150
At the Front 88

AVF
  Bophuthatswana coup 193–194, 198, 202–203
  constitutional negotiations 157
  elections of 1994 178, 185, 188–189, 208–209
  formation of 136–139
  Mandela's view on 3
  SADF and 176–177
  secret talks 173–175
AWB
  AVF and 136
  Boere Vryheidsbeweging and 133–134
  Bophuthatswana coup 191–199, 201–203
  Constand Viljoen and 140–141, 176, 189
  elections of 1994 201
  influence of 126
  World Trade Centre, storming of 165

Baker, Herbert 227
Bakkes, Cas 95
bantustans *see* homelands
Barnard, Ferdi 105
Barnard, Marie (née Haasbroek) 33–34
Barnard, Niel 111, 171
Basson, Japie 110
Basson, Wouter 91
Battle of Blood River 41, 118
Battle of Cassinga 85–87, 89
Belhar Confession 146
Bellary camp 14
Berkhof, Hendrikus 61
Betel (farm) 79–80
Beukes, Gerhard 83–85
Beyers, Andries 125
Beyers, Christian Frederick 20–23, 96
Bilheimer, Robert 58
Bischoff, Dries 136
bittereinders (bitter-enders) 15
black people 18, 35, 40, 51, 120, 229
Blanke Bevrydingsbeweging 127
Bloemfontein Conference 8–9
Blood River, Battle of 41, 118

Boere Krisis Aksie (Boer Crisis Action) 122–123, 130, 193–194
Boere Vryheidsbeweging (Boer Freedom Movement) 133–135
Boere Weerstandsbeweging 127, 136
Boer Freedom Movement *see* Boere Vryheidsbeweging
Boer War *see* Anglo-Boer War
Boipatong massacre 154–155
Bophuthatswana 125, 191–198, 201–203
Boraine, Alex 103
Boshoff, Carel 127, 151, 181, 217–218
Boshoff, G.J.J. 39–40
BOSS 76, 111
Botha, Louis 6, 14, 18–21, 23–24, 31–33
Botha, Pik 78, 169, 198, 210–211
Botha, P.W. 76, 78, 90, 92, 95, 105, 110–117
Botha, Roelof 'Pik' *see* Botha, Pik
Botha, Willem 214
Botha, Willie 214
Brand, Robert 200
Breytenbach, Andries 125, 201–202, 223
Breytenbach, Jan 81, 83, 85–87, 94, 98, 194, 196, 199
Brink, C. 54
Britain 20–21, 28–29, 48
  see also Anglo-Boer War
Brits, Aletta 128
Brits, Coen 23, 32, 128
Broederbond *see* Afrikaner Broederbond
brothel on base, 32 Battalion 81–83
Bruwer, Dries 122–123, 129, 134, 136–137, 176, 200, 214
Bureau for Racial Affairs *see* SABRA
Bureau for State Security *see* BOSS
Burger, Die 42
Burger, Schalk 15
Buthelezi, Mangosuthu 125, 139–140
Butler, Anthony 178

Cape Times 64
Carlisle, Robin 101
Carnegie Commission of Investigation on the Poor White Question 6

INDEX

Cassinga, Battle of 85–87, 89
Central Intelligence Agency 77, 117
Chamberlain, Joseph 8
Chamber of Mines 24
Chiole, Joseph 176–177, 179–183, 185–186, 199, 214, 219, 222–223
Christian Institute of Southern Africa 63, 65–66, 70
Christian Science Monitor 201
Christian Student Association 54, 57, 59–60
Churchill, Winston 48
CIA *see* Central Intelligence Agency
Ciskei 125, 175, 192
Citizen, The 110
Civil Cooperation Bureau 105
Cold War 77–78, 117–118
Commando 29
communism 69, 111–112, 114, 117, 136, 160, 169, 177–178, 209
Communist Party *see* SACP
concentration camps, Anglo-Boer War 10–16, 31, 33
Concerned South Africans Group *see* COSAG
Conservative Dialogue Project 157
Conservative Party *see* CP
constitution of South Africa 47, 223
COSAG (later Freedom Alliance) 125, 175, 182, 192, 198
Cottesloe Declaration 57
CP
  agricultural sector and 122–123
  AVF and 176
  Boere Vryheidsbeweging and 134
  Chris Hani assassination 132
  Constand Viljoen and 129–130
  constitutional negotiations 157, 161
  COSAG and 125
  elections of 1994 179–181, 183, 209
  HNP and 125–126
  Mandela's view on 140
  Mulder family and 110, 113
  referendum of 1992 123–124
Credo van 'n Afrikaner 41

Cronje, Dolf (kind oubaas) 79–80
Cuba 77, 85–86

DA *see* Democratic Alliance
Dakar meeting, IDASA 104–105, 146
Days of the Generals 120, 228
death squads 91, 105
De Jager, Chris 125, 128–129, 133, 134, 223
De Klerk, F.W.
  Abraham Viljoen and 107
  agricultural sector and 122–123
  Constand Viljoen and 107, 121–122
  constitutional negotiations 117–119, 164
  as leader of NP 114, 116
  referendum of 1992 123–124
  right wing and 140
  SADF and 127, 178, 228–229
  secret talks 171
  Theron family and 169
De Klerk, Marike 164
De Klerk, Willem Abraham 25, 30, 40, 47–50
De la Rey, Koos 15, 21, 22, 50, 210
Democratic Alliance 221
Democratic Party *see* DP
Derby-Lewis, Clive 132
Derby-Lewis, Gaye 132
De Ville, Rosier 125, 134, 214, 219, 221–222
De Wet, Christiaan 6, 19, 20, 23
De Wet, Danie 23
De Wet, Piet 14, 55
Die Burger see Burger, Die
Diederichs, Nico 47
Dis nou ek 217
Dönges, Eben 45–46
DP 219
Dreyer, Hans 163
drought of 1932/33 5–6, 33–34
Du Plessis, Danie 26
Du Plessis, Wentzel Christoffel 49
Du Preez, A.B. 62, 65–66, 70, 100
Du Preez, Max 138, 159
Durand, Jaap 145–155, 223–224
Dutch Reformed Church

251

Abraham Viljoen and 63, 70–71, 100
apartheid and 55, 59–60
Belhar Confession 146
Constand Viljoen and 224
constitutional negotiations 144
influence of 39–42
Ossewabrandwag and 43
secret talks 145–147, 151–154, 158–160
Viljoen family and 32, 36–37, 39–40
Dutch Reformed Mission Church 146
Du Toit, Z.B. 145

elections
of 1994 138–139, 179–180, 199–201, 209–214
of 1999 219
Electoral Act 182
Elizabeth, Queen 48
English- and Afrikaans-speakers, hostilities between 45, 74, 114–115
ethics of warfare 89

FAK *see* Federasie van Afrikaanse Kultuurvereniginge
farmers *see* agricultural sector
Federasie van Afrikaanse Kultuurvereniginge (Federation of Afrikaans Cultural Associations) 26–27
FF *see* Freedom Front
First World War 20–24
FitzPatrick, Percy 7
FNLA 76–77, 81
food security 166
see also agricultural sector
Fourie, Brand 78
Fourie, Joseph 'Jopie' 22
Fourie, Nicolaas 195
Freedom Alliance (formerly COSAG) 175, 182
Freedom Front 181–189, 200, 213, 218–219, 221

Gaum, Frits 153
Geingob, Hage 163
Geldenhuys, Jannie 88, 90
George VI, King 48

German South-West Africa 20, 23
see also South West Africa
Germany 5, 42–43, 59, 117, 171
Gerwel, Jakes 213–214
Gesuiwerde Nasionale Party (Purified National Party) 27–28
Geyser, Albert 63–64
gold mines 7–8, 24–25
Gouws, Lloyd 163
Gouws, Pieter 134, 214
Gqozo, Oupa 125, 139–140
Grant, Wally 133–134
Great Depression 5–6
Great Trek, centenary commemoration 28, 41
Greyling, Koos 39–40
Grobbelaar, Pieter 214
Groenewald, E.P. 60–61, 68, 100
Groenewald, Jan 133
Groenewald, Pieter 200, 214
Groenewald, Tienie 114–119, 133–134, 136–137, 161, 176, 179, 188, 214, 216
Group 36 83–84
Gumede, William 167
Gunners Artillery Association of South Africa 74

Haasbroek, Petrus 33–34
Haasbroek, Saartjie 34
Hamann, Hilton 120, 212–213, 228
Hanekom, Braam 151–153
Hanekom, Christof 152
Hanekom, Sonja 151, 154
Hani, Chris 1, 91–93, 131–133, 156, 167
Harmse, Retha 131
Harrington, Eric 66
Hartbeespoort Dam 99
Hartzenberg, Ferdi 176, 178–181, 185, 188, 193, 197, 202, 209–210
Havenga, Nicolaas Christiaan 50
Herstigte Nasionale Party *see* HNP
Hertzog, Albert 113–114
Hertzog, James Barry Munnik (J.B.M.) 18–20, 24–25, 27–30

INDEX

Hervormde Kerk 57
Het Volk (People's Party) 18–19
Heyns, Johan 158–159
History of the War in South Africa, The 9
Hitler, Adolf 5, 29
hit squads 91, 105
HNP 113–114, 125–126, 134, 201–202, 216–217, 223
Hobhouse, Emily 10–11
Hoekendijk, Johannes 58–60
homelands
    Bophuthatswana 125, 191–198, 201–203
    Ciskei 125, 175, 192
    impact of 139–140, 191–192
    KwaNdebele 105
    KwaZulu 125, 175, 192

IDASA 103–105, 157, 216–217
IDASA-komplot teen Afrikanernasionalisme, Die 216–217
IEC 181, 186–187
IFP 125, 140, 157, 187–188
Immorality Act of 1927 18
Independent Electoral Commission *see* IEC
Information Scandal (Muldergate) 110–111
Inkatha Freedom Party *see* IFP
Institute for a Democratic Alternative for South Africa *see* IDASA
Institute of Race Relations 65
Ireland 212
Iron Guard *see* Ystergarde
Israel Defense Forces 80

Jaffer, Zubeida 213–214
Jenkins, Ivor 157, 159, 168–171
joiners 14–15
Jong Suid-Afrika (Young South Africa) 26
Jooste, Chris 151, 154–155
jukskeibrekers (yoke-breakers) 35, 224

Kameeldrift 65–66
Katutura, South West Africa 89–90
Kaunda, Kenneth 78
Kemp, Jan 20

Kerkbode, Die 57–58
Kestell, Father 41
Khula Consultancy 164
Klopper, Henning 26
Kloppers, Phil 193
Kögl, Jürgen 162–168, 171, 209, 216
Koppie Alleen (farm) 33
Kotze, Constand Laubscher [grandfather] 33, 38
Kotze, Geesie Maria *see* Viljoen, Geesie Maria (née Kotze) [mother]
Kotze family 37–38
Kriegler, Johann 186–187
Kriel, James 95–96, 98
Kruger, Paul 7–9
KwaNdebele 105
KwaZulu 125, 175, 192

Labour Party 25
Lautenbach, Dale 200
League of Nations 23, 48
Leibbrandt, Johan 183–186
Leibbrandt, Karin 183, 185–186
Leon, Tony 219
Lombard, Ivan 26
Lombard, Johannes Antonie 'Dot ie' 67–68
Long Walk to Freedom 139
Louw, Deon 222
Louw, Leon 214
Lubbe, Willie 133
Lyman, Princeton 206–209, 211–212
Lyttelton, Alfred 9

Malan, Daniel François (D.F.) 22, 27–28, 29, 41–42, 50
Malan, Magnus 75, 78, 80, 90, 112
Mandela, Nelson
    Bophuthatswana coup 202
    Chris Hani assassination 132–133
    Constand Viljoen and 222–223, 225
    elections of 1994 201, 214
    Pieter Potgieter and 160–161
    release from prison 114
    on right wing 139–140, 155

secret talks 1–3, 159–162, 165–167,
    206–209, 224–225
sworn in as president 227–228
Mangope, Eddie 198
Mangope, Lucas 125, 139–140, 191–193,
    196–198, 202–203
Marais, Augusta 55–56
Marais, Ben 55–57, 62–63, 67
Marais, Jaap 113–114, 125, 134, 201, 216–217
Marais, Org 101–102
Marais, Sebastiana 55–56
Maritz, S.G. 'Manie' 20–21
Martin, Deon 193
Matola raid 168
Mbeki, Thabo 155, 162, 164–168, 170,
    173–174, 207–208, 211, 221
Mbeki, Zanele 165
McWilliams, Ronnie 74
Mdlalose, Frank 187
media access, of political parties 174
Meiring, Georg 176–180, 196, 201, 228
Mentz, Moolman 125, 128–129, 134
Menyatsoe, Ontlametse Bernstein
    195–196
Merriman, John X. 18
Meyer, Roelf 183
Military Intelligence 91–93, 114–117
Milner, Alfred 7–9, 45
mineworkers' strike in 1922 24–25
MK 91–92
mobile warfare 90–91
Mobutu Sese Seko 76–77
Modise, Joe 170
Momberg, Jannie 222
MPLA 77, 87
Mulder, Connie 22, 109–111, 113
Mulder, Corné 21–22, 109, 111, 113, 124–126,
    129–130, 182, 214
Mulder, Frederik 21, 109
Mulder, Pieter (father) 21–22
Mulder, Pieter (son) 22, 109, 113, 124, 185,
    214, 218–219
Muldergate see Information Scandal
Mushimba, Aaron 163

Namibia see South West Africa
Nasionale Pers 110
National Front for the Liberation of Angola
    see FNLA
National Intelligence Service 111, 170–171
National Interpretation Branch see Tak
    Nasionale Vertolking
nationalism
    Afrikaners 15, 24, 47
    blacks 51
    South African 18–19, 47
National Party see NP
National Union for the Total Independence
    of Angola see UNITA
National Union of South African
    Students 65
Natives Land Act of 1913 18
Naudé, Beyers 63–66, 71, 146, 216
Nazism 42–43, 46, 59, 126
Neethling, Lothar 136
Netherlands 58–59
New Order 42, 46
Nhlanhla, Joe 149–150, 158, 170
Niehaus, Carl 2, 159
NIS see National Intelligence Service
Nooitgedacht (farm) 38
NP
    apartheid 18, 41–42
    Boere Vryheidsbeweging and 134
    constitutional negotiations 123, 144, 174
    divisions in 109, 112–114, 117–118
    Dutch Reformed Church and 55
    elections 25, 27, 37, 40, 46–47, 49–50,
        113, 219
    formation of 19–20
Nujoma, Sam 163–164
NUSAS see National Union of South
    African Students

OB see Ossewabrandwag
Oelofse, Japie 193
Olivier, Nic 101
O'Malley, Padraig 197
Oosthuizen, Abrie 218

INDEX

Operation Savannah 80
Operation Smokehill 87–88
Orangia Unie (Orange Union) 18
Orania 151, 217
Order Boerevolk 127
Order van die Dood 127
Ormond, Miss 115
Ossewabrandwag 42–43, 46

Pakenham, Thomas 7–9
Partner to History 206
People's Movement for the Liberation of Angola *see* MPLA
People's Party *see* Het Volk
Perskor 110
PFP 99, 101–104, 106, 113
Philadelphia Inquirer 176
Pienaar, Pine 85
Pirow, Oswald 42
Pont, Adriaan 133
poor-white problem 6, 25, 33–34, 41
Potfontein (farm) 31–32
Potgieter, Pieter 159–161
poverty of Afrikaners *see* poor-white problem
Pretoria News 185, 189, 200–201
Pretoria University 54, 73
prisoner-of-war camps, Anglo-Boer War 14, 17
Progressive Federal Party *see* PFP
prostitution *see* brothel on base, 32 Battalion
Pro Veritate 65
Purified National Party *see* Gesuiwerde Nasionale Party
Puritans in Africa, The 25

Radio Pretoria 174
Ramaphosa, Cyril 145, 167, 178
Rand Daily Mail 110
Rand Rebellion *see* mineworkers' strike in 1922
Rebellion of 1914 20–23, 96, 179
Reconstituted National Party *see* HNP
referendum of 1992 123–124

Reformed Church 57
Reitz, Deneys 29, 43
religion 17, 36–37, 47–48
Resolution 435 163
Retief, Piet 118
Rhodesia (Zimbabwe) 119–120, 160
Rhoodie, Eschel 110
right wing 1–3, 126–128, 139–140, 143, 147, 175–176, 222
Roberto, Holden 76
Roslin Castle 14
Rothman, Gert 76, 78
royal family, visit to South Africa 48
Rundle, Fred 201
Russia *see* Soviet Union
Rusthof (farm) 32

SAAF *see* South African Air Force
SABC 185
SABRA 151–152, 154
SACC 69–70, 106
SACP 92, 166–167
SADF
  ANC and 3
  in Angola 78
  Bophuthatswana coup 196, 202
  Constand Viljoen and 90–91, 93, 138
  constitutional negotiations 176–180, 228–229
  politics and 93, 119
  P.W. Botha and 111
Saloojee, Yusuf 211–212
Savimbi, Jonas 76–77, 78, 178–179
Schlebusch Commission 65
Schlemmer, Lawrence 220
Scope 83
Second Anglo-Boer War *see* Anglo-Boer War
Second World War 28–30, 35–36, 44, 59, 109
secret talks 1–3, 143–156, 158–162, 165–168, 170–171, 173–175, 178–179, 205–214, 216, 223–225
segregation *see* apartheid
Sharpeville massacre 60, 63
Sisulu, Walter 167

Slabbert, Frederik van Zyl *see* Van Zyl Slabbert, Frederik
Slovo, Joe 166–168
Smuts, Jan 10, 18–25, 27–29, 37, 40–51
Smuts, Koosie 10
Smuts, Sybella 10
Snyman, Willie 176–178
South African Air Force 177
South African Army College 78
South African Broadcasting Corporation *see* SABC
South African Bureau for Racial Affairs *see* SABRA
South African Communist Party *see* SACP
South African Council of Churches *see* SACC
South African Defence Force *see* SADF
South African Party 18–20, 23, 27, 32, 51, 210
South African Women and Children Distress Fund 10–12
South West Africa 80–81, 120, 162–164
  see also German South-West Africa
South West Africa People's Organization *see* SWAPO
Soviet Union 77–78, 117–119
Soweto protests 78–79
Spaarwater, Maritz 94–95
Sparks, Allister 145
SSC 92, 115–116
Standerton 12–13, 23, 25, 31–33, 37, 49–50
Standerton concentration camp 12–13, 31
Standerton High School 35
State Security Council *see* SSC
Stein, Callie 177
Stengel, Richard 139–140
Storey, Peter 107
Stormjaers 43
stretcher-bearers 84
Strydom, Adriaan 104
Strydom, Barend 127
Sunday Times 64
SWAPO 80–81, 85, 90, 163–165
Swart family 12–13

swart gevaar (black peril) 35, 40
Swartman, stad en toekoms 154

Tak Nasionale Vertolking (National Interpretation Branch) 115
Tambo, Oliver 165
Tebbutt Commission of Inquiry 195–196, 202
Terre'Blanche, Eugène
  Bophuthatswana coup 194, 197–198, 202
  elections of 1994 178, 187, 189, 201
  influence of 126, 130, 133, 135, 140–141, 156
  secret talks 160
Terreblanche, Solomon Johannes 'Sampie' 152
Thabo Mbeki and the Battle for the Soul of the ANC 167
Theron, Annatjie 169–170
Theron, Dawid 169–170
Thirion, Chris 88–94, 127
total-onslaught concept 111–112, 114–115
traitor Boers *see* joiners
Transitional Executive Council 197–198, 202, 206
Transvaler, Die 26, 42, 43, 47
TRC *see* Truth and Reconciliation Commission
Treaty of Vereeniging 15, 23
Treaty of Versailles 23
Treurnicht, Andries 41, 58, 61, 112–113, 124, 134–135, 140, 209, 222
Truth and Reconciliation Commission 73, 212

UDF *see* United Democratic Front
Umkhonto we Sizwe *see* MK
UN 163, 191, 224
Union Buildings 227–228
Union Day celebrations 74
Union Defence Force 75, 109
Union of South Africa, formation of 18, 120, 213
UNISA 63, 67–68, 101
UNITA 76–77, 178–179

INDEX

United Democratic Front 165
United Nations *see* UN
United Party 27, 49–50
United States *see* US
University Christian Movement 65
University of Pretoria 54, 73
University of South Africa *see* UNISA
University of the Western Cape *see* UWC
urbanisation 25, 46
US 57, 77–78, 118, 206
UWC 146, 214
Uys, Jacobus Stephanus 195
Uys, Piet 176–177, 194, 199

Van den Bergh, Lang Hendrik 64, 110–111
Van der Schyff, Louis 203, 217
Van der Walt, Tjaart 198
Van der Westhuizen, Captain 64
Van Heerden, Cynthia 36
Van Heerden, Eric 36
Van Rensburg, Hans 43
Van Rooy, J.C. 26
Van Wyk, Theo 101
Van Zyl Slabbert, Frederik 102–103, 164
Vercueil, Herman 129, 136–137, 194, 200
Verwoerd, Hendrik 43, 57
Viljoen, Abraham Carel (Braam)
  Anglo-Boer War 13, 32–33
  birth of 5–6, 32–33
  Constand and 106–107, 143–144, 157–158, 215–216, 223–224
  Dutch Reformed Church and 62–63, 65–67, 70–71, 224
  family of 17, 32, 36, 68–69
  at IDASA 103–105, 157
  known as Braam 102
  in KwaNdebele 105–106
  letter to *Die Kerkbode* 58, 61–62
  mistaken for Constand 98, 105, 150–151
  on NP 51
  political career 99–106
  SACC and 69–70
  secret talks 2–3, 143–148, 150–151, 153–156, 158–159, 161–162, 170, 214, 216, 223–224
  at UNISA 67–69
  in United States and Netherlands 57–62
  at university 38–40, 53–58
  youth of 34–39, 53
Viljoen, Abraham Carel [grandfather] 12, 14, 17, 31, 33, 39–40
Viljoen, Andresina Cecilia [aunt] 12
Viljoen, Andries [father] 12–13, 23, 31–33, 35–39
Viljoen, Andriesina Zezilia [grandmother] 12, 32
Viljoen, Braam *see* Viljoen, Abraham Carel (Braam)
Viljoen, Christina Sussanna (Ristie) [wife of Constand] 80, 95, 97–98, 211, 220
Viljoen, Constand Laubscher
  32 Battalion 82–83
  Abraham and 106–107, 143–144, 157–158, 215–216, 223–224
  Afrikaner Broederbond and 75–76, 127–128
  Anglo-Boer War 13, 96
  birth of 5–6, 32–33
  Bophuthatswana coup 191, 193–194, 196, 198–200, 202
  conservatism of 85
  constitutional negotiations 175–178
  Dutch Reformed Church and 224
  elections of 1994 199–202, 210–214
  farm of 38, 79–80, 90, 96–98
  known as Stofstrepie 94
  Mandela and 225
  military career 73–78, 80–96
  political career 128, 135–140, 157, 181–189, 202, 205–206, 215–223
  on politics and military 93–94, 119–122
  Radio Pretoria 174
  secret talks 2–3, 158–162, 166–168, 170, 173–175, 178–179, 205–208, 210–213, 224–225

Truth and Reconciliation Commission
  73, 212
  at university 38, 53–54
  wife of 97–98
  youth of 34–36, 53
Viljoen, Francois [uncle] 12
Viljoen, Geesie Maria (née Kotze) [mother]
  32, 35–38, 106
Viljoen, Magel Margaretha [aunt] 12
Viljoen, Marietjie [wife of Abraham]
  68–69, 71, 223
Viljoen, Ristie see Viljoen, Christina
  Sussanna (Ristie) [wife of Constand]
Viljoen, Sannetta [sister] 32
Visser, Kobus 136
volkstaat issue 137, 206–208, 210, 212, 213,
  218, 221
volkstaatraad (volkstaat council) 210, 212,
  213, 221
Vorster, John 43, 76–78, 110–111, 114
Vryheidsfront see Freedom Front

Waluś, Janusz 132
Webster, David 105, 223
Weltz, Betty 186

Wenkommando 126, 136
Wernher, Beit & Co. 8
Werth, Carl 214
White Liberation Army 127
Wilson, Harold 200
Wit Kommando 127
Wolfaardt, Alwyn 195–196
Wolfaardt, Johan 99–102, 106–107, 223
World Apartheid Movement 127
World Council of Churches 57, 100
World Trade Centre
  IEC offices 186
  storming of 141, 156, 165
World War I see First World War
World War II see Second World War

yoke-breakers (jukskeibrekers) 35, 224
Young South Africa see Jong Suid-Afrika
Ystergarde (Iron Guard) 126

Zaire 76–77
Zambia 78, 87
Zhukov, Georgy 168
Zimbabwe (Rhodesia) 119–120, 160
Zuma, Jacob 155, 162, 164–166, 168, 207–208

Do you have any comments, suggestions or
feedback about this book or any other Zebra Press titles?
Contact us at **talkback@zebrapress.co.za**

*

Visit **www.randomstruik.co.za** and subscribe
to our newsletter for monthly updates and news